Posthumanism

This book is part of the series Themes in Twentieth- and Twenty-First-Century Literature and Culture:

Series Advisor: Rod Mengham
Tim Armstrong, *Modernism: A Cultural History*
Alex Goody, *Technology, Literature and Culture*
Suman Gupta, *Globalization and Literature*
Richard Lane, *The Postcolonial Novel*
Pramod K. Nayar, *Posthumanism*

Posthumanism

Pramod K. Nayar

polity

First published in 2014 by Polity Press

Polity Press
65 Bridge Street
Cambridge CB2 1UR, UK

Polity Press
350 Main Street
Malden, MA 02148, USA

ISBN-13: 978-0-7456-6240-4
ISBN-13: 978-0-7456-6241-1(pb)

A catalogue record for this book is available from the British Library.

Typeset in 10.5 on 12 pt Bembo
by Toppan Best-set Premedia Limited
Printed and bound in Great Britain by Clays Ltd, St Ives plc

For further information on Polity, visit our website: www.politybooks.com

Contents

Acknowledgements

This book owes numerous debts to institutions and individuals, and select individuals within institutions.

At the University of Hyderabad (UoH), Saradindu Bhattacharya unearthed essays and materials with scrupulous speed and method. Neeraja Sundaram added her bit when called upon to do so. Also, at UoH, Anna Kurian's now-legendary reading of early drafts, conversations and productive disagreements (mostly over the human nature of posthumanism) have with affection and attention shaped this book in ways too many to number.

V. Premlata of Dayalbagh Institute of Education, Agra, invited me to speak on posthumanism at a seminar on interdisciplinarity, following this up with the generous sharing of her collection of books and materials on consciousness studies.

The Indian Council of Cultural Relations gave me a travel grant that helped me take up the Visiting Scholar position for a short but productive period at the University of Dayton, OH, USA in October 2012. Much gratitude goes to the indefatigable Harish Trivedi of the India Foundation, Dayton, OH, for setting the wheels in motion and extending, along with Sharon Trivedi, his superb hospitality. Without him and the India Foundation the trip would not have happened at all. Amy Anderson of the Center for International Programs, University of Dayton (CIP-UD), with customary warmth and quiet efficiency, ensured a perfect stay – her friendship, and Bill's, has been singular. Thanks also are due to Tina Manco Newton and Charlotte Hansen at CIP-UD for all the efforts directed at my comfortable stay. Faculty in the English Department of UD, notably Sheila Hughes and Andy Slade, made sure that my lectures and student consultations would not interrupt my (manic) work schedules. Also at Dayton, thanks go to Alpana Sharma and the English Department of Wright State University, and Susana Peña, Dan Shoemaker, Kristen Rudisill, Jeremy Wallach, Esther Clinton, Marilyn Motz, Khani Begum and Matt Donahue at Bowling Green State University for their hospitality and enthusiastic interaction during the stay there in October 2012.

It is a pleasure to sound a special note of gratitude for Ibrahim, the continuingly loyal friend of my school days, for his warm hospitality during the Ohio stint, an effort in which he was aided admirably by his mother, and of course the team of Sadiya, Adil, Aamer and Salman.

Parts of the book appeared in incipient form in various places. Shalmalee Palekar invited me to contribute an essay on William Gibson to *Westerly* (56.2, 2011: 48–61, now incorporated into chapter 3) and R. Radhakrishnan invited me to work on biological citizenship for the special issue of *Modern Fiction Studies* (58.4, 2012: 796–817, now manifest in fuller form in chapter 6). An essay on posthumans and vampires that I first published in response to Nandana Dutta's invitation in *Margins* (1.1, 2011: 65–84) is grafted into chapter 6 as well. Posthumanism and species cosmopolitanism was the subject of a plenary talk delivered, thanks to Himanshu Mohapatra's generous invitation, at the Utkal University's Department of English seminar on 'Topographies of Mind, Society, Culture: Identities and Crossovers' in November 2012.

The section on biometrics in chapter 3 began life as an essay in *Economic and Political Weekly* (96.32, 2012: 17–22). The analysis of Lessing's *The Fifth Child* will appear in *Samyukta*. My argument about the deracination and domestication of vampires using Stephenie Meyer's trilogy as a case study appeared first in *Nebula* (37.3, 2010: 60–76), and in the case of Octavia Butler's *Fledgling*, in *Notes on Contemporary Literature* (41.2, 2011: 6–10). *Notes on Contemporary Literature* will also publish my reading of posthumanism in *Never Let Me Go* in a 2013 issue. The arguments on Frantz Fanon find their origins in my *Frantz Fanon* (Routledge, 2013). Much gratitude to Nandana, Shalmalee and Radhakrishnan for inviting me to contribute and the journals' referees for incisive comments on early drafts of the essays.

I am grateful to Andrea Drugan, Lauren Mulholland (then at Polity) and Jonathan Skerrett, my cooperative and encouraging editors at Polity. And to Leigh Mueller's careful copy-editing, I owe many thanks.

To Nandini, Pranav, parents and parents-in-law, for their unstinting support and uncountable prayers, my gratitude, as always.

1 Revisiting the Human: Critical Humanisms

Shori, the genetically modified vampire, is able to tolerate sunlight and cohabit easily with humans in Octavia Butler's *Fledgling* (2005). Shori represents a hybrid race, neither human nor vampire, both human and vampire. It is a postgender world in Ursula Le Guin's *The Left Hand of Darkness* (1969), and one can choose to be man or woman when coming into heat. Le Guin complicates the supposed distinguishing feature of the 'normal' human race, where each body is of a single biological sex, and speculates about genders being interchangeable. In Marge Piercy's *Woman on the Edge of Time* (1976), 'troublesome' inmates of the mental hospital are implanted with neurotransmitters – a theme Piercy borrows from a real-life incident in which, in the 1960s, the staff at Atascadero and Vacaville (California), prisons for the criminally insane, used the drug succinylcholine to modify their patients' behaviour – that would enable the doctors and nurses to control patient behaviour, mainly by rendering them passive, inert. The inmates remain arguably human but minus the several cognitive, intellectual and emotive abilities we have associated with the 'normal' human. Vampires turn vegetarian and stop feeding off humans in Stephenie Meyer's now-cult *Twilight* series (2005–8), and even begin considering a life where they merge into the human race through procreation. In Anne Rice's vampire fiction, vampires live in covens and replicate the family structures of humans. Arnold Schwarzenegger, the alien cyborg, develops, inexplicably, emotional capacities and affiliations in the later *Terminator* films (1984–2009). In *Gattaca* (1997), an individual's fates are almost entirely determined by her/his genetic codes. Those whose DNA is acceptable become the upper classes ('valids') and those who fail the genetic tests become, naturally, the 'in-valids'. Cloned individuals constitute a segment of the future society in Kazuo Ishiguro's novel *Never Let Me Go* (2005). The cloned 'individuals' are essentially designed to be organ donors to the humans who need certain organs in order to live on. So-called 'normal', self-contained and sovereign humans are 'converted' into life forms living on through their incorporation of, and blurring corporeal borders with, other bodies and organs. Animals in fables around the world exhibit anthropomorphic tendencies, while humans routinely turn into werewolves in horror cinema and fiction. Individuals with special powers – mutants – have to battle for rights and dignity against humans in the *X-Men* (2000–9, with more sequels and prequels in the offing). Yrr, a sentient life form – essentially single-celled organisms that have developed hive intelligence – empower various underwater life forms to attack human civilization in Frank Schwatzing's *The Swarm* (2006) for having destroyed the marine habitat of millions of species. Michael Chorost in his autobiography, *Rebuilt: How Becoming Part Computer Made Me More Human* (2005), states unequivocally that his cochlear implant – essentially a computer chip in his head that helps him hear – makes him a cyborg, a *Homo faber*, but it also makes him more human. Mutant babies blur the sex-difference as well as animal–human differences in Katherine Dunn's controversial novel, *Geek Love* (1989). Dunn makes a political critique of the very idea of the 'person' in a world where individuality and 'personhood' are perceived, in the case of impaired individuals, only in terms of their 'disability' or difference from the 'normal' human anatomy or physiology. In Wendy Mass' novel *A Mango-shaped Space* (2003), the synesthetic protagonist is addressed as 'freak', because she is able to *see* music and numbers in terms of colours. From a different field, the Tissue Culture and Art project makes sculptures out of lab-manufactured organic materials, where life and its matter are transformed into a work of art in order to show how the vitality of life runs across humans, animals and things.[1]

These texts focus on the construction of the 'normal' human with specific biological features and abilities, sex, form and functions. A particular physiology, anatomy, intellectual ability and consciousness, they implicitly propose, gets defined as the marker of normalcy. The compulsory humanity of the human, as defined by and essentialized in these features, is interrogated by drawing attention to the constructed nature of the human 'person'. More significantly, these texts emphasize the blurring of bodily borders, identities (gender, species, race) and even consciousness, in which isolating the 'human' from a human–machine assemblage, cadavers or another form of life is impossible. Critical posthumanism, as we shall come to call this philosophical and political theme in literature, popular culture and theory, is the *radical decentring of the traditional sovereign, coherent and autonomous human in order to demonstrate how the human is always already evolving with, constituted by and constitutive of multiple forms of life and machines.* Literary texts that have since the Renaissance always shown us how humans behave, react and interact – indeed it has been said that literature 'invented' the human – have now begun to show that the human is what it is *because* it includes the non-human.

Outside and yet within these literary and popular representations of corporeal–physiological fluidity, ontological liminality and identity-morphing that have firmly placed the man–machine linkage, trans-species bodies and organic-inorganic hybrids within the cultural imaginary, are the rapid advances in technology.

Technologies of cloning, stem-cell engineering, cryogenics, Artificial Intelligence and xenotransplantation blur borders of animal, human and machines in what might be thought of as a new organicism (or even 'organism'?). Human Rights activists worry that prisoners, comatose patients and asylum inmates, along with ethnic/linguistic/religious minorities, differently abled and developmentally challenged people are treated as less than human, long after slavery has ostensibly been abolished. Cognitive ethologists and biologists have demonstrated that those features we take to be uniquely human – altruism, consciousness, language – are also properties exhibited by animals. Human consciousness itself, they have demonstrated, is an epiphenomenon.

As even this very short and selective inventory demonstrates, previously taken-for-granted categories of the human/non-human are now subject to sustained, controversial examination since the late twentieth century. Philosophers, literary and cultural studies scholars, scientists across various disciplines have fought, often acrimoniously, over what it means to be human in an age like this. Ethicists, animal rights activists, medical experts quarrel with theologians, lawyers and governments in order to establish the 'rightness' or 'wrongness' of new forms of hybrid life forms, mostly synthesized and curated in the vat, the operating theatre, the hard drive or the petri-dish.

Even when fiction does not explicitly detail contemporary science, it does explore the *nature* of the human in the age of advanced biotechnology, genetic engineering and computers. From much of the sci-fi, the dystopian novels and other popular expressions, we understand that a new cultural history of the human needs to deal with the question: what forms of the human are now extant and existent? Sci-fi also calls upon us to speculate on the future course of human evolution: what will the human *be* like tomorrow? What comes after (post-) the human? Posthumanism is, at first glance, a temporal marker indicative of this later, perhaps more advanced, human.

Two important frames for the term need to be explicated right away.

'Posthumanism' on the one hand merely refers to an *ontological condition* in which many humans now, and increasingly will, live with chemically, surgically, technologically modified bodies and/or in close conjunction (networked) with machines and other organic forms (such as body parts from other life forms through xenotransplantation).

'Posthumanism', on the other hand, and especially in its *critical* avatar, is also a new *conceptualization* of the human. Posthumanism studies cultural representations, power relations and discourses that have historically situated the human *above* other life forms, and in control of them. As a philosophical, political and cultural approach it addresses the question of the human in the age of technological modification, hybridized life forms, new discoveries of the sociality (and 'humanity') of animals and a new understanding of 'life' itself. In a radical reworking of humanism, *critical posthumanism* seeks to move beyond the traditional humanist ways of thinking about the autonomous, self-willed individual agent in order to treat the human itself as an assemblage, co-evolving with other forms of life, enmeshed with the environment and technology. It rejects the view of the human as exceptional, separate from other life forms and usually dominant/dominating over these other forms. Critical posthumanism begins with the assumption that the human incorporates *difference* in the form of other DNA, species and forms of life, so that its uniqueness is a myth.

Critical posthumanism rejects the 'ableism' of traditional humanism to include variant bodies – such as the differently abled – as well as the animal. By focusing less on ability and agency and emphasizing shared vulnerability, posthumanism calls for a radical rethink of species uniqueness and boundedness of the human. In each of the literary and popular texts cited in the opening paragraph, for instance, the author is interested in looking at the normative human before demonstrating how the non-human or someone who does not fit the taxon of the 'normal' human is constituted.

Critical posthumanism seeks a more inclusive definition of the human and life, and, for its theoretical-philosophical methodology, draws upon all those discourses, representations, theories and critiques of traditional humanism in which the marginalization of 'other' bodies as infrahuman or non-human has been deconstructed. Disability studies, animal studies, monster studies, cybernetics and consciousness studies all contribute to posthumanism because these redefine the boundaries of the human, and call into question the hierarchies of human/non-human, human/machine and human/inhuman. When humans are speciesist and treat non-human life forms as expendable, then some species of humans are also – as history shows in the form of genocides, racism and slavery – excluded from the category of the human to be then expendable. Cary Wolfe makes the comparison of forms of speciesism that is so central to critical posthumanism's multispecies citizenship:

As long as this humanist and speciesist *structure* of subjectivization remains intact, and as long as it is institutionally taken for granted that it is all right to systematically exploit and kill nonhuman animals simply because of their species, then the humanist discourse of species will always be available for use by some humans against other humans as well, to countenance violence against the social other of *whatever* species – or gender, or race, or class, or sexual difference. (2003: 8)

This perception of the intrinsic link between a speciesist humanism and discriminatory practices such as racism or sexism is at the heart of the new humanism that critical posthumanism seeks.

Thus posthumanism is not simply about a human with prosthetic implants/additions that enhance human qualities and abilities (this is the *popular* sense of posthumanism, and is more in line with the ontological basis of the term, as opposed to what I have been calling *critical* posthumanism).

Rather, critical posthumanism sees the uniquely human abilities, qualities, consciousness and features as evolving in conjunction with other life forms, technology and ecosystems. This means critical posthumanism does not see the human as the centre of all things: it sees the human as an instantiation of a network of connections, exchanges, linkages and crossings with all forms of life. Its roots lie in disciplines and philosophies in which modes of describing/ascribing difference and categorizations (human/non-human, human/machine and human/inhuman) historically – whether in philosophy or political science – that create The Human as a category have been revealed to be exclusionary. To phrase it differently, critical posthumanism finds its roots in those critico-theoretical projects in which the constructed and *exclusionary* nature of the systems of segregation, difference, purity, coherence and separation – of bodies, subjectivities, identities – in biology, literature, philosophy or politics is rejected in favour of mixing, assemblages, assimilation, contamination, feedback loops, information-exchange and mergers. In lieu of traditional humanism's species–identity, treated as self-contained and unique, critical posthumanism focuses on *interspecies* identity; instead of the former's focus on the human, critical posthumanism sees the *humanimal*. All evolution and human development is less about Being than a 'becoming-with', in Donna Haraway's memorable phrasing in *When Species Meet* (2008).

In this chapter I first examine the many definitions of the terms 'humanism', 'transhumanism' and 'posthumanism'. I then survey, briefly and mainly by way of a scene-setting exercise, three major critiques of humanism: Foucauldian poststructuralism, feminism and technoscience.

TERMS AND DEFINITIONS

Humanism

Before we define 'humanism', we need to understand what we mean by the term 'human'. The human is traditionally taken to be a subject (one who is conscious of his/her *self*) marked by rational thinking/intelligence, who is able to plot his/her own course of action depending on his/her needs, desires and wishes, and, as a result of his/her actions, produces history. The human has traditionally been treated as male and universal. It is always treated in the singular (*the* human) and as a set of features or conditions: rationality, authority, autonomy and agency.

Humanism is the study of this individual subject and the composite features we now recognize as the human. It treats the human subject as the centre of the world, which is influenced by the human's thoughts and actions. The freedom of the individual to pursue his choice is treated as central to the human subject. The human's awareness of his self – to recognize himself for what he is – or self-consciousness is also treated as a sign of being human.

More importantly, concepts of human dignity, Human Rights and debates over the human 'condition' are premised upon this idea of the universal human. It treats the common human condition. Morality, ethics, responsibility in the modern era (roughly post-1600) all emerge from this view of the autonomous, self-conscious, coherent and self-determining human. The essence of the human lies in the rational mind, or soul – which is entirely distinct from the body. Change and improvement therefore are deemed to be possible through this power of the rational mind. Rationality is also this 'essence' of the human – his ability to think about himself, be sure of himself – that distinguishes him (supposedly) from all other forms of life, and aliens.

Transhumanism

Posthumanism – I use the term to signify not only the ontological condition but also a vision of the human – has two visible strands, stemming from very different views of the human, today. The first strand is the pop posthumanism of cinema and pop culture (*Terminator*, *The Matrix*, cyberpunk fiction). This strand, more a hagiography of techno-modifications of the human, argues that technological and biological modifications will improve the 'human'. This implies that *there is a distinctive entity identifiable as the 'human'*, a human 'self' or 'person' which can do with some improvement. This strand of posthumanism refuses to see the human as a construct enmeshed with other forms of life and treats technology as a means of 'adding' to already existing human qualities and of filling the lack in the human. This version of posthumanism is usually referred to as 'transhumanism'.

Transhumanism is accurately defined by Cary Wolfe as 'an intensification of humanism' (2010: xv). Transhumanists believe in the perfectibility of the human, seeing the limitations of the human body (biology) as something that might be transcended through technology so that faster, more intelligent, less disease-prone, long-living human bodies might one day exist on Earth. Nick Bostrom, a leading philosopher of the transhumanist condition, defines it thus: 'It [transhumanism] holds that current human nature is improvable through the use of applied science and other rational methods, which may make it possible to increase human health-span, extend our intellectual and physical capacities, and give us increased control over our own mental states and moods' (2005: 202–3).

Transhumanists see existing forms of the human as an intermediate stage before the arrival of the advanced *human* form in which bodies and their intelligence might be enhanced for greater utility and purpose. ('Enhancement' has been most recently defined as 'an intervention designed to modify a person's traits, adding qualities or capabilities that would not otherwise have been expected to characterize that person': Bess 2010: 643.) Transhumanism relies on human rationality as a key marker of 'personhood' and individual identity, and sees the body as limiting the scope of the mind. While early transhumanists rarely addressed the moral issue, more recent transhumanist philosophers like Ingmar Persson and Julian Savalescu (2010), James Hughes (2010) and others deliberate the issue of a morally advanced human with greater abilities of empathy, selflessness and ethical responsibility, for whom the enhancement of abilities without a moral enhancement (as Persson and Savalescu see it) would mean that a cognitively enhanced but morally backward minority could inflict greater harm. The debate whether modifications enhance or diminish humanness continues unabated (Wilson and Haslam 2009, Harris 2007 and 2011, Koch 2010), even as bioethicists disagree over the treatment-enhancement approach (where certain medical interventions are to be considered treatment for impairments or illness and therefore *necessary*, as opposed to other interventions that 'simply' enhance existing qualities and abilities: see Sabin and Daniels 1994, Bostrom and Roache 2007, O'Mathúna 2009, Buchanan 2011).

Transhumanism continues to believe in the Enlightenment ideals of the human/animal divide. It treats humanity as a species separate and self-contained. The philosopher Giorgio Agamben summarizes it best when he notes how the human has been defined by the expelling of the animal, whereby 'something like an animal life has been separated' from the human and a hierarchy created between vegetal, animal and human life (2004: 15–16).

In transhumanism, and especially in its popular manifestation in sci-fi, there is an overarching emphasis on the machination of humans and the humanization of machines. The near-obsessive exploration of superintelligent computers that threaten to overwhelm the humans and the robotic implants that rearrange and derange the human in popular culture treats the posthuman as an advanced human, a congeries of human and machine. A paradigmatic definition of the posthuman as this human–machine interface is Katherine Hayles': '[The posthuman] implies not only a coupling with intelligent machines but a coupling so intense and multifaceted that it is no longer possible to distinguish meaningfully between the biological organism and the informational circuits in which the organism is enmeshed' (1999: 35).

W. J. Mitchell, another hagiographer of this form of posthumanism that believes in advanced humanity, characterizes the posthuman as 'Me++', where humans 'routinely exist in the condition . . . [of] "man–computer symbiosis" ', and where they 'now interact with sensate, intelligent, interconnected devices scattered throughout [the] environment' (2003: 7).

This version of posthumanism is techno-deterministic, and techno-utopian, in its faith in technology's ability to ensure a certain kind of future. To cite Bostrom once more: 'the wisest approach to such prospects [indefinite health-spans, greater intellectual abilities] is to embrace technological progress' (203). Transhumanism also sees a *telos* for humanity's future that is achieved almost exclusively through technology. This view of the future of mankind in transhumanism draws, not unjustifiably, the criticism that it is another 'white mythology' because it retrieves the myth of the white man's technological superiority and progress (see Dinerstein 2006, for example).

Popular posthumanism does not see the human as just another construct. It retains the key attributes of the human – sensation, emotion and rationality – but believes that these characteristics might be enhanced through technological intervention. This implies traditional views of the human persist in popular posthumanism: it only seeks an enhancement of the human. It is this belief in the innate, essential qualities of the human that critical posthumanism disputes by demonstrating how the human is a congeries, and human qualities or characteristics have co-evolved with other life forms.

Critical Posthumanism

The second strand of posthumanism might be termed 'critical posthumanism'. As an immediate two-part definition of this strand of posthumanist thought, one can say with Maureen McNeil (2010) that it rejects both human exceptionalism (the idea that humans are unique creatures) and human instrumentalism (that humans have a right to control the natural world). This strand is far more critical of the traditional humanism, and treats

(i)   the human as co-evolving, sharing ecosystems, life processes, genetic material, with animals and other life forms; and
(ii) technology not as a mere prosthesis to human identity but as *integral* to it.

Critical posthumanism calls attention to the ways in which the machine and the organic body and the human and other life forms are now more or less seamlessly articulated, mutually dependent and co-evolving. It critiques the humanist and transhumanist centrality of reason and rationality (with its fantasies, sustainedly articulated in cyberpunk fiction and cinema, of disembodiment), and offers a more inclusive and therefore ethical understanding of life. In the place of the sovereign subject, critical posthumanism posits the non-unitary subject (the non-unitary subject has been theorized extensively by feminist philosophers such as Luce Irigaray as we shall see, and in the case of posthumanism by Haraway 2008 and Braidotti 2013).

Posthumanism as a philosophical approach involves a rethinking of the very idea of subjectivity because it sees human subjectivity as an assemblage, co-evolving with machines and animals. It also calls for a more inclusive definition of life, and a greater moral–ethical response, and responsibility, to non-human life forms in the age of species blurring and species mixing. Posthumanism therefore has a definite politics in that it interrogates the hierarchic ordering – and subsequently exploitation and even eradication

– of life forms. Normative subjectivity, which defined and categorized life forms into 'animal', 'plant' and 'human', is now under scrutiny for its exclusivism, and it is this that more than anything else marks critical posthumanism. Critical posthumanism draws the connections between traditional humanism's exclusionary strategy and women, races or ethnic groups, but also animals, being kept out as slaves, monsters or mere providers of meat, entertainment or labour. It is in the exclusionary definition of the human that we can find the origins of sexism, racism and other exclusionary practices.

Unlike the transhumanists who wish to overcome the human form, critical posthumanism does not seek to do away with embodiment. Critical posthumanism sees embodiment as essential to the construction of the environment (the world is what we perceive it through our senses) in which any organic system (the human body is such a system) exists. But this embodiment is *embedded* embodiment, in which the human body is located in an environment that consists of plants, animals and machines. Critical posthumanism, adapting work from cognitive sciences, biology and philosophy, sees the complexity of the human system, with its 'unique' consciousness or cognitive/perceptual processes, as emerging from this embeddedness, where human complexity, with all its internal organization and operations, is a *consequence of its openness to the environment* (we shall look at this crucial line of thought in cognitive sciences and systems biology in chapter 2). Systems, including human ones, are in a state of emergence rather than in a state of being when the system is constantly traversed by information flows from the environment. When biological sciences tell us that bacteria sustain what we consider to be the self-contained human body, or that many of the evolutionary characteristics of the human were responses to other organic forms on Earth, then critical posthumanism recontextualizes the human system as having 'become-with' other life forms.

Critical posthumanism sees the human as a congeries, whose origins are multispecies and whose very survival is founded on symbiotic relations with numerous forms of life on earth.[2] Critical posthumanism thus favours co-evolution, symbiosis, feedback and responses as determining conditions rather than autonomy, competition and self-contained isolation of the human. It sees human experience, modes of perception and even affective states as essentially derived from, influenced by and formed by the sensoria of numerous other living beings first, and then becoming autopoietic later. Human biological processes are, as the work of Lynn Margulis has shown, enabled through the absorption *into* the human body from the environment, of bacteria and organelles, over centuries of evolution. What we understand as uniquely human, therefore, is *the consequence of hybridization and exchange of material and immaterial – data, such as in the genetic code – across species, skin and function of animals, plants and humans.* The human in this critical posthumanist outlook is a 'dynamic hybrid' of 'ontologically different elements' (Jöns 2006: 572).

The human as a dynamic hybrid in critical posthumanist thought focuses not on borders but on conduits and pathways, not on containment but on leakages, not on stasis but on movements of bodies, information and particles all located within a larger system. Under the influence of second-order cybernetic theory (or neocybernetics), critical posthumanism is less interested in the great human subject than in the human as (i) a system situated in an environment, and (ii) an instantiation of networks of information (say DNA, but also memories) and material (say bacteria or viral forms) exchanges between systems and environments. Human perception that creates the world – the hallmark of the humanist subject – is made possible through this exchange.[3] Finally, critical posthumanism sees the autonomy of the human as the system's self-regulation in response to the environment. As we shall see in the section on neocybernetics in chapter 2, this simply means the internal complexity of the human is not a marker of self-contained autonomy but rather an attempt on the part of the system to *regulate itself, close itself and its operations off from the environment in which it is embedded.* This means the human is always already engaged with the environment. The human, in the words of one commentator, is 'fuzzy edged', 'profoundly dependent into its surroundings' (Pepperell 2003). It sees the human's subjectivity as in-formed by lived (biological, embodied) experiences in an environment and the lived experiences as shaped by the subjectivity in a reciprocal relationship. Both biological living and subjectivity are 'emergent' conditions, the result of dynamical interactions. What is 'natural' to the human is, therefore, *the product of natureculture in which materials (bodies, both human and non-human), immaterials (information, data, memories) and the hybrid dynamics – flows, processes – linking these constitute the human even as the human is an instantiation of this hybridization.*

If humanism posited a self-contained, exclusive and bounded human, critical posthumanism recontextualizes the human into its setting (both organic and inorganic), and locates the human's structure, functions and form as the result of a co-evolution with other life forms.

Hence critical posthumanism poses the ethical question:

Since our origins, histories and evolutionary trajectories are all merged, and when we share mortality and vulnerability with animals, how do we live *with* other life forms?

This book focuses on the critical posthumanist strand.

Critical posthumanism shifts away from the moral transhumanist position in one very significant way. Moral transhumanism believes we can accentuate and enhance specific human qualities (such as compassion) for the greater good of life on earth – but with this it retains a *very clear idea of the desirable qualities of the human.* The human is still the centre of all things desirable, necessary and aspirational. In the case of critical posthumanism, it treats the 'essential' attributes of the human as always already imbricated with other life forms, where the supposedly 'core' human features, whether physiology, anatomy or consciousness, have co-evolved with

other life forms. Where moral transhumanism seeks enhancement of supposedly innate human features and qualities, critical posthumanism rejects
the very idea of anything innate to the human, arguing instead for a
messy congeries of qualities developed over centuries through the human's
interactions with the environment (which includes non-organic tools and
organic life).

CRITICAL HUMANISM AND THE ORIGINS OF POSTHUMANISM

Twentieth-century philosophy, critical theory and biology have radically
undermined the very idea of the human and Enlightenment humanist ideals.
In this section I shall survey, briefly, some of the major moves in the decentring – where the human is no longer the centre of life on Earth – of the
human.

Critical humanism has questioned:

- the myth of the human as the centre of the universe;
- the so-called 'autonomous rationality' of the human mind;
- the agency of the individual in effecting changes in his life, and influ-
  encing history;
- the belief in the transparency of language as a medium of expression of
  individuality and experience;
- the exclusion of certain groups and races – Jews, blacks, women, slaves,
  untouchable castes – from the very category of the human.

Critical humanism proposes that the very idea of the universal human (or
Human) is constructed through a process of exclusion whereby some of
these ethnic and religious groups or races are categorized as less-than-
human. In addition, the very idea of the 'person' as a self-conscious subject
ranks the human above the animal because it is assumed that the animal is
not aware of being an animal, whereas the human is aware of her/his
'humanness'. Thus the universal category of the 'human' is not really universal at all because several forms of life have been throughout history
subordinated to the human as sub-human, non-human and inhuman in the
system of classification. Human history, for the critical humanists, has consistently referred to homosexuals, madmen, slaves, Jews, women as being
outside the category of the human, just as it has treated animal life as less
important than that of the human. Humanism was always linked to Europe's
'imperial destinies' of exclusion, exploitation and conquest (Davies 1997:
23).[4] Humanism, when it appeared in Renaissance Europe, was, paradoxically, very attentive to biological mutants and medical anomalies – deemed
to be 'monsters', about which more in a later chapter – because these
seemed to not fit into the category 'human': they were formed differently,
they behaved differently. 'Universal' humanism was ironically, therefore, a

system of *differentiation* in which some forms of the body were treated as 'human' and others as 'not-human'. When, for instance, Arty, the limbless child who becomes the patriarch of the family in Dunn's novel *Geek Love*, persuades 'norms' to amputate their limbs so that they can become 'special', like him, he deliberately blurs the normal/deviant binary of the human species. The in-human, or questionable 'person', of *Geek Love* is the product of the differentiation process that has strict norms about what constitutes the 'normal'.

Humanism centres the white male as the universal human, and all other genders, differently formed bodies and ethnic types are treated as variants of this 'standard' model, and also forms/models that *lack* something. Critical humanism treats humanism as a politically significant philosophy because it enabled Europeans, upper classes, professionals (like medical doctors or psychiatrists) to categorize some individuals as inhuman or sub-human and confine them or deny them rights. Animals and some ethnic groups have been the victims of this form of classificatory paradigm in which the universal Man was defined.

The deconstruction of humanism in the twentieth century has come from multiple sources. Of the major critiques of humanism examined here – poststructuralism, feminism and queer theory, technoscience studies and critical race studies – most focused on the following domains within humanism: subject/subjectivity, the body, the idea of the rational human. We might, at the risk of simplification, summarize the deconstruction of humanism as a two-step argument:

- there are no essential features of the human subject because 'human nature' is socially constructed and enmeshed in the very systems of observation that characterize it as 'human';
- knowledge cannot be grounded in the human subject and its cognitive processes because knowledge, like human nature, is socially constructed.

Poststructuralist Anti-humanism

Michel Foucault traces the emergence of the human, as we know it now, to the set of ideas and concepts that evolved during the European Enlightenment. Toward the end of *The Order of Things*, Foucault would famously write: 'man is an invention of recent date' (1973: 387). What Foucault is referring to here is a way of *perceiving* the human cognitive processes, human behaviour and actions. The human was 'invented' when these ways of perceiving and talking about these processes, behaviour and actions became codified in the 'human sciences'.

The human was investigated, studied, written about and pronounced upon. Foucault focuses on man in three domains: life (therefore as a biological category, as an animal), labour (as a productive creature in economics) and language (in culture).

The human's cognitive processes and their characteristics which constitute its subjectivity are treated as the foundation of all knowledge within humanism. Foucault argues that the foundation of humanism is its belief that these processes and characteristics can be analysed. It is this belief that leads to the creation of the 'human sciences', according to Foucault. Foucault's own project – genealogy – involved an investigation of the histories of disciplines in the social sciences in which the human subject was formed. Thus the very idea of a 'human nature', for Foucault, is open to doubt. It is not what human nature is, might be or ought to be: for Foucault, it is about how the very category, the concept of 'human nature' works in specific cultures and contexts.

The human subject as the origin of knowledge is demolished by Foucault when he proposes, in a famous conversation with Noam Chomsky:

I have . . . given very little room to . . . their [individuals'] attitude for inventing by themselves, for originating concepts, theories, or scientific truths by themselves . . . And what if the understanding of the relation of the subject to truth were just an effect of knowledge? What if understanding were a complex, multiple, nonindividual formation . . . ? One should . . . analyse the productive capacity of knowledge as a collective practice. (cited in Barker 2003: 73–4)

Foucault here is situating the so-called 'sovereign', autonomous, free-willed human subject within a network of social forces and power relations. All knowledge that the human subject possibly possesses proceeds from the social forces. Hence, where humanism believes that the human subject, the agent of historical consciousness, will generate meaning, Foucault proposes that we need to look at the institutional structures that allow any subject to see something as true or false. That is, 'truth', as Foucault put it, is 'the ensemble of rules by which the true and the false are separated' (1972: 132). Every society, writes Foucault, has its 'regime of truth' (131).

When Foucault demolishes the human subject as the origin of and authority over meaning, he also calls into question the foundational assumption of humanism: of the overriding significance of rationality. Foucault demonstrates how the very idea of rationality or Reason hinges upon the categorization of 'unreason' and madness. Thus, what we take to be the 'natural' rationality of the human emerged from a set of historical social processes through which specific criteria of the 'sane' and 'insane' evolved. Scientific rationality, a key cog in this process of defining Reason, ensured that the human could be defined in biology and medicine. This scientific rationality was accompanied by new 'regimes' whereby segments of population would be defined and described as 'deviant' – criminal, insane, homosexual – and could be, and were, placed under surveillance by the Church, psychiatric hospitals, medical doctors and the police. Economics and sociology examined the human for her/his utility, participation in social activities, and categorized them. What Foucault is suggesting here is that the very idea of the human was bound up with an *investigative* modality whereby knowledge about the human was generated through particular scientific, social and philosophical apparatuses. Health, the mind, religious beliefs, habits and hobbies, abilities and needs were all studied by individuals and 'experts' tasked with identifying criteria of 'good' health, acceptable beliefs and needs. Thus the human subject became a subject *to* these regimes.

With this Foucault has rejected the centrality of human cognitive processes in the production of knowledge. What he is calling attention to is the institutional processes, the rules and regimes, the discursive structures within which the human subject develops meaning. There is no single rational route the human subject takes. No human subject can realize an 'essential' or 'true' (human) nature free from the constraints and restrictions of power (embodied in the institutions mentioned in the paragraph above).[5] This means that self-identity is constituted within power, and so one cannot ever know one's true humanity, one's true identity, independent of power's distorting effects (Ingram 1994: 221). The subject does not pre-exist the discourses: it can exist only within the modalities established by the discourses. And discourse is always about power. Any kind of subject – a listening subject, a thinking subject, a suffering subject, a loving subject, a questioning subject – is formed only within these discourses.

Having established that the subject is formed within (and subjected to) the orders of discourses in the human sciences, Foucault proposes that we treat humanism as a set of techniques or processes. Humanism functioned to 'differentiate' between individuals and ethnic groups. Thus Foucault sees humanist philosophy as a device through which powerful groups and institutions were able to control other individuals and groups. Humanism, in this view, was inextricably linked to practices of treatment, administration, surveillance and regulation of individual and collective bodies.

Governments, having acquired knowledge about the individual or group, could, Foucault writes, 'expose, mark, wound, amputate, make a scar, stamp a sign on the face . . . in short, seize hold of the body and inscribe upon it the marks of power' (1997: 24). Subjectivity was thus subject to technologies of power acting upon the body (say, in medical science or the prison) or the mind (say, in psychiatry).

But power was also asserted on the body through what Foucault termed 'technologies of the self'. He meant that an ethics of living was being put into place, whereby the self becomes a project, to be constantly modified, transformed and upgraded. Thus the humanist notion of the self as sovereign and unitary and therefore in control of its action and its future resulted in multiple practices of the self that the human inherited from traditions. The human, in other words, accepts and assimilates these technologies of the self because s/he comes to believe that the care of the self indicates a sovereign self. In fact, as Foucault argues, these styles, rules and practices of the care of the self are practices of subjection that generate the illusion of freedom.

When Foucault presents the individual as the effect of discourses rather than as a sovereign, self-regulating, self-willed subject, he erases the foundations of humanism itself. There is no more a sovereign subject.

Feminist Critiques

Says a character in Marge Piercy's *Woman on the Edge of Time*:

'Cause as long as we were biologically enchained, we'd never be equal.
And males never would be humanized to be loving and tender. So we all became mothers. Every child has three. To break the nuclear bonding. ([1976] 1983: 97)

The biological 'enchainment' of Piercy is motherhood, which traps the woman in a particular role, and casts her biology in a particular role as well. Considerable feminist thought, in both 'western' and postcolonial theory, focuses on this biological determinism that traps women.

In a magisterial study of norms of femininity and eating practices, Susan Bordo (*Unbearable Weight*, 1993) builds on Foucauldian ideas of the subject. Bordo demonstrates how eating disorders in women are cultural practices that stem from normative ideals of 'the feminine'. Bordo, like Foucault, treats the body, especially the female body (it must be noted that Foucault had little to say on the gendered body), as a site where multiple discourses intersect. Power relations between the genders are maintained through particular models of femininity. Dieting, cosmetic surgery and fitness regimes are technologies of the self that constitute the female subject, under the guise of a normative standard of the healthy, fit and beautiful female form. Bordo's work foregrounds both the question of subjectivity and the body, locating both within cultural practices and discourses.

Other feminist critics have adopted Foucault differently. Nancy Hartsock objects to Foucault's rejection of the very idea of the subject. Hartsock argues that when marginalized groups such as women, or people of colour, seek justice and identities as themselves, Foucault denies them the chance of subjectivity by treating them as instances of discourses over which they have no control. Hartsock instead proposes that 'we need to engage in the historical, political and theoretical process of constituting ourselves as subjects as well as objects of history'. She also proposes that women need to develop 'standpoint epistemologies', in which their 'practical daily activity contains an understanding of the world' (1990: 171–2). Hartsock's emphasis on the performance of subjectivity to generate standpoint epistemologies takes on a slightly different colour in the work of poststructuralist feminist adaptations of Foucault – as in the case of Judith Butler.

Judith Butler, like Foucault, rejects the idea of a founding, or foundational, subject that is female. Such a foundational subject, she writes, 'presumes, fixes and constrains' (1990: 148). Butler argues that feminine and masculine dispositions are the result of an internalization of assimilation of loss. This loss and prohibited desire – and here we recall Foucault's emphasis on the social construction of deviance, normalcy, etc. – is inscribed (Butler's term is 'incorporated') on the body, which results in the efforts to be ultra-masculine or feminine. The prohibition continues in cultural and legal taboos against homosexuality. One goes through life enacting this loss, and striving to stay heterosexual: 'Gender is the repeated stylization of the body, a set of repeated acts within a highly rigid regulatory framework that congeal over time to produce the appearance of substance, of a natural sort of being' (33).

In Butler's now well-known formulation: 'to understand identity as . . . a signifying practice, is to understand culturally intelligible subjects as the resulting *effects* of a rule-bound discourse' (145). Gender as ontology, for Butler, operates within 'political contexts', contexts that determine 'what qualifies as intelligible sex' (147). Butler calls for 'practices of repetitive signifying' to ensure the subversion of gender (145). 'Masculine man' and 'feminine woman' are *signifiers* and acts that, in the very act of naming, construct these identities. The act of naming identifies some body as a masculine one. In other words, there is no gender identity that precedes language. Like Foucault, Butler is anti-foundationalist in her rejection of a pre-discursive 'I' that can be the ground of all feminist politics. Such a notion of a pre-discursive 'I', for Butler, as for Foucault, returns us to the foundationalism of humanism.

When we view a body, we view it as male or female because we are seeing it from within a set of discourses that have determined a set of features to be male or female. This situatedness of our position when we view the human is what Le Guin seeks to avoid in her androgynous tale, *The Left Hand of Darkness* (1969). We do not know if Ai, the narrator, is a man or woman, although, as critics note (Pennington 2000), the clues indicate Ai is a man. Ai admits that he is unable to escape his own contexts when viewing the gender-shifting people of Gethen: 'I was still far from being able to see the people of the planet through their own eyes. I tried to, but my efforts took the form of self-consciously seeing a Gethenian first as a man, then as a woman, forcing him into those categories so irrelevant to his nature and so essential to my own' (12). What Ai is stating here is that he can only see Estraven and the Gethenians through the gender categories he is used to, from his own culture, even if these categories are 'irrelevant' to Gethen.

If Butler follows Foucault and rejects the foundational grounds of identity formation, other feminists reject the humanist universalization of subjectivity. The 'universal' human, the French feminist philosophers complain, is invariably coded as male. This means the woman's subjectivity is always seen as a derivative, secondary and incidental to any discussions of the human subject: the feminine is marginalized as the

Other of masculinity. Encapsulating the feminist critique of humanism is Lila Abu-Lughod:

There are certainly good reasons to be wary of [a] philosophy that has masked the persistence of systematic social differences by appealing to an allegedly universal individual as hero and autonomous subject; that has allowed us to assume that the domination and exploitation of nature by man was justified by his place at the centre of the universe; that has failed to see that its 'essential humanism' has culturally and socially specific characteristics and in fact excludes most humans; and that refuses to understand how we as subjects are constructed in discourses attached to power. (1993: 28)

Or, in Catherine Belsey's words, humanism assumes that ' "man" . . . [is] . . . the origin and source of meaning, of action, and of history' (1980: 7).

In this (poststructuralist feminist) view, the difference of the two genders is structured around power relations in which whatever is different from the masculine is treated as inferior and different. By positing the feminine as the negative Other of the masculine, gender power relations ensured that the feminine would always be the marginal gender, the lesser one of the two. This binary of superior-masculine versus inferior-feminine naturalized the difference and erased its constructed nature. (A similar move was made with regard to the marginalized races, classes and ethnic groups.) As the investigator in Le Guin's novel, *The Left Hand of Darkness*, puts it:

There is no division of humanity into strong and weak halves, protector/protected, dominant/submissive, owner/chattel, active/passive . . . The whole tendency to dualism that pervades human thinking may be found to be lessened, or changed, on Winter . . . You cannot and must not . . . cast [the Gethenian] . . . in the role of Man or Woman. Our entire pattern of socio-sexual interaction is nonexistent here. (1979: 100)

Sexual difference was built into language and representation and subjects are made through their participation in language. Thus the humanist idea that subjects produce language is subverted here when poststructuralists and feminists show identities and subjectivities emerging in language, and not preceding it. Even the experiential understanding of the body is mediated by language and discourse. There are no fixed or stable identities – identities have to be constantly performed within language and representations.

It is within these poststructuralist and psychoanalytic trends that the work of Luce Irigaray and Hélène Cixous might be understood in their rejection of the humanist ideal.

Luce Irigaray, interrogating the myth of the sovereign and autonomous, coherent and unified self of classical humanism, developed a theory of fluid selves. Focusing primarily on the fluid, leaky body of the woman, Irigaray proposed that sexual desire is fluid, and its dynamic flow, like all flows, cannot be contained within a self's boundaries. We need to think of a more fluid sense of the self/identity.

Addressing the question of sexual difference, Irigaray argued that we cannot see 'male', 'female' as oppositional and different. Instead, we need to see each as constitutive of the other.

Irigaray was also alert to the constitutive role of language in the construction of identities based on difference. 'I', 'me', 'you' are identities primarily embedded in language, notes Irigaray. However, each of these terms, and their possessive forms ('mine'), is understandable only in a relation with their Other. Thus 'mine' makes sense only because it automatically positions it as opposed to 'not-mine'. Every linguistic sign and name thus names a relation. She then argues that no self is unitary, neither is any gender. It is in the dialogic relation between these that a sense of the self evolves. 'Masculine' and 'feminine' are not either-or terms in opposition: these are mutually constitutive where the flows of desire, or morality, emerge in the dialogic space between them. Irigaray also argues that the human always reaches out to the Other, as the need to 'touch' is an integral component of our 'selves'. Ethics, she suggests, is not built upon the individual's sovereignty, but upon the dialogue of the masculine and the feminine, in the becoming of 'we' rather than the being of 'I' or 'me'.

For the feminists, the humanist idea(l) that change, improvement and emancipation can occur through Reason is suspect. Thus models of femininity and masculinity are passed off as 'standard' or normative within humanism: 'Man' or 'Woman'. For feminists this naturalization of what is essentially the effect of hegemonic discourses of gender roles erases the possibilities of multiple kinds of femininity. Women rarely have the choice of femininity outside these normative and so-called 'universal' models, and hence they lack sovereignty over their bodies, minds and selves. The woman's self is what is prescribed for it within hegemonic discourses. By naturalizing the woman's 'self' in this fashion, humanism glosses over the processes through which certain models of the feminine are *constructed*, and the power relations and authority that are the determinants in these processes.

Hence some novelists work toward eliminating gender altogether. Ursula Le Guin says about her controversial novel *The Left Hand of Darkness*, in an interview titled, provocatively, 'Is Gender Necessary?': 'I eliminated gender, to find out what was left. Whatever was left would be presumably, simply human. It would define the area that is shared by men and women alike' (1979: 163). Le Guin is drawing attention to the constructed and influential nature of sex differentiation and gender roles here, where differentiation and roles based on biological sex *detract* from the human. (Although this retains the idea of an 'essential' human, albeit ungendered.)

If Irigaray focuses on the dialogic nature of all identity and Butler on the discursive construction of identity in their critiques of the humanist notion of the subject, the work of Hélène Cixous deconstructs the idea of a coherent, unified subject by proposing that femininity is marked by excess flows, fluidity and borderlessness. Her work refuses to accept something like 'a' female sexuality which is uniform and homogeneous. Cixous proposes a model of femininity that is full of spillage, flows, raptures and pleasure: 'I, too, overflow, my desires have invented new desires, my body knows unheard-of songs', as she puts it in her famous essay 'The Laugh of the Medusa' (1976: 876). Unlike the traditional humanist emphasis on ordered, rule-bound and logical writing as an index of the rational mind – which Cixous dismisses as a phallic model that restrains creativity – Cixous proposes a free-flowing, excessive and elliptical mode of expression. In a particularly fervent passage, Cixous writes of the nature of woman's writing and its link to subjectivity and identity (and one must recall here the argument made above of the 'performance' of identity in discourse and language):

Her libido is cosmic, just as her unconscious is worldwide. Her writing can only keep going, without ever inscribing or discerning contours, daring to make these vertiginous crossing of the other(s) ephemeral and passionate sojourns in him, her, them, whom she inhabits long enough to look at from the point closest to their drives; and then further, impregnated through and through with these brief, identificatory embraces, she goes and passes into infinity. (889)

Where humanism preached rationality, reason and order, Cixous clearly emphasizes the passions, emotions and fluidity. While she does romanticize the emotions to a considerable extent, she proposes a return to our less controllable selves as a site of identity.

Such critiques, however, lead to more conceptual confusions within feminist theory and practice. On the one hand, feminist practice and activism stress the need for the sovereignty of the female subject, autonomous and in control of her-self. Emphasizing the feminine, as Irigaray and Cixous do, does entail a certain kind of biological determinism. Where earlier feminists such as Nancy Chodorow and Michele Barrett worried about the biologism that restricted the woman to the task of mothering, contemporary feminist writers have sought to rethink the entire question of motherhood.

Despite this incipient biological determinism, the theoretical underpinnings of Irigaray, Cixous and Butler also seem to indicate a (postmodern) position in which they see the subject itself as created out of discourse, and hence possessing little autonomy. While practice demands a belief in the sovereign subject and her rights, theory, drawing upon postmodernism, disavows these discourses of the subject's rights. As Sara Ahmed points out, this entire confusion proceeds from the entity the theorists and the practitioners are trying to theorize: the subject (1996). Contemporary feminism is keen on exploring relations (gender, class, race – and thus contexts) that create specific kinds of subjectivities for women, and thus deny or grant rights: 'pointing to the arbitrary nature of the liberal formal self . . . undermines the concept of the subject as a self-identity' (75) – and this is feminism's most effective break with humanism. Such feminist readings refuse to essentialize gender simply as 'the woman', treating subjects as enmeshed in multiple strands and contexts. Materialist feminism (Haraway 1988, Braidotti 1991), despairing of the discursive turn, focused instead on embodied and embedded subjectivities of women, choosing to address questions of power relations, wages, situated knowledges and socio-economic marginalization as the contexts in which the woman's body, being and consciousness are forged.

Closely aligned with the feminist critique of humanism is the queer/transgender one. Individuals seeking gender reassignment surgeries and theorists of transgender build on the humanist argument of self-actualization. Traditional humanists have argued that the human is characterized by the need and capacity to actualize himself. If this is so, then, ask the trans-gendered individuals: 'in a society that valued self-expression and self-transformation, why not permit people to decide whether they wanted to live as men or as women, and why not allow them to change their bodies in the ways they desired?' (Meyerowitz 2006: 363). The liberal humanist sovereign subject, for queer thinkers, is abstract, and universalizes the subject with no attention to local social locations – such as gender and sexuality. By focusing on the constructed nature of the liberal subject, queer theory, like feminism, makes a case for the situatedness of identity and subjectivity within and as the *effects* of social–material conditions, discourses, institutions and power relations (Butler 1990, Brown 1995).

Identity in the feminist and queer critiques of humanism is multiple, fractured and unstable. It is not self-contained but relational, enacted within language and discourse, and enmeshed in power structures.

Technoscience Studies

If Foucault was interested in the history of the construction of the self, and the feminists saw the woman's self as constructed within discourses that denied it sovereignty, for only the male self was universal and sovereign, technoscience studies and cyborg theories see the human and the human self as always already imbricated with technology.

Technoscience studies argues that *Homo sapiens* was always *Homo faber*, man as maker, the user of tools, of which the body was the first. Bernard Stiegler puts it best:

I am already and have always been constituted by my relation to the *mēkhanē* and, through it, to all possible machines. It was around four million years ago, according to the dating of Leroi-Gourhan (since reduced to 2.8 million years ago), that a new form of life appeared, one supported by prostheses. . . . This living being that we call man and that this myth [of Prometheus and Epimetheus] soberly designates as *mortal* (that is to say: the being who anticipates his own end and his *difference* from the immortals, from whom he receives, albeit by theft, his power, his fire, that is to say *tekhnē* and all its possibilities, and who therefore endures, in the ordeal of non-predestination that results from this, the experience of a difference marking his origin, which is thus essentially the difference between the sacred and the profane) is a being that, to survive, requires non-living organs. (2003: 158)

We have always been cyborgs in this sense, even if the term itself was not invented till the mid twentieth century. Thus historian David Channell proposes that contemporary technoculture thinking merely climaxes a much older western tradition in which ideas of organic order and hierarchy merge with the post-Newtonian/Cartesian notion of mechanistic rationality (Channell 1991). Thus 'the Great Chain of Being' – that view of the world as hierarchic and ordered persistent since at least the medieval age in Europe – combines with the idea of the 'clockwork universe' (Gray 2001: 10). Cultural studies and the history of ideas locate other antecedents to the contemporary technologically crafted posthuman hybrid. While not, strictly speaking, situated within technoscience studies, medievalists, for instance, trace genealogies of man–machine linkages and different conceptualizations of the human form.

Jeffrey Jerome Cohen has carefully traced in medieval and early modern medical treatises, science-writing, philosophy, art and autobiography the insistence on 'machines': the mind as machine, the human body as machine, the cosmos as machine, etc. Gregory the Great called love the 'machine of the mind' and referred to contemplation and allegory as *machinae* that take identity out of the merely corporeal (Cohen 2003: xiv). Cohen notes how, in Villard de Honnecourt's thirteenth-century designs for perpetual motion machines, the energy from wind or water was to be harnessed to/with the human body (xvii). Myra Seaman notes how the Middle Ages also conceptualized scenarios with human–Other hybrids. Seaman writes:

they, too, examined and extended their selfhood through a blend of the embodied self with something seemingly external to it – not the products of scientific discovery, but Christ, as well as the promised embodiment after death his sacrifice ensured. In this way, the contemporary popular posthuman is (perhaps surprisingly) tied to the premodern, the time before the 'discovery' of the human that thus might be labeled 'prehuman'. In both cases (medieval and modern) the posthuman is not a distinct 'other', an entirely new species; instead, the posthuman is a hybrid that is a more developed, more advanced, or more powerful version of the existing self. (2007: 250)

The 'new' developments in technology and prosthesis, these commentators note, are prefigured in myth and legend, folk tales and animal fables in which the human/non-human boundaries are blurred. In one sense, then, technoscience merely instantiates the stuff of older human dreams, aspirations and nightmares wherein the very nature of the human as an isolated, coherent and autonomous being has been interrogated. Feminist technoscience studies have offered powerful critiques of the gendered nature and inequality of biopower relations that contemporary technoscience has produced.

Donna Haraway's critique also sees human history as one of the human body's imbrication with technology. Haraway treats the human as a hybrid of machines and the organic body, thus marking an end to the idea of the sovereign human individual. Haraway proposes that the human evolved *with* the machine, and to separate the two as 'origin' and 'prosthesis' respectively was to negate the co-dependency of both.

For Haraway the cyborg is a liminal creature, between the human and the machine, neither human nor machine, both human and machine. She finds the cyborg significant because it breaks these categorical boundaries. In one of the more popular statements from her classic essay (anthologized too many times to require anything less than a few terabytes to document) 'A Cyborg Manifesto' (1991), the cyborg is a creature or life form in a postgender mode. The cyborg has multiple origins, and cannot be pinned down to any one, and disturbs, as Haraway demonstrates, the categories and statuses of men, women, artefact, racial identities but also bodies and the categories of living/non-living. But Haraway is also alert to the power relations that enmesh the cyborg, demolish the origin stories and suggest new/ alternative futures for the human race. Early experiments with cyborgs were meant to prepare humanity for space travel but were also connected to Cold War politics and the Star Wars agenda later, as Haraway detailed (Haraway with Goodeve 2000: 129).

She sees technology, therefore, as something that has the emancipatory powers to free humanity from rigid categories. Even when human diversity is foregrounded (Haraway is reading UNESCO's The Family of Man exhibition of 1955 in her *Modest_Witness@Second_Millennium*, 1997), she argues, fundamental humanist notions of the family, heterosexuality, childrearing remain the cornerstone. Haraway is also emphatic about a postgender world where the cyborg dismantles the biological categories of sex and gender. In her reading, nature/culture, human/cyborg binaries break down. Haraway accepts the feminist position in which 'essential' identities – the man, the woman – are destroyed. While Haraway concedes that essentialisms cannot be relevant any more, she is also wary of the postmodern 'play' of endless difference and relativism.

In the world of today, with the global domination of informatics and informational technologies, Haraway calls for attention to the new roles essayed by women. She insists that we see how new divisions of labour come into being, how women are integrated into global production and how domains of intimacy, leisure and the home are, for women, reconfigured through the technologies of today.

Thus Haraway, while denying the humanist idea of an 'original' (sovereign) human and a (derivative) prosthetic technology, sees the human–inhuman linkage as offering the possibility of a new genderless world. Toward the end of 'A Cyborg Manifesto', therefore, Haraway argues that the machine is *us*, built into our bodily processes and constituting our very embodiment.

Haraway's cyborg feminism destroys the dualisms and binaries of traditional humanism: animal/human, man/woman, man/machine. (Later she would revive the figure of the vampire as such a border-crossing, category-transforming figure, whose 'categorical ambiguity and troubling ambiguity' make it difficult to classify it simply as 'good' or 'bad' – 1997: 215.) What is important is that the cyborg, as envisaged in a later work by Haraway, is female:

> the cyborg is a bad girl, she is really not a . . . she is a shape-changer, whose dislocations are never free. She is a girl who's trying not to become Woman, but remain responsible to women of many colors and positions, and who hasn't really figured out a politics that makes the necessary articulations with the boys who are your allies. It's undone work. (1991b: 20)

Here Haraway smartly overturns the hypermasculine cult of the cyborg as well – where *Terminator* or *Blade Runner* had embodied the pumped-up masculinity of the man–machine interface.

If traditional humanism was built on the exclusion of some individuals, groups and races from the very category of the human, cyborg feminism retrieves the excluded, and becomes a more inclusive idea(l) whereby gender, race and ethnicity are rendered 'immaterial' in some sense. Race itself, writes Haraway, becomes the object of bioscientific knowledge (1997: 235), a process Foucault would readily recognize as instituting identities with so-called 'rational' categories. This cyborg critique of (patriarchal, white) humanism in Haraway inaugurated a whole new field within cyberculture studies, one often associated with cyberfeminism and feminist studies of technoscience.

While critiquing the humanist emphasis on normative masculinity, scientific rationality and gender roles, Haraway also rejects the structures within which these norms and standards evolve: the family, labour, kinship and sexuality. Haraway proposes alternative modes of kinship: in friendship, labour, work and shared mortality. She seeks new ways of belonging, of associations in which 'competition' is not the only way of evolution.

In more recent work, Haraway (2008) has drawn attention to what she calls 'companion species': humanity co-evolves with other species, shares space with them, and hence ought to offer a different response to them.[6] 'Response' for Haraway is a 'response-ibility', an ethical relation to the fellow-species. With this, I propose, Haraway offers a radical posthumanism in which the category 'human' is one that is inextricably always othered: linked to, dependent upon, supportive of the other. She proposes that 'to be one is always to become with many' (4). Species interdependence is what 'makes' the world, in Haraway's reading.

Other commentators such as Sandra Harding (*The Science Question in Feminism*, 1986) call for attention to science itself as a social institution whose division of labour marginalizes the woman but is constantly projected as 'objective' and erases the unequal nature of relations within itself. Combining feminism with science and technology studies, Harding notes that women are called upon to be 'more like men', thus effectively 'degendering' them. But there is no corresponding degendering for men! Others, like Evelyn Fox Keller, see a close link between the so-called 'objectivity' demanded by 'rational' science and the construction of gendered subjectivities and identity within technoscience. Keller writes: 'Modern science . . . is based on a division of emotional and intellectual labour in which objectivity, reason, and "mind" are cast as male and subjectivity, feeling and "nature" are cast as female' (cited in Smith Keller 1992: 14). Keller is pointing to the refusal of objectivity to women, whereby the woman's perception, intellect and modes of engaging with objects of study are dismissed as irrational and unscientific.

Cultural studies of science in the age of globalization note how the latter and its digital component are made possible *by* and *through* the bodies of women workers, especially in Third World nations, as feminist critiques note (Braidotti 2007). Capitalism works through bio-power, the control of bodies. However, 'bio-power has already turned into a form of bio-piracy in that it aims at exploiting the generative powers of women, animals, plants, genes and cells. The self-replicating vitality of living matter is targeted for consumption and commercial exploitation' (2007: 70). Vandana Shiva, as early as 1997, anticipating the work of Braidotti and others, spoke of 'biopiracy' whereby capitalism now colonizes the interior of bodies – animals, plants, humans – for their *reproductive* potential (embodied in seeds, for instance). The insistence on the value of Life and life-generating material, for Shiva and later feminists, is part of the bio-power complex produced by techno-globalization. In the new biological citizenship (of which more later, in chapter 3) engendered by techno-globalization, women remain subalterns. More recently, and mostly in keeping with the arguments forwarded by Haraway, theorists are proposing a humanism, as manifest in the humanities, as a project of taming the human, a self-domestication (see Bergthaller 2010). Philosophers such as Gilles Deleuze reject the idea of a human evolution as simply anthropocentric. Deleuze thus proposes a biotechnogenesis, with technology and biology symbiotically co-evolving (Pearson 1997: 182). This humanities, with its form of anti-foundationalist humanism, seeks to imagine a whole new world and way of life where man will be *Homo faber* (who seeks to convert everything around him into instruments to serve his needs and desires) driven less by self-interest than by a sense of care for others – a scenario projected in fiction like Margaret Atwood's *Oryx and Crake* (2004) in the character of Snowman/Jimmy (DiMarco 2005).

The work of the feminist philosopher of science Karen Barad demonstrates that the human, like the non-human, emerges in the interaction (relationality, cross-overs and mergers) of discourse and materiality. Barad proposes that the relationship between the social (which includes language) and the scientific is not one of 'static relationality but a doing – the enactment of boundaries – that always entails constitutive exclusions' (2003: 803). For Barad the very apparatus of science (that produces particular forms of things, including humans or life forms) is 'constituted through particular practices' (817). What is significant is that Barad sees these practices as ena-bling the construction of boundaries: 'the differential boundaries between "humans" and "nonhumans", "culture" and "nature", the "social" and the "scientific" are constituted' (817). The very sense of being is the conse-quence of the 'intra-actions' within the apparatus, but also of the apparatus situated in laboratories and even geopolitical spaces. Instead of 'things' or 'objects', Barad calls them 'phenomena' which *emerge* in the intra-actions. Barad therefore calls attention to literary and other discourses as *material* practices (820–1). Materiality, conversely, is discursive: 'material phenomena are inseparable from the apparatuses of bodily production: matter emerges out of and includes as part of its being the ongoing reconfiguring of boundaries' (822).

This is an important contribution to posthumanist thought because Barad seeks to demonstrate how discourses, material practices and meaning-making cannot be disentangled easily. Each is constitutive of the other, and being, with all its gendered, sexualized, racialized, normalized 'meaning' and identity, is to be seen as a *phenomenon*, not simply as the 'effect' or 'cause' of discourse. The human body – matter – emerges as a phenomenon *within* these intra-actions. By refusing to separate the material (human or non-human) bodies from meaning ('the human', 'the non-human') and mean-ing-making apparatuses, and by showing how meaning-making is material even as material is an emergent condition, Barad proposes that the 'human' and 'animal' (as in the meaning of 'human' or 'animal' as particular forms of life with specific properties) are also emergent phenomena. Boundary-marking – human versus animal – is meaning-making, even as the matter (human, animal) emerges within the discursive–material dynamics. The material is already, as she puts it, 'material-discursive' (2003: 824). In Barad we see a reiteration of *process*, of *emergent* conditions, of the intertwining of apparatuses, relations, contexts, matter and semantics that produce what we have come to identify as the human, distinct from animal, plant, bacteria, machine or even other humans. It is in the intra-active process of making boundaries of matter and meaning that the human or animal 'matter' emerges. It is this emphasis on dynamics and process – merging, conver-gence, fusions and fissions – that critical posthumanism will also demon-strate. To cite Barad's posthumanist vision one final time: 'bodies are not objects with inherent boundaries and properties; they are material-discursive phenomena. "Human" bodies are not inherently different from "nonhuman" ones' (823–4).

Critical Race Studies

In Margaret Atwood's *Oryx and Crake* and Octavia Butler's Xenogenesis trilogy, citizens of a new world, or a new age on Earth, first have to lose some of the features of an older humanity – features that eventually led the human race to ecocide. Atwood writes:

What had been altered was nothing less than the ancient primate brain. Gone were its destructive features, the features responsible for the world's current illnesses . . . For instance, racism . . . the Paradice people simply did not register skin colour . . . Since they were neither hunters nor agriculturalists hungry for land, there was no territoriality . . . Their sexuality was not a constant torment to them . . .: they came into heat at regular intervals, as did most mammals other than man . . . They were perfectly adjusted to their habitat, so they would never have to create houses or tools or weapons, or, for that matter clothing. They would have no need to invent any harmful symbolisms, such as kingdoms, icons, gods, or money. (2004: 358)

The Oankali in Octavia Butler modify the humans so as to increase their longevity but also tone down their 'natural' (human?) aggressive instincts. This question of dehumanizing humans or humanizing clones (or should that be re-humanizing?) is best exemplified in Ishiguro's *Never Let Me Go*:

We challenged the entire way the donations programme was being run. Most importantly, we demonstrated to the world that if students were reared in humane, cultivated environments, it was possible for them to grow up to be as sensitive and intelligent as any ordinary human being. Before that, all clones – or students, as we preferred to call [them] – existed only to supply medical science . . . Shadowy objects in test tubes. (2005: 256)

Debating the extent and exact nature of the 'human' in clones, this 'guardian' at Hailsham points to the processes of socialization that make one human, or not. The above statement not only refutes the very belief in an innate, or immanent, humanity, it also demonstrates how socialization and the environment might well alter genetic predispositions. Even clones, designed from gene upwards, can be made into something else, something more, given the right contexts. By speaking of acculturation into humanity, Ishiguro focuses on becoming rather than being, and the measures undertaken to bring clones into the fold of the 'citizenry'.

Elesin's complaint in Wole Soyinka's play *Death and the King's Horseman* captures the dehumanization of the native at the hands of the colonial: '[It] turned me into an infant in the hands of unnamable strangers . . . My will was squelched in the spittle of an alien race' (1984: 11–12). Not only is the black man in the colonial age not a citizen, he is not even human, suggests Soyinka. Colonialism functions by dehumanizing the subject races.

Citizenship and identity predicated upon racial and ethnic identity in human history and the contemporary age are best examined within post-colonial studies. The work of postcolonial thinker Frantz Fanon and later Critical Race Studies (CRS) theorists like Stuart Hall and Henry Louis Gates, Jr, among others, has pointed to the undeniable link between Enlightenment humanism, racism and capitalist modernity, dating back to the early modern period's great slaving voyages, whereby members of particular races or ethnic groups were denied their citizenship, rights and dignity.

CRS shows how, armed with biological theories about the inferiority of the black races, European colonials relegated the Africans to the domain of the non-human and the animal. Fanon argued that the violence of colonialism dehumanizes the native, making him lose his sense of Self. This dehumanization begins when the black man is simply treated as a black body, and is trained to be ashamed of it. There is no attempt to engage with something deeper than the colour of the skin. Because of a violent reductionism, the colonized were reduced to stereotypes of evil (a 'quintessence of evil', as Fanon puts it in *The Wretched of the Earth* – 2004: 6), freezing the native in a static mould, and this reductionism in turn dehumanizes the native: he is made to feel like an animal because he is addressed, described and believed to be an animal by the colonial apparatus. Fanon writes: 'He [the colonizer] speaks of the yellow man's reptilian motions, of the stink of the native quarter, of breeding swarms, of foulness, of spawn, of gesticulations' (7). The act of classifying and naming serves to dehumanize the native into an animal, and therefore something *less* than the human.

As a result of this dehumanization, the black man is forced to do something to restore his sense of Self. Fanon argues that the route to a retrieval of the Self is violence. But what is important for our purposes here is how Fanon sees this retrieved Self of the thus-far dehumanized black man as a means of humanism itself.

Humanism, as we have already noted, divided and ranked people on a scale where the European was at the top and all other races were lower down. This ranking meant the 'lower' races would be dominated or eliminated; in other cases, they would be 'improved' and 'reformed'. In both cases, the word 'human' was attached only to the white races.

Fanon is suspicious of such forms of humanism, and not of humanism in general. Thus, while acknowledging that European humanism did have some relevance (2004: 237), its racist system (colonialism) defeats any humanist programme. Fanon seeks nothing less than the complete overthrow of a humanism based on exclusion and traditional categorizations. In its place he seeks a humanism in which difference is respected.

The human cannot, Fanon suggests, be defined (as classical humanism has done since the Enlightenment) only in opposition to the European model of the 'human'. The African (and, by extension, women, Asians and members of any racial group) must be a human in and of himself, and not evaluated from the European perspective. This humanism involves an ethical recognition: recognizing the identity, personhood and cultural identity of all *Others*, a *mutuality* of recognition, and respecting, but neither erasing/homogenizing nor penalizing, *difference*.

Fanon offers his own brand of humanism here when he *entrusts the task and the project of a more inclusive humanism to the formerly colonized*, i.e., the 'Third World' (Nayar 2013). Fanon's humanism, rather than an individualism, is focused on a collective ethic. It is the solidarity with the *world's* suffering, irrespective of race, colour or geography. Fanon even aligns the colonizing white man with the colonized black, both as victims of a cruel process (1970: 32). Suffering and oppression are unifying factors for his thoughts about humanism – and these factors enable him to call for a consciousness beyond nationalisms. In another essay, 'Letter to the Youth of Africa', Fanon writes: 'It is essential that the oppressed peoples join up with the peoples who are already sovereign if a humanism that can be considered valid is to be built to the dimensions of the universe' (1967: 114). With works such as Fanon's, European humanism's exclusionary biases and beliefs have been exposed.

Revisionist views of humanism such as Fanon's continue to possess considerable relevance today. Take, for instance, the status of the refugee or immigrant in twentieth-century global geopolitics. Individuals and their families seeking asylum or citizenship are treated not simply as members of the human species but as members of particular biological categories. In the USA, Aihwa Ong notes, whiteness is established as a category for citizenship through its contrast with black slaves. Chinese and Asian immigrants were 'cleansed' of ethnic tendencies through paternalistic care, welfare measures and disciplining. That is, they were 'normalized' into Americanness by ensuring they lost some of their ethnic characteristics (2003: 70, 79). Ong argues that, for the immigrants, welfare measures, citizenship, rights and identity itself were premised upon racial polarities: 'The legacy of racializing expectations with regard to market potential, intelligence, mental health, and moral worthiness came to influence at the practical, everyday level the experiences and understanding of both the newcomers and the long-term residents who assisted them' (82–3).

Citizenship projects, Nikolas Rose and Carlos Novas point out, 'have linked their conceptions of citizens to beliefs about the biological existence of human beings, as individuals, as families and lineages, as communities, as populations and races, and as a species' (2005: 440). Citizenship or national identity is defined (and limited) in biological terms. The status of 'person' or citizen remains, therefore, contingent upon biological markers and identities.

Biometric identification – the newest version of cyborgization – and genetic testing bring back into the cultural imaginary and social practices older questions of biological identities and the corporeal foundations of citizenship and belonging. Biometrics – to which I return in chapter 3 – rematerializes the body and its identity in very different ways in this age of electronic dissemination and dematerialization. In the USA, television shows like *African American Lives* – hosted by African American literary theorist Henri Louis Gates, Jr – *Who Do You Think You Are?*, *Faces of America*, etc., have been hugely successful. Tracing ancestry and family history of the African Americans has mushroomed into a very profitable business as well. One can acquire an ancestry kit, use some saliva and discover one's genetic roots. *African Ancestry* offers an 'Ancestry Certificate' at the end of the check. The new genetic determinism that this suggests also ends up reiterating the older biological determinisms that governed racial profiling and stereotyping, but occasionally also throws up surprises (as happened when quite a few of the African American clients discovered that there was some white ancestor in their blood as well). More importantly, those who discovered their roots broadcast their racial selves in what has come to be known as the 'roots and revelations' culture (Nelson and Hwang 2012).

Late twentieth-century critical humanism, as this chapter has demonstrated in its abbreviated survey of critical positions within feminism, technoscience critiques, race studies and poststructuralism, has demolished the myth of the unified, coherent, autonomous, self-identical human subject. It has posited the subject, and biology, as a construct of discourses, of enmeshed and co-evolved species and technologies. Consciousness, rationality, 'normalcy' are all now treated as instantiations of power relations, differentiations achieved through technologies of control and self-regulation that result in inequalities of gender, race, sexuality and ethnicity. By demonstrating the end of the sovereign human subject, critical humanism prepares the ground for the new form of the human, the posthuman.

Critical posthumanism in this book is a *critical-philosophical project* that unravels the discursive, institutional and material structures and processes that have presented the human as unique and bounded even when situated among all other life forms. (In the rest of this book I examine critical posthumanism, although for brevity I shall simply refer to it as 'posthumanism'.) Its philosophical foundations are to be found in new developments in robotics and computer technology where new forms of the human, and the machine, emerge, and in the biological sciences where new theories of the emergence and evolution of life circulate. It also includes a systematic deconstruction of cultural representations that shows how particular discourses of animality, monstrosity and disability enabled the human species to define itself against its Other, the freak/monster, the animal and alternative body-forms.

Posthumanism as *critical approach* and *theoretical methodology* studies cultural representations and discourses that have historically situated the human above other life forms, treated the human as distinct and self-contained, valorized particular features – intellectual, linguistic, physiological, anatomical – as truly, authentically and completely human and constructed a relationship in which the human dominated other life forms. Its ethical reading practice and politics constantly draws attention to those representations and discourses in which, by situating the human above and in control of other life forms, the human species has exterminated animals, marginalized certain kinds of human bodies and, out of this process of exclusion and extermination, defined the human subject as unique. It proposes a 'non-anthropocentric' understanding of life (Hengel 2012: 3) in which human life has always been symbiotically connected to many life forms and technologies.

In its critical and theoretical methodology, critical posthumanism owes a considerable debt to the arguments forwarded by the critical humanism discussed in the preceding section. It, however, differs substantially from critical humanist thought in several ways, which I shall now outline.

First, from the more traditional critiques of humanism (the 'critical humanism' summarized above) critical posthumanism appropriates the idea of the constructedness of the 'normal' human, and its exclusionary definitions and practices. As we have noted, critical humanism argues that there are no *essential* features of the human subject because 'human nature' is socially constructed and therefore knowledge cannot be grounded in the human subject and its cognitive processes because knowledge, like human nature, is socially constructed. Critical posthumanism *begins* with this assumption of the constructed nature of the human – her/his body, functions, attitudes, behaviour, relations, consciousness – in which the very process of construction of the human by the human is exclusionary.

Second, critical posthumanism moves this argument about the constructedness of the normal human to the next, and higher, level by showing how such an exclusionary idea(l) of the human has always had to account for the non-normal human *as well as* the non-human indirectly. Where critical humanism (except the later feminist critiques of Donna Haraway and Rosi Braidotti, animal studies and disability studies) only argued for traditional humanism as excluding variant *human* bodies, races, genders and ethnicities, critical posthumanism proposes that the category of the human was constructed by expelling the animal, the plant and the machine. In other words, where critical humanism unravelled the exclusionary nature of the allegedly sovereign human, critical posthumanism proposes that the sovereign human is in fact a hybrid, constituted by the very forms of life that were excluded to define the limits and identity of the human.

Third, critical posthumanism amplifies the concerns of critical humanism, especially its concern with exclusion, difference and Otherness – racial, gendered, sexual, anatomical, species – and proposes that the human is constituted by difference. It deploys difference and Othering as the cornerstone of human identity. If critical humanism spoke of difference and Othering *within* the human race, critical posthumanism extends this to include the machine, the plant and the animal. It argues that the 'essential' human includes the non-human Others such as the machinic, the plant and the animal.

Critical posthumanism is not a simple binary of the humanist/antihumanist positions outlined above but a whole new conceptualization of the human as a more inclusive, non-unitary entity whose boundaries with the world, with other life forms and species, are porous.

Critical posthumanism is thus a *discourse* of life itself in which interconnections, messy histories, blurred origins, borrowings and adaptations, cross-overs and impurities, dependency and mutuality across species are emphasized over boundedness, self-containment, distinctiveness and agency. 'Life' in posthumanist discourse is discussed as a process of *becoming* through new connections and mergers between species, bodies, functions and technologies. These connections are not about transcendence but about embodiment in what Rosi Braidotti regards as a 'new materialist' notion of life (2006b). Human life is about becoming, but a becoming-with other life forms.

Critical posthumanism is an *ethical project* that asks us to ponder, and act, upon the acknowledgement that life forms have messy, intertwined histories. From borrowed, adapted, merged and mutually dependent origins to coop-erative evolution of species, life forms have always lived and become with others. It asks us to acknowledge that human hierarchization of life forms has resulted in catastrophic effects for/upon animals, forests and plant life and some groups of humans in the form of genocides. Thus critical post-humanism is an ethical position against hierarchization of life forms because such rankings have inevitably resulted in exclusionary practices directed at particular life forms, races and groups.

Further, as Wolfe never tires of reminding us through *What is Posthumanism?* (2010), we share mortality, vulnerability and finitude with animals. In such a context, critical posthumanism calls for an ethical question: how do we live with others on Earth? Val Plumwood's simple yet trenchant declaration about ecological crisis gestures, in posthumanist fashion, at the need to rethink not only what it means to be human but also what modes of the human we need to discard, modify and retain: 'If our species does not survive the ecological crisis, it will probably be due to our failure . . . to work out new ways to live with the earth, to rework ourselves . . . We will go onwards in a different mode of humanity, or not at all' (cited in Roelvink 2012: 3). This does not centre the human, as one might suspect. Joanna Zylinska addresses this suspicion in her study of bioethics for the new media age in explicitly critical posthumanist terms (without calling it such) and in a way anticipates much of this book's key thesis:

alternative bioethics also takes as its task an examination of the historical formation and ideological structuration of 'the human', and of many of the concepts positioned as the human's 'other', such as the animal and the machine. The human does not disappear from the kind of nonhumanist bioethics envisaged here: in fact, it func-tions as its strategic point of entry. (2009: 176)

The human is constituted by difference, with different species, forms of life and systems incorporated into itself. Our empathy toward others, founded in imitation but also perhaps in biology and conditioning (as we shall see in the chapter on the body), suggests that our very consciousness is *embedded* in the social, our minds a part of the social brain.

Finally, posthumanism's ethical vision also poses a *politics* of response and responsibility toward all forms of life, toward difference. When we empathize with a suffering other, we respond (not react), seeing ourselves in the vic-tim's shoes, and this response itself arises from evolutionary processes whereby we have had our consciousness and imitative responses conditioned through embeddedness in a community of several species.

Life, whether of the human or the non-human, is about relationality, difference and connections rather than about isolation, separation and boundedness. If we can use the human as the point of departure to then cognitively and ethically revaluate difference and acknowledge the intrinsically differentiated, different and differential nature of the human, we have a critical posthumanist position. In lieu of the traditional humanist idea of the centrality of the human, posthumanism proposes a 'trans-species egalitarianism' (Braidotti 2006a: 41).

Only when the human recognizes that the Other is within, that the Other shares life with its-self, can the human be more responsible to life itself. The human, in the critical posthumanist vision, always emerges in multiple encounters, relations and transverse connections of vitality with what it deems not-human. It is this sense of connectedness, cross-overs, mergers and relationality that constitutes critical posthumanist politics.

Yet, to see critical posthumanism as founded only in critical theory and/or philosophy – where the nature of the human has been rigorously debated – is to ignore the major contributions made by popular culture, and literature, to the radical rewriting of the idea of the human. This book, while tracing critical posthumanist ideas in popular culture, technoscientific developments and critical theory, and disciplines like animal studies and disability studies, focuses extensively on literary texts. The rationale for constantly bringing back the ethico-political project of critical posthumanism to literature and literary texts must therefore be outlined briefly.

Literature as a humanistic discipline is, the book assumes, the field where the 'nature' of the human in all its experiences, attitudes, behaviour and *possibilities* might be best witnessed. Literature is the domain in which the human is defined, described and debated. Yet, as Geoffrey Galt Harpham presciently points out to us in *Shadows of Ethics*, literature is also the site where we can witness the Other and the different. 'Literature as a genre seems especially committed to an exploration of outsiderhood', writes Harpham (1999: 7). It is the space where Otherness is assigned to some individuals, races and ethnicities, but also where Otherness is engaged with. Conversely, one could say that an engagement with Otherness also effects a certain consciousness about the nature and limits of the Self. When we are preoccupied in the immersive environment of a text with all its affective and sensuous constituents, as we read about the Other, we are also simultaneously aware of our-selves reading. In immersive engagement with the (human, non-human) Other in a literary text, I am made aware of my-self as a human.

From this awareness of the Self and the Other it is possible to speculate, within the immersive experience of the text, upon versions of engagement with the Other as well. Cultural texts (of which surely literature is the pre-eminent form), says Elizabeth Goldberg, speculate about 'how to create cultural images that will not perpetuate cycles of violence and revenge' (2007: 14), and therefore, I might add, *not* perpetuate images of Otherness.

Literature and other cultural texts, continues Goldberg, enable 'a deeper consciousness' that would encourage the readers/audiences to 'act in a way that would contribute to efforts to decrease the occurrence of such events in the future' (14–15), i.e., the occurrence of horrific events to the Other. They contribute to a 'collective consciousness about torture, genocide, and other such violations' (15), or violations of the Other.

Harpham and Goldberg both point to the key role literary texts play in defining the nature of the human, the construction of Otherness and offering up possibilities of different modes of engaging with the Other so that the Other might one day be seen as constitutive of Me or I or Us. It is in literature, argues Andy Mousley, that we can seek an 'upsizing' where particulars in a character's life might be seen to reflect a larger condition, even the 'nearly-universal', as Mousley calls it. 'Different, person-specific' metaphors might indicate, if 'upsized', a metaphysical condition (2010: 832). Mousley proceeds to argue the case for literature as a space where the so-called 'irreducibility' of difference and individualism can yet merge with the desire for connection and the nearly universal. He writes:

Discourses of difference which emphasise the resistance of the local and the particular to the totalising perspectives of grand narratives will continue to exist – and with good reason – but if we are to combat the ongoing dehumanisation, objectification, and commodification of human beings, we need to re-build a 'bigger picture' than discourses of difference tend to allow, of what human beings are like. Literature is one of the places where this larger vision is richly and subtly elaborated. (836)

To adapt Mousley's argument about the humanistic discipline and urges of literature and locate it within the claims made by Harpham and Goldberg cited above, this book locates a whole new attitude toward the human and its so-called 'Other' (whether differently abled humans, animals or machines) emerging in late twentieth-century *literature*. The 'larger vision' of a more inclusive life-being which resists the 'dehumanisation, objectification, and commodification' not just of humans but also of animals, plants and bacteria is to be found in literature. Technoscientific developments that have enabled the rise of posthuman bodies or theories in evolutionary studies and biomedicine that reconceptualize the 'nature' of the human, and their ethico-political implications in terms of the human–non-human relation, are addressed, this book assumes, in the humanistic discipline of literature.

As this book demonstrates, critical posthumanism and its present apotheosis, species cosmopolitanism, manifests in select late twentieth-century literary texts. Marge Piercy, Doris Lessing, Kazuo Ishiguro, William Gibson, Katherine Dunn, Margaret Atwood, Stephenie Meyer, Anne Rice, Ursula Le Guin and Octavia Butler offer various modes of humanistic engagements with the non-human Other. Relying occasionally on the primacy of the human capacity for adaptation, mixing and recognition-response to the Other, these authors speculate about the possibilities of the human. They posit a species cosmopolitanism in which the non-human Other is inextricably a constituent of the human, and where difference and alterity of species, races, bodies and functions (physiologies) is desirable, necessary and integral to the human. 'Humanism' therefore, in this literature, seeks to redraw the boundaries of the human, to see inclusivity in difference and integration/ity with Otherness, even as this literature constantly alerts us to the power relations that haunt all ontology, whether singular or multispecies. The realist utopianism of, say, Octavia Butler refuses a simple valorization of multispecies belonging for precisely this reason: it warns us of new forms of bio-power that produce empowered and subaltern subjects in the new biological citizenship as well, whether for vampires, animals or humans.

2 Consciousness, Biology and the Necessity of Alterity

This chapter traces key moments in biological, philosophical and computational theories that contribute in significant ways to the rise of posthumanist thought.

Critical posthumanism, the concern of this book, sees the human as embedded within an environment, an instantiation of a series of information exchanges, transfers of data and feedback mechanisms that cause the system to close itself off operationally in order to regulate itself as a response to the complexity of the environment. The autonomous human is seen in critical posthumanism as a fiction. The human has co-evolved with both technology and other organisms, and even human perceptions and consciousness are structural changes wrought in the biological system as a response to the neighbourhood.[1] It is therefore an emergent condition. The human is a congeries, a moment in a network. Contemporary critiques of traditional humanism, as noted in the preceding chapter, draw upon various schools of thought – race studies, poststructuralism, social studies of technoscience – to demonstrate how the very notion of the human has been exclusionary, and built upon a process whereby the differently abled, women, particular races and ethnicities, and animals have been treated as inhuman and non-human. Critical posthumanism's philosophical and political purchase emerges from recognizing this exclusionary principle behind all humanist thought. Critical posthumanism is about greater inclusivity, interconnections, co-evolution and mutualities.

This new vision of the human as co-evolving, as an instantiation of a network of connections and exchanges and as embodiment embedded in an environment has been influenced by developments in the domains of cybernetics, consciousness studies, cognitive sciences and computer sciences, and the development of new domains within biomedicine, genetic science and biology such as systems biology.

The present chapter focuses on cognitive studies and systems biology as two domains from where all related developments in philosophy (especially phenomenology, to which biologist Francisco Varela made significant contributions in his later work) and social theory have found their inspiration.

COGNITION, CONSCIOUSNESS AND AUTOPOIESIS

Cybernetics, whose first key moments are to be found in the pioneering Macy Conferences running from 1943 to 1954, sponsored by the Josiah Macy Foundation, was a key early development in thinking about consciousness, information circulation and systems. It was during this series of Conferences, attended by Gregory Bateson, Norbert Wiener, John von Neumann, Claude Shannon, Margaret Mead and others, that ideas about the feedback loop and new theories of cognition and information processing first emerged. Later, a second-order cybernetics in which the focus shifted from individuals to social systems emerged with the work of Heinz von Foerster and Niklas Luhmann, the later work of Humberto Maturana and Francisco Varela and Evan Thompson, whose ideas have found resonance in Cary Wolfe, Mark Hansen, Bruce Clarke and others.

Information Flows, Feedback Loops

The first generation of cybernetic theory emphasized behaviour rather than structural units. Thus the 'human' was characterized by Norbert Wiener (who coined the term 'cybernetics') as driven to communicate. The focus, argued Wiener, Claude Shannon and others, ought to be the *flow* of information and its patterns rather than the materiality of any entity. 'Immaterial' information is of paramount importance in this scheme of things. Human beings, in this view, were no different from any intelligent machines, because they were simply information-processing entities.[2]

This, the first-order cybernetic theory, therefore took the radical step of declaring consciousness, cognition and perception (integral components of human subjectivity) to be constructed: cognition as the effect of an information flow from the environment, and contingent upon the feedback mechanism, upon a *process* rather than material or structural elements.

The focus on information flows across human biology and the environment, machine and man in cybernetic theory marked a major blow to the idea of the unified and self-contained humanist subject, the human. Suddenly, information theory had shaped the human differently, and the human's boundaries with the world were not sacrosanct. The human, it was now proposed, is situated in a continuous feedback loop in which information flows into, out of and across the human and the environment. The feedback loop was essential to ensuring the safety of the system/ entity. Just as the body regulates its internal temperature depending on the rise/fall of temperature in the environment – that is, the body receives the information that the neighbourhood temperature has altered and so changes its internal rheostat by sweating, for example – systems regulate their internal states to adjust to the world outside. The feedback loop therefore is the flow of information from the environment to the body and back again.

Extending this idea of feedback loops in the course of the Conferences, there emerged the notion of reflexivity. Reflexivity is the action whereby the processes through which the system has been made become part of the system. In the last years of the Conferences this reflexivity debate coalesced around the figure of the observer. Heinz von Foerster argued that the observer standing outside the system watching the processes also becomes a part of the feedback loop and therefore a part of the system he/she is observing. Second-order cybernetics was initiated, according to current histories (Hayles 1999), with Foerster's work, and would gather strength most notably in the work of Maturana and Varela.

Autopoiesis

The information feedback loop theory dismantled boundaries by arguing that information flowed into and out of the human body or system into the environment. The radical shift in this view came about with new work in the biology of cognition. In this later view, information did not cross into the body: it triggered changes in the internal structure but changes that were determined by the internal structure itself. That is, it is the internal dynamics of the system that determines the changes in how it observes the world, although the internal dynamics might be 'perturbed' by the information coming from this world. This internal dynamics and interactions of the system that determine what it sees of the world were the focus of autopoietic theory.

A term invented and popularized by Humberto Maturana and Francisco Varela in their 1972 work, autopoiesis is literally 'self' ('auto') and 'creation' or 'production' ('poiesis'). This was the definition provided:

An autopoietic system is organized (defined as a unity) as a network of processes of production (transformation and destruction) of components that produces the components that
1. through their interactions and transformations continuously regenerate and realize the network of processes (relations) that produced them; and
2. constitute it (the machine) as a concrete unity in the space in which they [the components] exist by specifying the topological domain of its realization as such a network. ([1972] 1980: 135)

A 'unity' (defined as 'that which is distinguishable from a background, the sole condition necessary for existence in a given domain. The nature of a unity and the domain in which the unity exists are specified by the process of its distinction and determination' − 138) that meets these two criteria is an autopoietic system.

Simply put:

• An autopoietic living system has identifiable boundaries that separate it from its domain or environment and every system strives to maintain its 'organization' (the set of relations that constitute it as a 'unity'). A system is 'closed' when its processes amongst the components depend only on each other to maintain these processes. Even the changes of state in the system are realized *within* the network of processes.[3]

- The system's properties are not the effect of the individual components of this system but rather the effect of the interactions of the components (the boundary itself is the effect of components' interactions, or of the transformations resulting from the entry of other components into the unity through its boundaries).
- These interactions also, often, change the components of the systems in what is known as 'emergent' behaviour.
- The other components of the unity are also produced by the interactions between the components.

The major contribution of this theory is its reworking of the very idea of 'autonomy'. 'Autonomy' is, for Maturana and Varela, the network of interactions of the components of a system that by their very interactions 'recursively' generate the networks that produced them. The word often used to describe the impact of the environment on the system is 'perturbation'. Contemporary theorists have, however, argued that 'when systems operate in any concrete context, they always and necessarily do so in conjunction with a technical environment whose agency cannot be reduced to mere perturbations – whose agency . . . remains beyond the scope and mastery of the systemic perspective' (Hansen 2009: 115). This last move holds considerable significance for posthumanist thought, and deserves sustained attention – I shall come to it later in this chapter.

The problem of consciousness, both human and computer, has been the concern of several roboticists, philosophers and biologists: Hans Moravec, Daniel Dennett, John McCarthy, Brian Cantwell Smith, Aaron Sloman, among others (for a quick summary, see Zelazo et al. 2007). Contemporary thinking and research has moved beyond the brain–mind model of human consciousness to propose an embodied consciousness that is dispersed. For the posthumanists, this has been a major shift in thinking because it does away with the mind/body dualism but also refuses a centralized mechanism of consciousness that has been the foundation of liberal humanism. It is therefore worth spending some time on these new ideas about consciousness.

If the brain cannot register sensation without inputs from the rest of the body and its sense organs, can we say the brain has consciousness of sensation? Intelligence and consciousness – though by no means are these synonyms – are now seen as existing beyond the brain. Recent research demonstrates that intelligence is not only embodied, it is also environment-dependent (Dourish 2001). Neural 'minibrains', research shows, work best when they are able to collate information from other 'minibrains' to which they are connected. More accurately, the brain's consciousness depends on the body's interactions with the world. The work of Rodney

Brooks, Mark Tilden and others in the field of Artificial Life has also a lot to offer in this thinking through of the distributed and embodied nature of consciousness. Robotics has shown how distributed modules of intelligence gather information and send it to a central processing unit. The central processing unit does not possess a unified view of the world: the view is determined entirely by the information coming in from its distributed network and modules (the robot's 'senses', so to speak). What this means is consciousness is not inherent to the mind/brain: it is an emergent property that is effected only through the collation of information and the interactions of the various parts with the world. The distributed components working randomly, occasionally in tandem, and *in the world*, generate this consciousness.

In Robert Pepperell's summary, then: 'the bodily vehicle and awareness of activity in the surroundings are crucial to good overall performance. This seems to imply some deep unity between the active world and the active, functioning mind' (2003: 18). It is the flow of information from the environment through the body into the brain, which then processes it, that constitutes intelligence or consciousness.

This view of consciousness as an 'epiphenomenon' shows consciousness as an *emergent condition* contingent upon

(i)   the interactions of the various distributed organs with the environment;
(ii) the interactions of these organs amongst themselves and with the brain.

This fits right in with the posthumanist vision of human embodied intelligence that draws its 'selfhood' – assuming that consciousness equals selfhood – from the sum total of the interactions of its parts within an environment. In place of the self-contained consciousness, we now have a consciousness that can only emerge within an environment and through distributed, beyond-the-brain networks.

Neocybernetics, or second-order cybernetics, rejects the idea of mere causal connections: in which the environment offers feedback to the organism and the organism responds through a self-transformation. In neocybernetics, every node in the network is at once a cause and an effect. This is known as pan-causality. There is no centralized structure. Even metabolisms and gene action have been studied through neocybernetics.[4]

Particular schools of philosophy, such as phenomenology, have distinguished between the living organism (the biological body) and living subjectivity. With the emergence of new thinking in philosophy and neurobiology (and the rise of a discipline called neurophenomenology, which is Francisco Varela's later work: 2001), theorists speak of the 'emergence of living subjectivity from living being, including the reciprocal shaping of living being by living subjectivity' (Thompson 2009: 81). This suggests a continuum of the mind, the body and the world. Evan Thompson, Varela's collaborator, offers a neat little schema for understanding this continuum, which links biology and its cognitive processes, the subjectivity of an individual and the world. The schema has five steps:

i.   Life=autopoiesis where the three criteria ([a] boundary-making that [b] contains the networked molecular reactions [c] produces and regenerates itself and the boundary) are sufficient for the organization of a life form.
ii. As a result of the dynamics within this operationally closed autopoietic system, a self emerges in the body.
iii. The emergence of a self implies the emergence of a world in which the self can exist, an environment suitable to that self.
iv. The world/environment of the organism is the sense the organism makes of that world – the sense of the world is the perception and interpretation of the world, as performed by the organism.
v.   Sense-making (Varela's term elaborated by Thompson) is cognition because meaning is not 'out there', but enacted by the organism in its interactions with the world. Living is this sense-making and sense-making is cognition. (2009: 82–3)

Even within the brain, the neurons – where, supposedly, consciousness 'happens' – are only nodes: they *pass on* information to the next neuron in the network. Further, each neuron works only in connection with numerous other elements: blood vessels, chemicals such as peptides and acetylcholine (neurotransmitters), hormones, etc. Susan Greenfield, neurobiologist, sums it up thus: 'One neuron could be a member of a number of different circuits; it would be the specific combination in each case that distinguished one circuit from another. Each circuit would contribute to the phenomenon of a memory, so that no single brain cell or exclusively committed group of cells is wholly responsible; instead the memory would be distributed' (cited in Pepperell 2003: 96).

Consciousness is therefore the interaction of multiple components of the human with the world, even as the world is produced for the human due to this consciousness. And, because we cannot demonstrate that any one component in isolation produces consciousness, we have a non-linear model of consciousness (as opposed to the linear model in which event X produces consciousness Y of the event). This non-linear model that sees consciousness as the result of multiple interactions and events also includes conditions such as the biology (age, sex, health) of the individual and the cultural contexts of the individual (cultural memories, for instance, that affect an individual's perceptions of the world or the event). We therefore have to think of consciousness as *distributed*.

A further discovery, much more recent, seems to suggest a biological foundation for characteristics like empathy – speculative fiction writer Octavia Butler's key theme in the *Parables* series (1993–8) – as well.[5] Mirror neurons in the brain of primates, biologists discovered (di Pellegrino et al. 1992) – thus making lives more complicated for psychologists in the process – are 'fired' not only when the animal picks up an object *but also when it sees another animal pick up an object*. When we learn by imitation, and we understand others' actions, it is possibly because of the work of the mirror-neuron system (Rizzolatti and Craighero 2004). Therefore, in experimental psychologist Cecilia Heyes' words, 'Mirror neurons seem to bridge the gap between one agent and another; to represent "my action" and "your action" in the same way' (2010: 1). Possibly – research in the area is still very new – it is the effect, Heyes proposes, of associative learning. By observing another individual, the fired-up mirror neurons enable one to plan or model one's actions to attain the same end (which is essentially associative learning). While these neurons have mostly been found in monkeys, some researchers believe that humans possess them too (Keysers and Gazzola 2010). Thus gestural communication involves the firing of mirror neurons in the passive observer (Schippers et al. 2010). Often referred to as 'resonance' – when one person's actions in their motor system trigger similar effects in the observer's – mirror-neuron activity is now being seen as a causal factor in empathy. Daniel Siegel speaks of 'resonance circuits' with their mirror-neuron system, superior temporal cortex, middle prefrontal regions that produce empathy and attunement and even create in our minds 'representations of other people's minds' (2007: 168). 'Empathic concerns', where one's feelings are affected by seeing the feelings of others (leading to idiomatic expressions about perspective such as 'I try to put myself in the other's shoes'), are perhaps rooted in such mirror-neuron activity (Gazzola et al. 2006). Although this involves seeing the other as 'rotated versions of ourselves', we do not attribute the observed action to ourselves: we do have cues for the self–other differentiation. Cognitive biologists argue that 'by transposing oneself to the location of the other, one sees things as she/he would see them', which relies 'on the mechanism that operates the translation of the egocentric coordinates at a different spatial location' (Jeannerod and Anquetil 2009: 360). This simultaneous transposition and differentiation is, the biologists now believe, the work of mirror neurons. Social interactions involve partners who are not 'agent' and 'observer' respectively, but both agents and observers simultaneously, suggesting a reciprocity of emotions and actions, further implying that the observation of other people's distress or pain 'activates regions [in the brain] involved in experiencing similar emotions' (Keysers and Fadiga 2009: 195–6). The leading researcher on mirror neurons, Christian Keysers, writes, in what is surely a posthumanist doctrine:

people around us are no longer just part of 'the world out there' . . . Through shared circuits, the people around us, their actions and their emotions, permeate into many areas of our brain that were formerly the safe harbors of our identity: our motor system and our feelings. The border between individuals becomes permeable . . . invisible strings of shared circuits tie our minds together, creating the fabric of an organic system that goes beyond the individual. (2011: 117)

This 'social brain' is precisely what we see in Butler's *Parables, Mind of My Mind* (1997), and films such as *Avatar* (2009).

If the mirror-neuron theory is true of humans, as it seems to be for several primates, then we have the biological basis of empathy. Further, if there is a biological basis to empathetic understanding, it is theoretically possible to argue that surgical and chemical interventions in the neurological structures of human brains can make them less or more empathetic toward others, thus suggesting that the arguments of John Harris and others (see chapters 5 and 6), which favour the making of a more *humane* human through posthumanist changes, are feasible.

BIOLOGY, SYSTEMS AND SYSTEMS BIOLOGY

Studies since the 1970s have redefined human biology and its evolution in very interesting ways for the posthumanist philosophers to build on. Of these, two particular developments stand out: symbiogenesis and systems theory.

Symbiogenesis

In Octavia Butler's climactic volume of the series *Xenogenesis, Imago*, we are told that the Oankali race had evolved through 'invasion, acquisition, duplication, and symbiosis' (1989: 23). This echoes almost exactly the new theories of evolution.

The work of Lynn Margulis has offered an entirely new way of looking at the evolution of life and life forms. In her *Symbiosis in Cell Evolution* (1981) Margulis wrote: 'The evolution of symbioses – that is, the formation of permanent associations between organisms of different species – has been the origin of some parts of eukaryotic cells' (1).

This apparently simple sentence means much more if we were to acknowledge its deeper significance: life and complex life forms have evolved because 'free-living' bacteria were symbiotically absorbed into certain host cells. Margulis' work shows that mitochondria, which generate the energy in cells, were once bacteria. Mitochondria 'developed efficient oxygen-respiring capabilities when they were still free-living bacteria' (3). The functions of particular cell organelles evolved long before the eukaryotic cell itself existed – these functions were later symbiotically absorbed into eukaryotic cells and thus furthered their functions and evolution. Margulis summarizes the entire evolutionary scheme through symbiogenesis (the term used to describe the symbiotic evolution of life):

The symbiotic complexes that became plant and animal cells have never stopped evolving. Metabolic and developmental innovations created new levels of organization impossible to the partners on their own. The symbioses became more and more integrated, and the partners more dependent on each other. The dependence between each organelle and the metabolic products of the others is now so complete that only with modern techniques of ultrastructural analysis and *in situ* chemistry can the metabolic pathways of the original partners be traced, and even now with difficulty. (5)

Margulis also proposes 'symbiotic complexes' which 'unite, in a single individual, genes that were once separate' (201). New life forms and individuals are formed, she argues, as 'products of the merging of independent genetic systems' (201). It is on these systems that the process of natural selection (the core of Darwinian evolution) acts, 'retaining and modifying it because the partnership leaves more offspring than the separate individual partners' (201). In other words (and since the reproduction of a species' genes is the cornerstone of all evolution, and indeed the very foundation for life), any system that offers more reproductive capabilities will be picked by natural selection. Symbiosis, which facilitates this extra reproductive mileage for many organisms, is therefore encouraged by natural selection, in Margulis' theory. Cells, writes Margulis elsewhere, 'evolved by "serial symbiosis"' which is 'the acquisition and integration of particular bacteria in a definite sequence' (2000: 143). In plants, both the key organelles, chloroplasts and mitochondria, were originally independent bacteria that were absorbed into the evolving life form. Thus what enables plant cells to perform their functions is their symbiotic relationship with these absorbed elements, although, as Margulis states above, the original bacterial functions (that is, in the pre-absorption state) can no longer be easily mapped. It is symbiosis that has produced higher forms of life, including the human.

The theoretical biologist Marcello Barbieri, working along the same lines as Margulis, has proposed that all organisms are networks and not sovereign, autonomous entities. Barbieri treats all organisms as the effect of a relational, interactive networking of genetic materials (the genotype), apparatuses and processes (ribotype) that transform genetic materials into proteins and higher, complex structures, and finally the embodiment (phenotype) of these two preceding processes. As Richard Doyle points out, in Barbieri's scheme, the DNA is the information code for life, but is never *adequate* for life to emerge. That is, Barbieri's model demands an entire network of processes and materials that can 'produce' life: the genetic materials are not the be-all and end-all of life (Doyle 2003: 22.3).

Exploring the origins of life through natural selection, Stuart Kauffman seeks an explanation within the self-organization of organisms. Kauffman proposes that the 'origin of life was a quite probable consequence of the collective properties of catalytic polymers . . . many properties of organisms may be probable emergent collective properties of their constituents' (1993: 22). Natural selection maintains complex biological systems that are 'poised on the boundary . . . between order and chaos' (xv). Kauffman further argues that selection only maintains this system, it does not determine the self-organization of the system: 'complex systems exhibit spontaneous order, that order can shine through not because of selection, but despite it' (xv). Kauffman's thesis, to which we return below, is that the self-organization of an organism is the result of its internal complexity in which change is only triggered by the environment, limited by the organism's internal complexity and constituents, and not determined by the environment. In fact the self-organization of the organism and the order it exhibits ensure that 'selection cannot ignore that order' (xvii). Kauffman also sees evolution as co-evolution and symbiosis (297).

Related studies and theories have come from Scott Gilbert (2002). Gilbert has proposed that the 'developing body', right from the embryo stage, is dependent on the environment, that genes manifest as body shape, function or behaviour based on their interactions with the environment. 'Epigenetics', as this branch of biology is called, links genes to environment. Gilbert writes: 'The developing body is dependent upon the bodies of other species and actually contains some of these bodies. In this appreciation of development, the genome is seen to have evolved such that it can interact with the biotic components of its environment, and that there are environmental cues that are essential in producing the particular phenotype' (203). One genotype does not produce just one phenotype, but a spectrum of phenotypes (a phenomenon called 'developmental plasticity'). The same population might have different phenotypes produced from a single genotype, depending on the environment. Thus, studies have shown how particular species modify their development in response to the presence of predator chemicals in their environment. Certain invertebrate species like *Daphnia* produce a different morphology when growing in pond water because the water contains predatory larvae (Gilbert 2002: 209).

The implications of this mode of development of phenotypes for theories of co-evolution – a central component, as I have suggested, of the re-envisioning of life, of the human, in critical posthumanist thought – should be obvious. To cite here Gilbert's summary of these implications:

development is regulated not only from 'below' (i.e., from our genome), but also from 'above' (from the environment). What we are depends on both endowment and experience . . . we find that two organisms are required for the development of a particular structure. This is even more striking in symbiotic associations during 'normal' development. Here, gene expression in one species is regulated by products from another species, and the species have co-evolved to maintain this developmental relationship. The two (or more) organisms work together to develop each other. (211)

The 'I', says Gilbert, is the 'permeable I' (211), thus drawing attention to life's cross-over, intersection, mergers and acquisitions of other life forms.

A major contributor to this idea of the 'permeable I' – and one which effectively dismantles the (humanist) notion of the self-contained 'I' that is distinct from the world – comes from recent research in immunology.

Models of immunology have, since the mid twentieth century, proposed that the human body's immune system (analogous to its Self) fights foreign bodies (the non-Self, or the outsider). The Self/non-Self model of the immune system therefore fits right in with the notion of the coherent, autonomous individual Self. In this model, elements of the body's immune system are activated only by the presence (or invasion) of foreign bodies: they are not activated by the Self. Pradeu and Carosella phrase it thus: 'the immune "self" consists of the unfolding of internal processes (self-definition), the result of which must always be defended against any external presence (enclosure)' (2006: 247). But it has now been proved that the principles that (i) 'no entity originating from the organism will trigger an immune reaction', and (ii) 'every foreign (originating from the outside) entity will trigger an immune reaction', are both false.

Phagocytosis of dead cells and auto-regulation of T-lymphocytes indicate that the immune system *does* react to the constituents of the Self. Pradeu and Carosella write:

> During the selection of lymphocytes in primary lymphoid organs (that is, thymus for T lymphocytes, and bone marrow for B lymphocytes), cells which react strongly to the patterns presented to them and those which do not react to these patterns are eliminated. Hence, a lymphocyte survives in primary lymphoid organs if, and only if, it reacts weakly to the 'self' constituents. (238)

Thus 'some immune cells interact with normal, endogenous components of the organism'. Interaction and activation of immune cells in many cases relies on other components of the Self, thus proving the principle that immune cells do not react to entities originating within the Self to be false.

Next, our bodies are made of millions of bacteria and other organisms. The gut alone has about 10^{14} microorganisms which help digestion. Several parasites, of malaria and other diseases, live in the human body for years, with no palpable effect. The foetal entity, usually, is not rejected by the mother's body (foetomaternal tolerance). More fascinating is the discovery that 'components originating from the child have been found in the mother's organism up to 27 years after birth' (Pradeu and Carosella 2006: 240). Clearly, then, the immune system does *not* react to these foreign entities, thus proving the principle that every foreign body triggers an immune response from the Self to be false.

Pradeu and Carosella propose, in lieu of the Self/non-Self model of immunity, a continuity model. Immune cells react to molecular patterns (called epitopes) when these epitopes are different from the patterns the cells *constantly* interact with, whether the patterns are Self-originating or foreign-originating. Any break in the continuity of the patterns, wherever the cause lies, is what triggers the immune system. The implications of this shift in conceptions of the immune system are interesting for us in our exploration of the symbiogenetic Self.

If the immune system is triggered by events within the Self, then it indicates that the Self cannot be treated as immune to itself. That is, destructive immune action is triggered not always by external causes but by internal ones as well. The Self is not sacred, coherent, and the foreign is not always invasive in this model. Identity therefore is not based on the *substance* (the material, presumably bounded) of the organism, but on its *continuity* with the world outside. As Pradeu and Carosella put it, 'identity as substance is based on the idea that, in spite of the changes that affect any individual entity, there is a metaphysical core that is preserved throughout time' (246). This model, as we have just seen, is clearly untenable. What Pradeu and Carosella forward, instead, is the view that 'Biological identity is . . . continuous and open, which means that it is defined as a succession of states without a permanent core, and that the integration of "foreign" elements is in many circumstances a normal and necessary process in organisms' (248). There is no bounded, coherent, autonomous self; even the immune system that makes the Self a 'fortress' (Pradeu and Carosella's term: 248) depends on the arrival of perturbations from the environment and the system's self-regulation by accounting for this continuity with the environment.

Alphonso Lingis notes that all life forms co-exist with other life forms: indeed in many cases the basic functions of life are possible only because of this symbiotic relationship. Sea anemones, for instance, digest food because a particular kind of algae resides in their orifice, which breaks down the food particles (2003: 165). In a quick summary of symbiosis and human life which is worth quoting in full, Lingis writes:

Human animals live in symbiosis with thousands of species of anaerobic bacteria, six hundred species in our mouths which neutralize the toxins all plants produce to ward off their enemies, four hundred species in our intestines, without which we could not digest and absorb the food we ingest. Some synthesize vitamins, others produce polysaccharides or sugars our bodies need. The number of microbes that colonize our bodies exceeds the number of cells in our bodies by up to a hundredfold. Macrophages in our bloodstream hunt and devour trillions of bacteria and viruses entering our porous bodies continually. They replicate with their own DNA and RNA and not ours. They, and not some Aristotelian form, are true agencies of our individuation as organisms. When did those bacteria take up lodging in our digestive system, these macrophages take up lodging in our bloodstream?

We also live in symbiosis with rice, wheat, and corn fields, with berry thickets and vegetable patches, and also with the nitrogen-fixing bacteria in the soil that their rootlets enter into symbiosis with in order to grow and feed the stalk, leaves, and seeds or fruit. We also move and feel in symbiosis with other mammals, birds, reptiles, and fish. (166)

Commentators draw attention to the depth, width and intensity of human interactions with other species and the environment:

We only have to consider the perpetual exchange of liquids, chemicals and energies in the form of urine, faeces, menstrual fluid, hair, air, sperm, food, water, skin, sound, light, and heat to recognise how deeply integrated into our environment we are. Because of this perpetual exchange between the living human organism and its surroundings, there can be no fixed state of a living human. (Pepperell 2003: 20)

In the early stages of development, there is greater interaction between species and genes. As the systems and life forms become more complex internally (a phenotypic differentiation, in biological terms), a species differentiation occurs and the boundaries harden, with the interactions becoming weaker. Phenotypic differentiation is 'amplified' by genetic difference (Kaneko 2006: 292). That is, in the early stages of the evolution of life forms, the two species co-exist. The third stage, when species are totally differentiated and their multispecies origins are now blurred (except when revealed through detailed studies of the chemical processes, as Lynn Margulis notes in the passage cited above) and they 'grow' differently:

Only at this third stage, each group starts to exist by its own. Even if one group of units is isolated, no offspring with the phenotype of the other group appears. Now the two groups exist on their own. Such a fixation of phenotypes is possible through the evolution of genes (parameters). In other words, the differentiation is fixed into the genes (parameters). Now each group exists as an independent 'species', separated both genetically and phenotypically. The initial phenotypic change introduced by interaction is fixed to genes, and the 'speciation process' is completed. (Kaneko 2006: 293)

If we were to perform a genetic reductionism and claim uniqueness of the *Homo sapiens* on the foundations of distinctive species gene make-up, then there is more trouble ahead. First, there is no uniquely human DNA. Second, humans differ genomically from chimps by about 1.2–1.6 per cent. Third, and much worse, we share DNA with yeast, worms and mice that (or should that be 'who'?) are therefore, genetically speaking, related to us.

This new biology erodes the idea of a self-contained human (or any life form, for that matter). It shows how dependency characterizes life itself. It erodes, also, the idea of a sovereign, autonomous, bounded life form, postulating, in its stead, a congeries of genetic sources, multispecies origins and multispecies evolution. Difference, multiplicities, networks, exchanges and mergers characterize all life. In Stuart Kauffman's words: 'the origin of life [is] an expected emergent collective property of a modestly complex mixture of catalytic polymers . . . which catalyse one another's formation . . . The origin of life was not an enormously improbable event, but lawlike and governed by new principles of self-organization in complex webs of catalysts' (1993: xvi).

In the posthumanist vision this means, simply, we acknowledge that we *are* Others, and therefore the human intolerance of the Other's difference – of ethnicities, life forms, species, bodies, skin colour, languages – is not simply untenable but also unethical since we have evolved *with*, and live because of, these 'others', and share more than just the Earth with them. Rosi Braidotti sums up the posthuman vision of life that such biological theories posit when she speaks of the self as an expanded relational self whose 'relational capacity . . . is not confined within our species but . . . includes all non-anthropomorphic elements. Living matter . . . is intelligent and self-organizing, but it is so precisely because it is not disconnected from the rest of organic life . . . the non-human, vital force of life' (2013: 60).

Systems Biology

The body is an autopoietic system of interactions that seeks to demarcate itself from the environment in which it is situated. Systems, like life forms, respond to the complexity of this environment by *reorganizing themselves internally*: 'As the complexity of a collection of polymer catalysts increases, a critical complexity threshold is reached. Beyond this threshold, the probability that a subsystem of polymers exists in which formation of each member is catalysed by other members of the subsystem becomes very high. Such sets of polymers are autocatalytic and reproduce collectively' (Kauffman 1993: 288). Kauffman is pointing to the ability of a system to regulate and reproduce itself as a result of the interactions amongst its constituents.

Contemporary theories in biology argue that bodies are simultaneously open and closed. They are systems that are 'open' because the effects of the setting/environment – such as flows of energy or information – enter the system. But they are 'closed' because the system's organization is self-referential (its components interacting with each other within). The system is *different* from, bounded from, but in interaction with, the environment.

Ludwig von Bertalanffy, a biologist, developed a 'systems' view of biological organisms in which he proposed that one cannot hope to understand an organism by reducing it to its constituent elements. As he put it, 'constitutive characteristics are not explainable from characteristics of isolated parts' (cited in Doyle 2003: 147). Bertalanffy goes on to state: 'the characteristics of the complex, therefore, compared to those of the elements, appear as "new" or "emergent"' (cited in Doyle 2003: 147).

In systems theory, of which systems biology is an offshoot, it is not enough to study individual components of any organism or system. One has to study the interactions of these components amongst themselves but also with their environment. Older systems biology theories therefore rejected, as can be imagined, genetic studies for their reductionism because, in their view, to reduce life to only its genetic 'code' is to ignore the articulation of this code in particular settings (environments). As a recent textbook puts it, 'the existence of certain molecules or some chemical structure is not a sufficient condition for life' (Kaneko 2006: 1).

To take one example, systems biology demonstrates how cell metabolism demands the coordination of multiple elements – from information transfer to energy and chemicals. It sees metabolism or any activity as a result of 'perturbations' coming from the environment or proximate conditions that then affect the particular elements in a system. When perturbations affect one element, that element's interactions with another in the metabolic pathway are also affected, and those affected elements affect others, and so on. This means a particular effect emerges from the perturbation travelling along multiple pathways within an organism. The elements therefore function not only because of their structural features but because of this set of perturbations traversing them. Once again, what we see here is systems biology's emphasis on *relational* behaviour and functions rather than isolated elements and structures.

Suppose we were to take cell division as an example of this principle of interactions and relational behaviour. Cells that make up the heart or liver divide till the organs reach a certain size – and then they stop dividing. If a section of the liver were to be removed, the remaining cells would multiply till such time as the original size was acquired. So how do the cells in these organs know when the right size is reached and therefore they can stop dividing? Cell division is a localized process but somehow the cells in these organs know their 'connections' with the whole organ/body. It is almost as though the organ, with its many cells, is able to transmit the information about the right size to each of the cells, so that every cell has a sense of the organ as a whole. Complex systems biology will tell us that this simply means we cannot study the properties of individual cells: we need to study them in their interactions with the whole, as *local, immediate and individual practices and functions are determined through the interaction of part and whole.*

Systems biology refuses to grant any primary importance to genetic structure or the informational code (DNA). It sees the biological body as a system open to the environment in which it resides, and with which it is in constant interaction (energy transfer, information transfer, etc.). It is a set of processes constituted by multiple elements in interaction.

To summarize systems biology:

- it focuses on the interactions and relations between elements rather than the structural features and properties of elements in any system;
- it sees metabolism and such activities of the system as emergent conditions, emerging through this set of networks and interactions of elements and not inherent in any particular structural feature of the organism;
- it focuses on the many intersections and pathways the elements form, and through which the perturbations of the environment impact the elements.

The body in systems biology is thus:
distributed within/across these pathways and interactions, with multiple nodes and intersectional processes, affected by many perturbations from the

environment that affect the elements which affect more elements (and so on) thereby producing metabolism, cell activity, consciousness and other effects, and is emphatically *not* a self-contained, bounded entity.

If we think carefully about this view of biology, it reiterates for metabolism or cell activity what consciousness studies has claimed about intelligence (as noted in the preceding section): that consciousness is an emergent condition that comes out of the interaction of networked elements in an organism and the interaction of these elements with the active world.

The stability and functions within a system, from this reading, are dependent upon the information coming from the external environment. Thus, the properties within a system emerge as a result of the interaction of components due to external stimuli (what is called 'first-order emergence'). This does not mean that all/any stimuli from the external environment, via the feedback loop, introduce the fluctuations in cell function. Rather, the amplification or 'reduction' in fluctuations in response to external stimuli is *dependent upon the internal state of the system*. The implications of this are interesting. If the internal complexity of the organism only selectively amplifies the fluctuations, it follows that 'the fluctuations appearing outside the cell too can be regarded to some degree as a product of the change of the internal state of the cell' (Kaneko 2006: 62).[6] To phrase this differently, *what count as perturbations and fluctuations in the environment is determined by the organism's structure*. Thus, to say that the environment impacts upon the nervous system is not accurate: the environment triggers certain structural changes in the organism but cannot determine the *direction* or *magnitude* of these changes, and the impact of the environment is determined by the limits set by the system itself (and here we see systems biology coming closer to the working of the autopoietic system of Maturana and Varela). As Stuart Kauffman puts it, 'life may have started with a critical complexity, then simplified under selection' (1993: 343), but with both complexity and simplification determined by the internal order of the system/organism.

Fluctuations might also be introduced as a result of the very process of the evolution of the cell/system. When the organ/organism/system has evolved the capacity to evolve, we have second-order emergence. The interactions of the components (in response to external information but limited by their structure) evolve in directions that cannot be predicted accurately. The interactions of the components mean simply its *potential* to evolve. 'Potential' becomes the keyword in latter-day posthumanist philosophy as well.

DEALING WITH/IN ALTERITY

I have already drawn attention to theories in biology, systems theory and cybernetics in which the human's boundaries, autonomy and coherence have been called into question. In this, the concluding section of the chapter,

I focus on a strand of thought that I believe is central to the philosophical position of posthumanism.

Posthumanism is all about the embedding of embodied systems in environments where the system evolves with other entities, organic and inorganic, in the environment in a mutually sustaining relationship. It is a philosophical position that sees alterity (Otherness and its concomitant characteristic, difference) as constitutive of the human/system. It is this role of alterity that I now turn to as a dry run for my more elaborate argument about posthumanism as being about companion species in the last chapter.

Alterity here is dealt with as the difference and separation of a system or entity such as the body from its Other or the environment. If theories of the autopoietic systems have spoken of the system as operationally closed-off, and therefore distinct, from its environments except for the perturbations impacting upon it, contemporary models of systems offer another account. This section looks at three thinkers who have reformulated the idea of closure in autopoietic systems: Mark Hansen, Andy Clark and Katherine Hayles.

Mark Hansen proposes that alongside systems that are closed to the impact of the environment they occupy, we can also think of 'system–environment hybrids' (SEHs) whose autonomy includes a 'constitutive relation with alterity' (2009: 115). What Hansen rightly emphasizes is that no system is completely closed autopoietically. In system–environment hybrid conditions, Hansen notes, the 'operation of an SEH does not involve all aspects and possibilities of a system or of each system involved and . . . it does not involve all aspects of the environment, all possibilities for environmental agency' (118). Hansen emphasizes that closure in any system occurs when the cognitive operations performed by either system or environment (or both) are 'selective'. Arguing for the environment as mere 'trigger', as theorists of autopoiesis do, is to ignore the considerable agency environment does possess, according to Hansen.

Andy Clark (2004) calls attention to the flexibility inherent in all living organisms. Clark notes that our relationship with, say, writing tools is not simply one of human+typewriter or human hand+pen. Rather, the 'merger' (his term) of hand and pen is beyond the physical relationship: we often *imagine* or *think* ourselves writing. This 'merger' is what Clark refers to as 'not just external props' but 'deep and integral parts of the problem-solving systems we now identify as human intelligence'. This is an important shift in thinking through the very idea of prosthesis and environment. What Clark is drawing attention to is the complexity of the system to have already rewired itself to consider the external prop or aid. The system is not closed operationally to the environment – on the contrary, the environment has a very real 'agency' (as Hansen calls it) in the system's reconstitution of itself. (This is, of course, biologically true of all organisms. The system/organism tries to maintain its internal complexity in a stable form – operational closure – but this act of maintenance requires that the system keeps a constant in-flow of materials and chemicals for the metabolic processes that keep the system alive. The operational closure of a system is always accompanied, in other words, by its openness to the environment.) The rewiring of the internal complexity of the system is a feature of the system's flexibility, and a system has the potential to rewire itself even when – and this is crucial – there is no information flow from the environment to the system. Such a 'merger' as a human thinking about writing is an excellent instance of the SEH that Hansen argues for.

One could consider cultural practices and props as functioning this way. Local cultural practices are integral to the way we think. There is no need for information flows, or even the immediate proximity of the event or practice, for the mind to process the event. Socialization over a period ensures that we have wired our system to think along specific lines. These are all instances of the SEH that Hansen sees as contradicting the idea of autopoietic systems.

Hansen makes one more important move here. Continuing the earlier theme in Maturana and Varela of the system configuring itself through an interaction of its elements, Hansen proposes that we see the human as possessing 'multiple and heterogeneous forms of autonomy' (2009: 129). Any organism (and here Hansen is building on the later work of Varela) in its process of emergence integrates the interactional domain into its processes. That is, emergent selfhood renders the interactional domain a factor in the 'ongoing evolution' of the system (129). What Hansen is getting at here is the necessity to see any sense of selfhood and emergence as always already incorporating the interactional environment. Evolution itself is a history of this incorporation–interaction in which a system or organism's teleology, or growth, is not the inherent, immanent feature of the organism but rather, in Evan Thompson's pithy formulation, 'an emergent relational one that belongs to a concrete autopoietic organization system interacting with its environment' (2009: 88).

The materiality of a system, especially a living system, is the effect of this SEH. Computation, as Katherine Hayles sees it, is at once technological, cultural and ontological. It is the process through which the materiality of the human body is possible, where the body and subjectivity are hybridized through the dynamics of play between physical objects, intentions and significations. Hayles notes how the mother's voice, telling stories that once gave 'life' to the writing that Mama read from, has now been replaced by the beeps and clicks of the computer: 'If the mother's voice was the link connecting subjectivity with writing, humans with natural environments, then the computer's beeps, clicks, and tones are the links connecting contemporary subjectivities to electronic environments, humans to the Computational Universe' (2005: 4). Subjectivity of the system in this reading is an emergent property that accounts for the environment – electronic, Mama's voice, writing, etc. – into its self-making. Hayles, like Hansen, sees the human–machine interaction as mutually constitutive, and subjectivity as a hybridized condition that emerges in this interaction when the 'subject' accounts for the alterity that is the machine, in-corporates it into itself. Hayles summarizes the alterity argument for machines and humans thus:

Human action and agency are understood as embodied processes sharing important characteristics with the processes taking place within computational media, including possibilities for evolution and emergence . . . An essential component of coming to terms with the ethical implications of intelligent machines is recognizing the mutuality of our interactions with them, the complex dynamics through which they create us even as we create them . . . The experience of interacting with them changes me incrementally, so the person who emerges from the encounter is not exactly the same person who began it. (243)

What emerges from this discussion is a sense of the living system not as an autopoietically closed system but one whose internal complexity accounts for the radically different external environment even when the environment is not exactly sending information into the system. The physical settings of our lives ensure that the rewiring of imagination and neural processes now incorporate the sense of anticipation ('I will have to drive', or 'I have to write that on a fresh Word doc') of using a machine. The 'change' that Hayles emphasizes is the emergence of systems. But it is also about potential – of the system to reformat itself in anticipation of a dealing with the Other.

Theories of cognition, consciousness, machine intelligence and biology contribute to posthumanist thought by emphasizing

- co-evolution and multispecies origins of life;
- the necessity of alterity to subjectivity;
- the linkage of embodied life with environments;
- the emergent (rather than immanent) nature of consciousness and the self;
- the stability of systems in dynamic interaction with environments.

To cite Pepperell on the new model of consciousness once more:

If we can start to see how the most 'sacred' of human attributes, such as conscious experience, creativity, and aesthetic appreciation, operate in ways not dissected from other functions in the universe, then we are moving away from the notion of humans as unique, isolated entities and towards a conception of existence in which the human is totally integrated with the world in all its manifestations, including nature, technology, and other beings. (2003: 100)

By refusing to see human or any subjectivity as self-contained, sovereign and independent, the new theories reject the centrality of humankind in the world. The constant reiteration of difference and multiplicities in these theories call attention to the necessary imbrication of the human with the world, where even subjectivity – the core of the liberal humanist project – is seen only as emergent when the feedback loops and the interactions of organism and environment are effected. Instead of linear tree-diagrams of ancestry, what we have now is the rhizome, interconnected networks wherein life emerges, sometimes in conjunction with the non-living. From this launchpad, posthumanism can now proceed to discuss alterity in its multiple forms, rejecting the human intolerance to Otherness or difference, showing alterity as constitutive of subjectivity and moving toward an entirely new conceptualization of the human, climaxing of course in the posthumanist vision of companion species (to which I shall come in the last chapter).

3 The Body, Reformatted

In Steven Spielberg's blockbuster *Jurassic Park* (1993), one of the terrifying dinosaurs hunting the children passes by a bank of monitors. The camera shows the text on the monitors reflected onto the creature. The text scrolling across the screen is A–G–T–C in various sequences. ATGC: the constituent nucleic bases of DNA and the manifestation of these in the form of the monster in a symbolic embodiment of the book of life. In Koji Suzuki's *Ring* trilogy (1991–8) – now successful films as well – a tape becomes the source of death. The electronic communication that is the tape is linked to the transmission of disease. The tape summons up a dead girl (Samara in the Hollywood version of the film), or a ghost, who uses television and contemporary technology to wreak vengeance upon the world. She mediates the medium in order to modify the codes of transmission. In the *Terminator* films, the threat is not from a machine that is ruthless in its intent but from the condition that the machine can *morph* into anything it wants to be: it is not in its radical difference from the human body or form that horror lies but in its *similarity* to the human, being taken for and passing as human. In the posthuman worlds of science fiction, machines and humans, intelligent robots and humans, all resemble each other. The ontological cross-over, articulated as passing bodies – passing here in the sense of masquerading as, taking the form, appearance and identity of, something/ someone else – is what frightens us. Another kind of morphing that suggests posthuman ontologies – again expressed in form – is seen in the Michael Bay *Transformers* films (2007–11). Ordinary cars, trucks and things that suddenly morph into gigantic machines are at war with each other – a whole tribal warfare among machine-races is at hand. Perfectly ordinary vehicles meant for human use are transformed into threats to the humans. All these examples from popular culture suggest a posthuman world of ontological fluidity at hand. Identities, including physiological and anatomical (i.e., biological) ones, are fluid, forms are open to change and modulate, often seamlessly (as in the case of *Transformers* and *Terminator*), into each other. The age of the integral/integrated, bounded body and identity is over: all are multiples, fluid, networked and capable of morphing into, or connecting with, some other body/ies as never before.

Science fiction and film have contributed much to our cultural imaginary regarding the nature of bodies. Cyborg bodies and clones have been the stuff of popular culture long enough for these bodies to become recognizable as variants of the normal human body. Posthumanist thought, which argues a strong case for the human as a constructed category built on exclusions even as its very identity is constituted through a close *assemblage* and *interface* with animals, machines and environments, in its most popular articulation often focuses on the body as a site for the new interpretations of the human.

The human body is generally taken to be a matter for biologists – pathologists, anatomists, physicians, among others. However, it is also a truism to say that the body has always been *mediated* by technological devices developed by various cultures: from paintings, sketches and etchings to photography and film. This means that common or medical, philosophical or speculative knowledge about – and interpretation of – the body is always already mediated by the structures that constitute the production of this knowledge. These structures are, of course, cultural and social. Certain tribes, for example, do not allow photographing of the body. Aesthetics generates particular forms of knowing of bodies. Even my sense of the self – this is *me* – and my subjectivity is mediated by how my historical and cultural moment has mediated my body for my own consumption. I recognize myself through the aesthetic, biological, medical, philosophical, religious paradigms that produce and mediate the idea of the normal, beautiful, sick or aged body for me. Even a biological understanding of the body is, in other words, never an isolated and objective understanding: biologism is a cultural condition through which particular views of the proper functioning of the body are produced within medical practices. Likewise, philosophical or psychological understandings of the body are also produced within particular social and cultural moments.

Before we proceed with the posthumanist version of the human body – and I homogenize all variant models of the human into one here – it is essential to trace the trajectory taken by the human body to bring it to the present moment in which its essence or boundaries are called into question.

BIOMEDIA, THE BODY MATHEMATIZED AND POSTVITAL LIFE

With the genetic revolution, initiated when James Watson and Francis Crick demonstrated that the so-called 'biological' features of the human could be traced to a set of chemicals working in assorted combinations, the genetic code emerged as the dominant paradigm through which not only biologists and medical practitioners but also the general lay public saw the body. The discovery of deoxyribonucleic acid, or DNA, radically altered medical and cultural perceptions of the human body, much as surgical and anatomical dissection did in the early modern period (see Sawday 1995). As Judith Roof (2007) has demonstrated in her admirable work, the human body began to be seen as an articulation of a code (the DNA), even as the DNA itself was textualized as the book of life (Erwin Schrödinger was the first to describe genetic material as a code-script, as far back as 1943). Genetics emerged as the dominant paradigm for viewing the human.

Since the 1960s, therefore, the body has been more or less effectively reduced to, summarized and metaphorized as a set of codes: the chemical codes within molecular biology, the numbered chromosomes of genetics and the mapping of the entire genome sequence. Life is reduced to a molecule. Biology suddenly was no more the preserve of the biologists. Or, more accurately, biologists found it essential to work alongside computer engineers to decode the human body's constituent molecular or genetic parts.

DNA is now a language that supposedly encapsulates the body. And because it is a language, it is scriptable, reproducible, storable and readable. In Roof's terms, DNA is the 'animating, originary Word made flesh' (2007: 73). Metaphors and analogies like DNA as the book of life or Matt Ridley's genome autobiography (the term used in the subtitle of his bestselling *Genome*) are common instances of the textualization of biology.

An eminently useful concept to describe this new paradigm within biology is Eugene Thacker's 'biomedia' (2004). Thacker defines biomedia as the 'technical recontextualization of biological components and processes' (11). It assumes that corporeality and biological materiality are aligned with an extratechnological moment that is consonant with the 'body itself' (11) so that the biological, biomolecular or patient body is 'compiled' through modes of visualization, modelling, data extraction and *in silico* simulation (13). These technologies prioritize the biological domain as a set of components in interactions with each other via various biomolecular, biochemical and cellular processes (14–15).

Thacker's vision of biology as biomedia gestures at the mathematization or informatization of life. The human body is reduced to a set of numbers that can then be stored, retrieved and reconstituted across terminals, screens and interfaces. There are two parts to this mathematization:

- first, the body *is* the data stored in the computers and databases: a dematerialization;
- second, the data can generate a body: a rematerialization.

The two parts firmly situate the body as biomedia: the genetic code to which the human form is reduced works with the computer code that compiles, sorts and interprets the data in order to identify a human body, or to develop an image of the human body through a set of numbers. The biological materiality of the human body becomes the bar code on the identity card even as the bar code, when swiped through the appropriate scanner, generates the human body for any identification. A common example that illustrates this mathematization of the body, and the flesh ↔ data ↔ flesh dynamics would be the new paradigm of surveillance commonplace to late twentieth-century life: biometrics, of which a case study would be the efforts of the Indian government to generate what it calls a unique identification number for all its citizens through iris scans and fingerprinting.

With biometric identification processes and technologies, the human body is also reconfigured differently: I am *me + my dataset* inscribed into the card I might be asked by the state to carry. The body cannot be separated from the dataset this body has generated for a machine. Biometrics also means that one cannot ever be disassociated from the database of the body. All bodies are mathematized.

This biometric technology produces a 'somatically legible subject' (Richard Nash's phrase: 2011). What this means is that every *body* is at once treated as unique in terms of its biological data and yet fits into a larger dataset of what all bodies are.

The significance of these technologies that somehow simultaneously dematerialize and rematerialize the body may be summarized as follows. The somatically legible subject is one who acquires two key characteristics once the dataset has been prepared.

(i)   Cultural legitimacy: through the incorporation of that body's socially, technologically and state-approved set of parameters – iris scans, for example – into the larger demographics. As the *Strategy Overview* document of the Unique Identification Authority of India, the organization that is in the process of preparing biometric identity cards for all Indian citizens, states:

In India, an inability to prove identity is one of the biggest barriers preventing the poor from accessing benefits and subsidies . . .
A clear identity number would also transform the delivery of social welfare programs by making them more inclusive of communities now cut off from such benefits due to their lack of identification. It would enable the government to shift from indirect to direct benefits, and help verify whether the intended beneficiaries actually receive funds/subsidies. A single, universal identity number will also be transformational in eliminating fraud and duplicate identities, since individuals will no longer be able to represent themselves differently to different agencies. This will result in significant savings to the state exchequer. (*Strategy Overview*, http://uidai. gov.in/UID_PDF/Front_Page_Articles/Documents/Strategy_Overveiw-001.pdf, 1)

It is the body's specific biological characteristics that enable it to be fitted into a larger social domain as a poor body. This is what I am referring to as cultural legitimacy whereby the biologicals determine, ascertain and validate access to resources, and only the biologicals approved as determining factors can be counted.

(ii)   Corporeal integrity is achieved through the compilation of datasets, even if the body exhibits wear and tear, ageing or injury. The parameters used in biometrics are the ones that do not change with age. A certain corporeal integrity is ensured at least in the form of the consistent dataset that is prepared and which only uses those biologicals that do not alter, remain coherent and integrated, even as the rest of the body alters with age and environment.

Biometrics is a popular instance of the mathematization of the body. Biologicals become a set of numbers, and datasets enable the assembling of an identity for any purpose. Biologicals cast in the form of such data also constitute a new form of biological citizenship. What this new biological citizenship entails I shall return to later in this chapter.

With advances in genome sequencing, the databasing of the human population, and the rise of systems biology, the perception of the body as a coherent, unified, well-bounded entity altered drastically. Systems biology showed how the body is essentially a collection of links in which even the DNA is one of several components with little more than an average role to play. What is interesting is how such a view intersects with the idea of life reducible to its chemical processes and components.

Biology is interpreted as the manifestation of a set of chemical processes and codes. It is also seen as a consequence of the networks of chemical, neurological and other processes. While the organism is reduced to, or mapped as, a genome, the genome itself must represent *life itself*. Linked to the mathematization paradigm described above, this view of life rejects the earlier idea of a bounded self/body and an invisible life *force*. This former view, which was called vitalism, saw the human as more than the sum total of its constituent parts: that life cannot be fully understood in terms of chemical processes or neural pathways. But with molecular biology (biology studied at the level of molecular reactions and interactions), this old vitalist view has altered.

We are in the age of postvital living. Where vitalism bestowed a certain mystique to the life force that was more than the molecule or the chemical, postvitalism reduces the life force to a set of information datasets of great complexity: the genome sequence. Richard Doyle (2003), a key theorist of a postvital view of life, argues that mathematization into the genetic code means that biology is now less concerned with the functions of living organisms than with the sequences of molecules in databases. The vitality of life is scattered through chemical bases (of the genetic code, but also hormones, enzymes, neurotransmitters and others) and the neurochemical pathways. To trace life is to trace the movement of chemicals, molecules, packets of energy and, of course, nucleic acids carrying information. Biology is the effect of networks of communication and the exchange of information (DNA as vital information) in the postvital paradigm. This distributed sense of the life force is postvital life. In this version of life, liveliness is a feature that emerges between multiple locations (or apparatuses, that involve laboratories, geopolitical locations as well as scientific and social discourses about the nature of life): the various chemicals and environmental factors

that energize the chemicals into particular interactions. This means, simply,
life does not have a sovereign origin in the postvital scheme of things. It
was never autonomous to begin with, nor has it evolved autonomously. Life
is the embodiment of multiple crossings of information/data and the linkages of these bits of data. At what point the chemical, motile and other
properties mean life is a matter of interpretation. The signs of vitality are,
in other words, attributes.

Postvital life marks a new order of convergence in which the subject
composed on-screen in the form of zeroes and ones constitutes, also,
my body and my personality. It assumes a convergence not only between
my iris or my DNA and my overall personality but also in the way
the digital subject (the body as data) and the flesh-and-blood subject
converge.

OTHER/ING BODIES

If bodies come into being without the usual procedure, would they be
human? Or, if a body has several of its parts replaced by machines or organic
parts from other species (xenotransplantation) or even made from genetic
material from assorted species, would the body be human? Do clones have
human rights? Are foreign parts within our bodies nativized, or do they
stay alien and foreign?

In the late twentieth century the cloning debate perhaps upstaged all
other biomedical issues – barring euthanasia – in the public debates. Fiction
and film, the two most influential media for organizing public perceptions
of science and technologies like cloning, have produced any number of
 works in which the ethics of cloning, the dangers of cloning and the
spectacular nature of cloning technology have been discussed, thereby
constituting our cultural imaginary around it.

Organ transplants alter our sense of self, in terms of embodied selfhood,
self-reflection (about the state of the body and the new organs inside) and
social identity (Svenaeus 2012). Clones disturb our sense of species self
because, while they are derived from humans – i.e., they replicate us – we
find it difficult to perceive them as human. Whether such beings, derived
from us, from our DNA, are to be treated as *persons* in the full sense of the
word is a subject explored in medical ethics, philosophy and politics. In
Kazuo Ishiguro's *Never Let Me Go* (2005), we find a detailed exploration of
clone life even as the novel explores the ethics of cloning, although, I shall
argue, the emphasis is somewhere else.

The clones in Ishiguro's novels are constructed as donors: reared so that
when they become adults their internal organs may be harvested to save
human lives. The donors usually die by the fourth 'donation' – though the
word 'die' is never used, and instead they are said to 'complete'. The completion of the clones implies a fulfilment of their human-determined destiny
and span of life. The clones, who can have sex but are infertile, seem indif-

ferent (Eatough 2011) to their bodies and to the conditions in which they are socialized to their destiny.[1] Their bodies are essentially organ farms, mere sites of supplying the goods the human race needs. Crucially, as I see it (and here my argument is in agreement with Shameem Black's, 2009), the clones in Ishiguro are what Giorgio Agamben (1998) identifies as *Homo sacers*: they are bodies and lives that may be terminated (by humans through legally and socially accepted procedures, in hospitals, in 1990s London, according to the novel) without attracting punishment, but they may not be sacrificed.

Bodies such as Tommy's, Ruth's or Kathy's in the novel are emblems of a new world order, and Ishiguro's novel explicitly sees *bodies* as place-holders in the shift from the old world to the new. Madame tells Tommy and Kathy that the new world that is rapidly coming is scientific and efficient. There are more cures for the old sicknesses, but it is also a harsh, cruel world (2005: 272). The cruelty of the new world that seems to go with its efficiency is directly linked to: (i) how diseased bodies may be treated and cured; (ii) the construction of bodies for this medical procedure. Once this premise of a new world has been accepted and indoctrinated into the clones, their perception of their bodies is significantly altered. Ruth thus is able to state quite unemotionally of her purpose as a donor: 'I was pretty much ready when I became a donor. It felt right. After all, it's what we're *supposed* to be doing, isn't it?' (227). The emphasis on a life-goal or mission seems to be common to humans as well as clones. Ishiguro therefore is not speaking only of cloned bodies but of the processes of socialization that bestow particular purposes and utility on bodies. This socialization is articulated in the guardian Lucy's speech to the clones: 'Your lives are set out for you. You'll become adults, then before you're old, before you're even middle-aged, you'll start to donate your vital organs. That's what each of you was created to do . . . You were brought into this world for a purpose, and your futures, all of them, have been decided' (81). Or, as Emily, one of their guardians, puts it toward the end of the tale: 'Their [the humans'] overwhelming concern was that their own children, their spouses, their parents, their friends, did not die from cancer, motor neurone disease, heart disease. So for a long time . . . people did their best not to think about you. And if they did, they tried to convince themselves you weren't really like us' (240).

Posthuman bodies are bodies designed for donation of organs, with pre-set life spans. Ishiguro, however, does not stop here. The novel ponders over the continued existence of the organs of the clones within other, human bodies. These other bodies that were dying have been given a new lease of life through the donations of organs from the clones. In effect, therefore, the identities of clones (derived from humans) and of the humans (whose organs are now from clones) begin to blur internally. Yet it is not certain that the end of the donations means the end of consciousness for the clones. Tommy says: 'You'll have heard the same talk. How maybe, after the fourth donation, even if you're technically completed, you're still conscious in some sort of way; how you find there are more donations, plenty of them, on the other side of that line' (279). If we take completion to mean also the fulfilment of the purpose of life, then Tommy is speaking of something – life? – that continues beyond the body's dismemberment. Admittedly, the clones live on in others, by virtue of their organs having helped humans to live. But Tommy is speaking of something else here. Michael Eatough argues that this body-without-organs state of life Tommy speaks of suggests a separation between his vocational progression as a 'donor' and the body's physical existence, *even though* his body's organs provide a concrete measure whereby he can track his progression to *Bildung* (Eatough 2011: 144). This is a new vision of the body and the self in which we see 'the forcible removal of organs that are both essential, and paradoxically, inessential to his path to *Bildung*: essential insofar as his goal is to grow and donate those organs, but inessential in that they can and must be removed without destroying his conception of self and purpose' (145). Eatough's argument that the novel proposes an indifference to one's body by identifying one's self with disembodied affective states rather than with a physical body (144) is, I believe, a vision of posthuman bodies. But Eatough misses a crucial point about these bodies.

It is important to note that in the novel vital organs are not, as is the case now, harvested from dead bodies: the *clones donate vital organs when still alive*. The clones are, after the first donation, 'living cadavers' (the term is used by Chris Hables Gray – 2001: 107–10). What we have then are cyborged bodies of clones: bodies kept alive under careful medical supervision for later donations until their fourth transplant. What Tommy is referring to in the passage cited above is this state of existence in which they are not fully alive – they lack some vital organs – or dead. They are *cyborged clones*, or posthumans. The clones do not have a full life even as clones: bits and pieces of them are removed until such time as the body cannot be kept alive any longer.

There is another, related point. Ishiguro calls into question the distinction between clones and humans through the very device of donation. While the larger technology is of xenotransplantation – the novel does not present the science behind the tale – it is significant that the organs donated by the clones are not from foreign bodies: the organs survive within humans, adapt to human bodies even as human biology supposedly (there being no mention of the human body's rejection of these transplants) assimilates the clones' organs (Griffin 2009). Thus we come full circle here: the clones are created from humans, they are brought up and treated as the Other but their organs are harvested and assimilated into humans so that eventually the clone body and the human body become one.

Organ transplantation, as noted above, seriously undermines the human/ clone distinction. It subverts the inter-human distinctions as well: of donor–recipient because the donor continues to exist, in some form, within the recipient. It also estranges the human self, or consciousness of one's body, from itself, a theme the philosopher Jean-Luc Nancy examines in his meditative memoir of his heart transplant. Nancy speaks of the new organ as an intruder in his body, even as he refers to his old, his original and own, heart as a betrayer: 'If my heart was giving up and going to drop me, to what degree was it an organ of "mine," my "own"?' (2002: 3). First, Nancy's original heart that betrays him functions as a 'stranger', says Nancy. Second, there is the intrusion by the foreign heart, the transplant, accompanied by the intrusion, into Nancy's body, of the medical apparatuses. Third, as a result of the immune-depressant drugs he has to take to ensure the transplant is not rejected by his body, the viruses and bacteria that have been long present in his system begin to assert themselves. Nancy puts it this way: 'I became familiar with shingles or the cytomegalovirus – foreigners/strangers that have always lain dormant within me, now suddenly roused and set against me by the necessary depression of my immune system' (9). Nancy is drawing attention not only to the transplanted organ as foreign body but to his own organs as having become stranger/foreign, and of various life forms inside him that also *become* foreign. This implies, to adapt Fredrik Svenaeus's argument, that his body is not the self he once thought it was: it contains, is constituted by, the foreign. Identity, says Nancy, is immunity, for it supposedly keeps the foreign out (9). As we shall see in the case of animal studies, this is a posthumanist view: that the human can emerge only with the expulsion of the improper or the animal within.

Yet again we reach the posthumanist conclusion: that the human body as a coherent, self-contained, autonomous self is no longer a viable proposition. We have to see the self as multiple, fragmented and made of the foreign. Nancy also offers another insight. Having endured the transplant and a subsequent cancer, Nancy discovers that: 'never has the strangeness of my own identity, which I've nonetheless always found so striking, touched me with such acuity. "I" has clearly become the formal index of an unverifiable and impalpable system of linkages' (10). And, more importantly, he discovers:

the general feeling of no longer being dissociable from a network of measurements, observations, and of chemical, institutional, and symbolic connections, which do not allow themselves to be ignored, as can be those of which ordinary life is always woven. On the contrary, these connections deliberately keep life constantly alert to their presence and surveillance. I become indissociable from a polymorphous dissociation. (12)

He is now cyborg, a node in a network, his body kept alive through these networks, his sense of self distributed across the network. Nancy is now an assemblage.

THE BODY AS CONGERIES, ASSEMBLAGE AND INTERFACE

Perhaps the most significant shift in thinking through the nature of life, the human body and subjectivity occurs when, in the aftermath of postvitalist theories and systems biology, the body begins to be treated less as a bounded entity than as a network or assemblage, evolving with technology and then environment, where identity emerges as a consequence of the layered flows of information across multiple routes and channels, and of course subject to social pressures and power relations. This view of the body as an assemblage with non-human and machine, and embodied but distributed subjectivity, is at the core of posthumanist thought.

Info-Flows, Distributed Subjectivity, Emergent Conditions

With advances in studies of consciousness (explored in the preceding chapter), the centrepieces of human subjectivity – consciousness and autonomy – are both seen as emergent and embedded conditions. Distributed intelligence and cognition are now seen as better descriptors of the human condition than the Enlightenment (liberal humanist) notion of the autonomous, self-contained, ordered human. Katherine Hayles summarizes the posthuman view of human cognition and consciousness: 'No longer is human will seen as the source from which emanates the mastery necessary to dominate and control the environment. Rather, the distributed cognition of the emergent human subject correlates with . . . the distributed cognitive system as a whole, in which "thinking" is done by both human and nonhuman actors' (1999: 290).

We need to see this distributed subjectivity, Hayles proposes (although Hayles' separation of the body into matter and information remains inherently problematic), not as a state of peril but of expansion and advancement, for human functionality expands because the parameters of the cognitive system it inhabits expands (290–1). In the posthuman, therefore

- consciousness, will, agency and subjectivity are emergent conditions;
- the autonomy of the human that marks, supposedly, its subjectivity is the consequence of relations and dynamics that cut across organic and non-organic actors, machines and humans – in other words, between the human and the environment.

This distributed subjectivity paradigm in posthumanism treats the human form as an *interface* rather than a self-contained structure, closed off and independent. More interestingly, the body is treated as a means of access to the virtual. The virtual is not simply a realm out there. Rather, the virtual envelops us just as the body becomes the means of access to that virtual. In this mixed-reality paradigm – in which all reality, virtual and physical, is mixed because the virtual is accessible only through the body – the materiality of the body is constitutive of the virtual even as the virtual is a means of developing our embodied subjectivity and experiential consciousness.

Much contemporary art focuses on this condition of mixed reality and interfaced bodies. Architectural artwork and installations like Diller and Scofidio's *Blur Building* (2002, http://arcspace.comfeatures/diller–scofidio–renfro/blur-building/), Monika Fleischmann and Wolfgang Strauss' works (*Liquid Views*, 1993, http://www02.zkm.de/you/index.php?option=com_content&view=article&id=64%3Aliquid-views-der-virtuelle-spiegel-des-narziss&catid=35%3Awerke&lang=en),[2] Myron Krueger's early experiments, the visitor-driven artwork (art responding to, shaping itself around visitor actions) which constitutes a major genre today in the Ars Electronica's CAVE experiments (late 1990s) and relational and liquid architecture (where spaces and settings shape themselves around individuals), offer a posthuman vision of the human as interface and of reality as mixed reality. Mike Hansen, who has produced the most persuasive study of this kind of art (2006), suggests a posthuman vision (the term itself occurs only once in his book!). Such artwork, suggests Hansen, demonstrates the biological substrate to all media. That is, the media support the human sensoria, even as the human senses are essential for the media to operate to full effect. It is through the corporeal that the virtual is accessed. Or, the virtual is actualized only through the corporeal sensoria. What Hansen calls bodies in code is the close linkage of the corporeal with informational flows in which 'embodiment . . . can only be realized, in conjunction with technics' (20). The body, in such artwork, is exteriorized and extended *into* the environment. Rather than a mere deterritorialization and disembodiment, one needs to see this as the 'dissolution of the divide between interiority and exteriorization, the flesh of my body and the flesh of the world' (91). Installation art of this interactive kind makes us aware of the primacy of corporeal access into the digital environment. Embodiment is never, therefore, about the limited flesh-and-bones but about the extended, expanded and interfaced corporeality that we all now experience.

Moving out of the domain of art into cities, William Mitchell proposes that the biological body is enmeshed with the city and the city itself is the 'domain of my networked cognitive system . . . the spatial and material embodiment of that system' (2003: 19). This means that, with video cameras, mobile communication, instant messaging, GPS and other technologies that bodies are now armed (or is that networked?) with, the sensorium is 'no longer localized by the inexorable laws of visual occlusion and acoustic decay, the range of my exploring fingertips, for there has occurred a radical de-localization of our interactions with places' (31). Yet, with such a de-localization in which one mediates the local through the machine, there is also an amplified rootedness because the body is informationally linked to the hot spots, the cellular network, the wi-fi that are hardwired into the environment. Though communications enable us to reach far beyond the immediately local, they also ensure – even with cloud computing – that one is always connected to a particular route or packet of information flow. Yet again, what we are seeing here is the breakdown of boundaries between the sovereign body and the environment because the body is now an interface, a node through which information flows and the info-flows themselves are instantiated through and as the body.

Info-flows are materially produced through a mix of human and non-human actors where the possibility of action is embodied as both territory and bodily locations. These bodily locations are 'knowing locations' (John Law and Kevin Hetherington, cited in Flusty 2004: 151), sites at which data is gathered, analysed and acted upon, points of passage or junctions from where knowledge, sociality and global flows emanate (151). This might be thought of as a corpo-realization of info-flows and is a posthuman condition. In order to demonstrate this argument about the body *as* interface producing its distributed subjectivity, and the necessity of the corporeal to the information flow, I return to my reading of William Gibson's 2003 novel *Pattern Recognition* (Nayar 2011b).

An intersection of the hyperreal world of signs (itself readable as the material-discursive) with concrete reality is the materialization of immaterial info-flows. In Gibson we discern a corpo-realization of the immaterial in which the materialization of info-flows demands a *body*. Immaterial info-flows that create smooth space demand embodiment. What Gibson does is to take the body as the site of this intersection of material and immaterial, but show the body as traumatized by this intersection – what I term the 'traumatic materialism' of info-flows. There are three crucial intersections of data and flesh in *Pattern Recognition*.

Cayce Pollard can immerse herself into the endless flow of signs in order to detect emerging patterns. She works, therefore, as a coolhunter. She says: 'manufacturers use me to keep track of street fashion . . . What I do is pattern recognition. I try to recognize a pattern before anybody else does' (Gibson 2003: 86). There is a simultaneity of two processes at work in this info-flow around Cayce.

The first process is the materialization of information. Cayce lives inside the flow of signs (or information), and yet remains outside it. She detects patterns within the flow of signs because *she* recognizes the meanings of these signs. She surveys and predicts brands and logos. Cayce can read, literally, the signs (logos, trademarks) of the future in the ebb and flow of signage around her, giving *form* to abstract trends, *materializing* signs, logos and cool. Signs remain immaterial in the sense that they are still abstract. What Cayce does is explained this way: 'I point a commodifier at it. It gets productized. Turned into units. Marketed' (86). The trend or fashion is the renewed flow of info through the Cayce-junction – the cumulative and tangible result of non-human (immaterial) info and human actors coming together.

The process of materialization of information requires a body – specifically, Cayce's material, corporeal body. It is entirely Cayce's interpretation that converts the sign into a marketable commodity, an object. Consumer products do not demand mere signage, they demand a corpo-realization. Signage is everted, it envelops her, even as she exists somewhere between the materiality of her body and the immaterial signage.[3] In a sense, then, the Cayce body is *de-materialized* when it becomes a part of the signage and *rematerialized* when her body becomes the means of actualizing the sign. Pattern recognition, then, is the intersection of the human body with the flow of information. The body discerns the patterns in the info-flow, even as the information patterns itself upon the discerning body.

A second instantiation of this intersection is the process of viral marketing. Magda, who works at viral marketing, describes her job this way: '[I] go to clubs and wine bars and chat people up. While I'm at it, I mention a client's product, of course favourably. I try to attract attention while I'm doing it' (Gibson 2003: 84). The listeners to this conversation go away and don't necessarily buy the product but what they do is: 'recycle the information. They use it to try to impress the next person they meet' (85). People remain the nodes in this transmission, conduits through which information flows. The product is constituted as a set of signs transmitted *through* bodies hired to do the job.

The fluidity of the present gets grounded through acts of cognitive (and therefore corporeal) interpretations. This theme of corpo-realization is also aligned, subtly, with the very project of advertising. Bigend tells Cayce that we 'cannot now anticipate the future any more, the present is too volatile and all we can do is prepare for the spinning [out] of a given moment's scenarios. Risk management' (57). Veronica Hollinger rightly reads this statement as addressing 'the challenge of . . . undertaking . . . cognitive mapping . . . adequate to the volatility and fluidity of the present moment' (2006: 462). Risk management is the cognitive mapping of patterns, it is about how we, as individuals or collectives, perceive, cognitively, meaning in fluidity. In Hollinger's terms, this is significant because pattern recognition is a particularly human trait (462). In effect it foregrounds the human.

A coolhunter who can detect patterns in street fashion and future trends, Cayce is allergic to labels and logos of any kind: 'What people take for relentless minimalism is a side effect of too much exposure to the reactor-cores of fashion . . . She is, literally, allergic to fashion. She can only tolerate things that could have been worn, to a general lack of comment, during any year between 1945 and 2000. She's a design-free zone, a one-woman school of anti' (Gibson 2003: 8). She navigates London's ubiquitous signage but logos still affect her viscerally when she wears them or comes into contact with them. She is immersed in signage and its ubiquitous flows, but she is outside it as well because of 'her talents . . . allergies . . . tame pathologies' (65). Apophenic Cayce can intuitively detect patterns, materialize them through her sensorium, but her body cannot assimilate them at all. To be consumed, an object must first become a sign, says Baudrillard (2005: 218) but, as Gibson will demonstrate, the sign works when cognitively (i.e., through the corporeal sensorium) perceived.

Signage brings home to Cayce that she is a vulnerable body as well, hers is a body that has to stay devoid of signage: 'She's gone to Harvey Nichols and gotten sick' (Gibson 2003: 17). Michelin Man logos make her throw up and want to scream (97, 98). Through these panic reactions the Cayce body responds, materially, to immaterial signs. She is the traumatic materialism of the signifier. Gibson thus complicates the body–signage, material–immaterial binaries by showing how they merge.

There is another example of the eversion of the human body vis-à-vis the virtual world of information. Nora, a maimed Russian woman, produces a mysterious footage by editing three short films she had made when at college. This footage, uploaded on the www, is now a cult sensation. However, it is not the footage itself that detains me here, but the Nora story.

Nora survives, more vegetable than human, with shrapnel in her brain. The entire account of the production of the footage reinforces the centrality of consciousness – embodied consciousness – to info-flows. The first comments made by Stella, Nora's twin, to Cayce gesture at the unbelievable but undeniable link between bodily trauma and digital art: 'The last fragment [of the bomb that killed the twins' parents]. It rests between the lobes, in some terrible way. It cannot be moved. Risk is too great . . . But then she notices the screen . . . When she looked at those images, she focused. When the images were taken away, she began to die again' (288–9). It is in the endless circulation of images – info-flows, signage – that she exists. Nora *is* the film she makes, in an extreme instance of eversion, one that also gestures at the material–discursive nature of posthuman bodies where her body's identity/meaning is a phenomenon produced through and in the interactions of numerous apparatuses (such as the film editing room, people, her chair and editing machinery).

Out of the injury in her head comes the minimalist footage that captures the world's imagination. Gibson builds on the link between bodily trauma and information later:

Her consciousness, Cayce understands, somehow bounded up by or bound to the T-shaped fragment in her brain . . . And from it, and from her other wounds, there now emerged, accompanied by the patient and regular clicking of her mouse, the footage . . . the headwaters of the digital Nile . . . It is here, in the languid yet precise moves of a woman's pale hand. In the faint click of image-capture. In the eyes truly present when focused on this screen.

Only the wound, speaking wordlessly in the dark. (305)

The Body, Reformatted 69

It is the wound that speaks to the world. In this, the climactic moments of the tale, Gibson reinforces the corporeal nature of information. Nora had wanted to be a film-maker. She now Photoshops the same films she had made years ago, paring them down relentlessly to their minimal images. The trauma of her injury creates the poetic visuals unfolding in short segments. Her consciousness, fragmented by shrapnel, achieves a flow of info, but a flow that is a-temporal, outside of history and geography (the footage has no markers of period or location, and its followers spend hours trying to figure out the story or the location). Nora does not recognize people, cannot identify her loved ones, all she recognizes is film image and the flow of info across her screen. She is rendered into the film, her consciousness is all film.

When the novel concludes, we understand that the footage is not 'outside' or extrinsic to Nora, it is her-self, everted. The signage *is* her body's apophenic pattern recognition: she internalizes the signs, materializes and corpo-realizes them. Images are not outside realities (or even symbols) for interior states, they constitute the interior states of people. Individual selves are everted – sometimes with creases, sometimes not – into info-flows. Traumatic materialism – as I have termed the intersection of bodies and info-flows in Gibson's novel – is the eversion of selves and information.

Assemblage

BioArt in the last decades of the twentieth century contributed in a major way to the rethink on ontology, technology and corporeality. Its philosophical assumptions draw particular attention to a state of becoming of all forms of life. BioArt – defined by one of its practitioners, António Cerveira Pinto, as 'play[ing] . . . with biology in general, be it wetware, digital biology or future nano "consortia"' (cited in Vita-More 2007: 174) – with its interest in chimeras, human–machine hybrids and interface projects that work with genetic principles, also contributes to the posthumanist vision. Very often, however, BioArt forms reflect cultural anxieties about hybridities, the grotesque and genetic experimentation.[4] The use of living tissue (SymbioticA, the Tissue Culture & Art Project), for example, in close conjunction with non-organic matter suggests a blurring of body boundaries. In addition, genomic arts, as Oron Catts and Ionat Zurr, both practitioners of tissue engineering arts, put it, 'blur the boundaries between what is born and what is manufactured, what is animate and what is inanimate' (2002: 366). Such art also offers a (prophetic?) insight into the future of human evolution, the many possible pathways that bodies, wetware and biology can take. Alexis Rockman's work (*The Farm*, 2000) is an excellent example of this. But most of all, many of the art projects locate wetware in particular environments and ecosystems in order to show how life in any organism is never independent of the setting. The human body is a congeries, or assemblage, of multiple species, machines and organic forms.

Evolutionary schema, such as the Darwinian one, says Ansell-Pearson, suggests that the entire process is self-directed: that evolution is the realization of the species-being of the human (1999: 141). However, as contemporary theories of cell evolution proposed by Lynn Margulis demonstrate, evolution has always been co-evolution. Therefore we need to see self-evolution and self-realization as a myth. The human evolves in relation with organic and non-organic forms: the state, the social order, plant and animal life. Genetic components also draw on other forms of life, and genetic changes that lead to evolution are very often *responses* to an environment. Thus we cannot see genetic changes as simply a process of self-regulation or self-evolution, but must visualize them as emerging from the feedback mechanism that links organisms to the environment. Any organism can therefore only be seen with reference to other organisms. This also implies that neither the organism nor its environment – which, it must be remembered, is at once organic and non-organic – are passive: each is in dynamic interaction with the other, influences the other and partakes of the other. Commentators like Richard Dawkins (1976) also posit a wholly different view of evolution. Dawkins argues, for instance, that we have to consider the possibility that the influence of any genetic replicator is rarely limited to the organism alone: the information travels along all available pathways and 'radiates' (his term) beyond the individual body. Thus even the genetic constitution of an organism is not, strictly speaking, bounded by the organism's body: it is in linkage with other organisms and the environment.

The evolution of the human, in this view, is less about filiation and genealogical routes than about rhizomes: lateral, cross-over, random connections across borders, species boundaries and genetic identities. Such a view also rejects the genetic determinism that informs much of twentieth-century biology whereby the human is reduced to the genetic code. The human is a network of multiple, criss-crossing relationships in which even the genes, despite their autonomy, find expression within a context. Thus, genetic activity, which supposedly defines our subjectivity, looks and identity as human, is to be seen as connected with the environment of the organism. Bits of DNA that get embedded from other organisms into the human, the elision of other bits and the combinations that produce particular DNA for organisms all originate outside the body/subject.

Such a reading deterritorializes human subjectivity and identity, and is an important step toward the posthuman. Posthumanism sees the assemblage of organic, machinic, natural and other circuits as *producing* subjectivity. There is no subjectivity that predates the circuit because there is no body that is *not* always techno-social.

Deterritorialization implies the becoming nature of subjectivity in which the human is always in process because the human is within a drift, or circuit, of chemicals, chromosomes and molecules that very often lie outside the biology of the human. Evolution is the exchange of information across biologies. In other words, the subjectivity of a human lies not within the interior but within the exchange and linkage the interior has with the exterior world. This exchange and linkage ensure the deterritorialization of human subjectivity because interiority is itself an *open* state: in constant communication with the exterior.

Posthumanism believes that the human is a congeries whose wetware, form and genetic structure have all evolved not as instances of self-realization but as the *instantiation of the connections between and across organic and non-organic forms*. The human as we know it cannot be reduced to its original parts (we cannot track each of the parts of the forms of life from which they emerged) or seen as independently evolved forms. The posthumanist view of the human as congeries is anticipated in Deleuze and Guattari's famous body-without-organs where they call for an opening of the body to connections and relations (Ansell-Pearson 1999: 154). This body is an assemblage made up of circuits, conjunctions, levels and thresholds, passages and distributions of intensity, and territories and deterritorializations (cited in Ansell-Pearson 1999: 154).

Posthumanist visions of assemblage and deterritorialized states of existence, with open borders across which information, consciousness and identities *flow,* might also be fruitfully aligned with new technologies and cultures of morphing. In the opening moments of this chapter, I cited the instances of *Terminator* and *Transformers* in which the ontological instability of beings and things invokes anxiety and fright. Now, posthumanist philosophy believes, a being is an assemblage produced out of networks and linkages. There is, therefore, no sovereign body because bodies and identities are the effect of distribution. Morphing in digital cultures – artwork such as the BBC's *Digital Faces* project (2005, available on YouTube at www. youtube.com/watch?v+XaRF27749Y) – and films like *Transformers* and *Terminator* propose *becoming* rather than *being* as the steady-state of existence where any identity can slide into, *become*, another in a process that does not need to end in a particular shape for all time. That is, human can morph into its Other – the machine – and carry over characteristics, and vice versa. The resultant form does not have to stay that way either. Advertisements in which faces morph into other faces and other identities have been around for some years now. Photoshop allows one to do the same. Stelarc with his extra arm or ear, Isa Gordon with the titanium glove for extra tactility, Kevin Warwick's implants (see www.kevinwarwick.com), but also people with pacemakers and other implants suggest we are seeing a *form in-between forms*: between machines and humans, between the organic and the inorganic, and in a process of *becoming*. This shift in perception of the human as morphable rather than fixed, sovereign and bounded is, according to Norah Campbell and Mike Saren (2010), a posthumanist vision: forms in a state of ontological fluidity.

From this recognition of the irreducible ontological fluidity of persons to an entirely new way of rethinking citizenship is but a step.

Posthuman Citizenship

The de- and re-territorialization of the body within circuits of information exchange and datasets constitutes the rise of a new biological citizenship that is posthuman. I locate this new citizenship not only in new forms of embodiment where we recognize that the body has co-evolved with technology and other life forms, but also in the mathematized, databased body producing biological citizenship.

Biological citizenship is defined as citizenship projects that 'have linked their conceptions of citizens to beliefs about the biological existence of human beings, as individuals, as families and lineages, as communities, as population and races, and as species' (Rose and Novas 2005: 440). Citizens, Rose and Novas argue, increasingly understand themselves in biological terms, and see themselves as possessing 'biovalue' (446; see also Sundar Rajan 2006), and the state or corporations become interested in specific bodies and organs of the population.[5] (And, as noted via Vandana Shiva and Rosi Braidotti in chapter 1, in this new biological citizenship, women, like stem cells, genes, tissues and such vital generative biologies, remain controlled, commercialized and exploited.)

I accept Chris Hables Gray's arguments in favour of cyborg citizenship in which he proposes that cyborg citizens are *real* political bodies and therefore need real political rights instantiated in technologies such as constitutions and operational tests of citizenship (2001: 29). What I wish to do here, while accepting the embodied nature of all citizenship that Gray proposes, is to elaborate the features of such an embodied citizenship, mainly with regard to new technologies of surveillance – which determine who is a citizen, and who is not – and databases of monitoring, archiving and retrieval that are based on biological data.

Biometrics, as I have argued elsewhere (Nayar 2012), constitutes a major shift in the construction of biovalues. At this moment in techno-history, biometrics includes fingerprints, ultrasound fingerprinting, iris scans, hand geometry, facial recognition, ear shape, signature dynamics, voice recognition, computer keystroke dynamics, skin patterns and foot dynamics. Future, or second-generation, biometrics will include neural wave analysis, skin luminescence, remote iris scan, advanced facial recognition, body odour, and others. Currently, passport controls, banking, social welfare, criminal investigation, state controls can all operate through biometric identification procedures.

Louise Amoore has argued that the body itself is inscribed with, and demarcates, a 'continual crossing of multiple encoded borders – social, legal, gendered, racialized' (2006: 337). The biometric border is a portable border, carried by mobile bodies at the very same time as it is deployed to divide bodies at international boundaries, airports, railway stations, on subways or city streets, in the office or the neighbourhood (338). Biometric borders, writes Amoore, 'extend the governing of mobility into domains that regulate multiple aspects of daily life' (338). Identity emerges in the seamless flow of information from the body through the ambient intelligence situated all around us, even as the machine intelligence signals a pass through, identified at the body. That is, in biometric identification processes, the data leave (and yet do not leave) the body, circulate within a network of information-processing machines and channels, and gain access. Ambient intelligence – whereby software and processing units are installed in everyday, and therefore inconspicuous, objects all around us rather than specific spaces marked/identified as hardware – ensures that the human in the vicinity is cyborged, being recorded, identified, verified through the info-flow.

A citizen's mobility itself is interestingly situated with these new technologies. Your access to, escape or diversion from, any path is now documented through the body revealing its passage to whatever checkpoints exist. Similarly, the geographical or territorial borders are marked on the body when it crosses them (the beep of recognition when the immigration officer's device records you have arrived at the border, the electronic tag on prisoners and parolees, etc.). It is possible, in other words, to prepare for the coming of a body well in advance because the progress of this body is marked and recorded – not unlike the Old Cumberland Beggar's progress in William Wordsworth's poem of that same title – through various points and scanners. The border is not out there, it is inside you, just as your body negotiates with the border beneath the level of conscious engagement. Whether you can cross a border or not is inscribed into your very body. The border's access points are buried in your body. (On cross-border migration and biometrics, see Ross 2007.)

I would now like to forward the suggestion that there is something akin to branding that biometrics works with. Historically, cattle and slaves, prisoners and criminals were branded. It marked what the African American critic Hortense Spillers (2003) called the theft of the body because the slave's body was resignified as the property of the white man. They could not escape and they could be easily identified by the numbers (the most horrific reminders of which remain the numbers tattooed on the concentration camp inmates in Nazi Europe). While biometric technologies are not the same as branding, there is something interesting going on here. Biometrics does not insist on inscribing a number/design/signature on the surveilled body. Instead, it assumes that the body is always already inscribed with tell-tale markers and marks. That is, the numbers, codes and signs are already within the body – what the technology does is to bring these to the surface. Thus biometrics remains within the larger ambit of branding in that it constructs the body as a site of enunciative practices. The difference is in the nature of the inscription. Branding *codes* the body as belonging to . . . X or Y. Biometrics *decodes* what is already inscribed in the body and then identifies it as belonging to X or Y structure/class/population. Just as the brand speaks up for the identity of the bearer – brands are essentially stories that the product/commodity carries upon itself – the biometric data revealed when we pass through a scanner pronounce our identities. Branding cuts into the skin, biometrics brings to the surface – epidermalizes – what is inside. This is the new biological citizenship in which the biometric data from within your body determine your biovalue to the organization, society and nation.

Biometrics foregrounds individuals' or populations' biovalue by constantly calling upon their bodies to identify, present, validate, show their ethnic membership, lineage and familial ties, all on one ID card. While the Unique Identification Number (UID) declares that the AADHAR guarantees identity, not citizenship (http://uidai.gov.in/UID_PDF/Front_Page_Articles/Documents/Strategy_Overveiw-001.pdf, 2), it remains unquestionable that your iris is your future. As the *Strategy Overview* document of the UID states:

For governments and individuals alike, strong identity for residents has real economic value. While weak identity systems cause the individual to miss out on benefits and services, it also makes it difficult for the government to account for money and resource flows across a country. In addition, it complicates government efforts to account for residents during emergencies and security threats. (*Strategy Overview*, 6)

This is biological citizenship, in which the genetic code, the iris or even the way you move might enable or hinder your access to services and the state.

Biometrics-determined biological citizenship embodied as UID assumes that social and political problems are resolvable through technology. In the UIDAI (Unique Identification Number Authority of India) document I just quoted from, it is stated that access to welfare and state services is facilitated by having a UID. If we were to take India as an immediate instance, the UIDA assumes that the unique biometric data facilitate the poor's access to, say, grain or health. It thus offers a technological hubris to a problem that has consistently plagued the country: its horrifically meagre public distribution systems and primary health services. The UIDA makes this clear in its document 'Envisioning a Role for Aadhaar in the Public Distribution System' (http://uidai.gov.in/UID_PDF/Working_Papers/Circulated_Aadhaar_PDS_Note.pdf).

The poetics of surveillance shifts the grounds of the debate: by focusing on the need for a number, it elides the absence of efficient delivery mechanisms for grain or medical services. It is almost as though it was only the lack of a UID that prevented the government from providing health care. But the main point, for my purposes here, is the entrenchment of biological citizenship through biometrics and other systems so that all of us, unwittingly, become posthuman: mathematized, networked, bar-coded.

Biological citizenship *minimizes* the body into a set of numbers, thus erasing the complicated nature of identity itself. This same set of numbers then offers the potential, and possibility, of *expansion*, of being used for various purposes. The UID is supposed to be multi-purpose. The UIDAI states:

> The UIDAI envisions a balance between privacy and purpose when it comes to the information it collects on residents. The agencies may store the information of residents they enrol if they are authorized to do so, but they will not have access to the information in the UID database. The UIDAI will answer requests to authenticate identity only through a Yes or No response. (*Strategy Overview*, 4)

The *Demographic Data Standards and Verification Procedure (DDSVP) Committee Report* of the UIDAI (2009) mentions that the UIDAI 'proposes to create a platform to first collect the identity details and then to perform authentication that can be used by several government and commercial service providers' (4). It does not specify who/what these commercial service providers are. Data stored in such databanks offer the potential of monitoring various individuals in multiple domains, a process now known as dataveillance. This means that the biometric data collected could be appropriated for other functions (a phenomenon called 'function creep', in which data collected for one purpose might end up serving an unintended or even unauthorized purpose). With ambient intelligence technologies – whereby the hardware for monitoring people is not always visible but absorbed into everyday settings, and the intelligence is distributed around us, constantly – our bodies are perpetually interfaced with the environs. When, for instance, our house starts recognizing my footfalls or the door my voice/face, we see the ambient intelligence networked with my body, and biometrics becomes merged into the *setting* (environs) of the body.

Yet this setting, on occasion, does not seem to matter. Databases and surveillance technologies that have stored biometric data can do real-time identification of citizens at a distance. The state or employer, the corporation or the legal apparatus can keep a metaphoric and literal eye on the citizen wherever s/he is through this process of biometric surveillance in which information about the citizen performing innocuous acts like crossing the street or making a phone call is quickly transmitted through networks into centralized databanks for processing. Posthuman citizenship, prophets of doom might rightly claim, is about continually performing good 'citizenship acts' because all your actions are being picked up – from ATM transactions to letters on email. Surveillance at a distance encourages, suggests Kelly Gates, citizenship acts (2006: 428). Once again this suggests a network identity of the human, where her or his actions are documented by a machine and transmitted onward.

Biometrics, even with its reliance on info-flows, reinstates the body at the core of all networks. This contributes to posthumanist thought by showing network and flows as constitutive of the human, the seamless merger of bodies and machines, data and flesh, each actualizing the other. Accounts of globalization and surveillance cultures (Braidotti 2007, Nayar

2012) note the Foucauldian 'bio-power' (bodies surveilled, controlled and commercialized) structures and relations that biometrics makes possible.

Reconfigured bodies and changing notions of the body that this chapter has discussed offer profound insights into the posthuman condition. The mathematization of bodies not only underscores the body's location within info-flows but also demonstrates how biological citizenship constantly moves *between* the biologicals and the informational. The reformatting of the body within new technologies and theories of corporeality emphasizes the body as the route into the virtual, even as the body itself is a networked body, interfacing with the environment, extending and expanding its sensoria through technology. Info-flows and the virtual are actualized through the corporeal.

Vitalist theories have now been modified in the posthuman age with a new view of the body and life itself: that life is distributed, embedded in and evolved from other life forms, genetic codes and info-flows. Bodies are not sovereign structures, bounded and coherent, but are congeries. Transplants call upon the self to recognize not only how its original organs had become foreign to it, but also how the organs transplanted give it a sense of the foreign added to it. Thus the interiority–exterior, original–prosthesis, self–other boundaries break down even as human–machine, organic–inorganic boundaries blur. Bodies are seen as *becoming*, whereby the so-called 'Other' is constitutive of the self, the Other is incorporated into the self (what Rosi Braidotti terms 'multiple becoming', 2006: 200). This body is not just a metaphor or a figure (that is, not just an effect of discourse). In every case, this cyborged, hybrid body is *embodied* even as its hybridity (like its boundaries, once) is produced in the material–discursive realm. Such a critical posthumanism, focused on the materiality of the body, is also alert to biological citizenship in which the material body is produced in and imbricated with technoscience and capitalist processes of exploitation (bio-power). By rejecting the view of the autonomous subject and instead proposing a subject that is essentially intersubjective and intercorporeal, posthumanism refashions the very idea of the human. The human is a node, one that is dependent upon several other forms of life, flows of genetic and other information, for its existence and evolution. Finally, it demonstrates that citizenship is embodied, but requires an interface with the info-flows of the environment.

4 Absolute Monstrosities: The 'Question of the Animal'

HUMAN . . . BORN OF NORMAL PARENTS
(sign at an exhibition of 'freak' foetuses in Dunn 1989: 54)

We're hormone robots anyway, only we're faulty ones.
(Atwood 2004: 166)

It [genocide of animals] is occurring through the organization and exploitation of an artificial, infernal, virtually interminable survival, in conditions that previous generations would have judged monstrous, outside of every supposed norm of a life proper to animals that are thus exterminated by means of their continued existence or even their overpopulation. As if, for example, instead of throwing people into ovens or gas chambers, (let's say Nazi) doctors and geneticists had decided to organize the overproduction and overgeneration of Jews, gypsies and homosexuals by means of artificial insemination, so that, being more numerous and better fed, they could be destined in always increasing numbers for the same hell, that of the imposition of genetic experimentation, or extermination by gas or by fire. In the same abattoirs.
(Derrida 2002: 394–5)

I think it entirely possible, if not likely, that a hundred years from now we will look back on our current mechanized and systematized practices of factory farming, product testing, and much else that undeniably involves animal exploitation and suffering – uses that we earlier saw Derrida compare to the gas chambers of Auschwitz – with much the same horror and disbelief with which we now regard slavery or the genocide of the Second World War.
(Wolfe 2003: 190)

Popular culture, since the early modern European interest in the monstrous and P. T. Barnum's circuses and exhibitions, has been fascinated by variations in the human form. The entire *X-Men* series of popular films positions the mutants with extraordinary talents as 'minorities' who need to defend their rights against the majoritarian 'normal' humans who cannot, of course, tolerate these creatures' difference from the norm (Reynolds 1992: 79; Fingeroth 2004: 106). In Katherine Dunn's controversial novel *Geek Love* (1989), an entire family is devoted to 'producing' mutant, deformed and 'different' bodies – with flippers instead of limbs, hunchbacks, Siamese twins – who could then be exhibited as 'freaks' for economic gain. Deformity and 'freakishness' of the body in the novel, argue critics, become means of empowerment, even as it explores the 'tenuousness' of the boundary between 'normal' and 'freak' (Hardin 2004) and the very idea of the 'individual' human. Ben in Doris Lessing's *The Fifth Child* (1988) is described as a 'throwback' to an ancestral race, an animal, and addressed very often as a 'thing' or 'it'. In Marge Piercy's *He, She and It*, the first responses to the coming-to-life of the Golem attest to the problematic nature of life which seems to cut across species and even the inanimate: 'He is a lizard-man, Itzak thinks, he is a man of shale' ([1991] 1993: 66). In Margaret Atwood's *The Year of the Flood*, Adam One's preachings focus on a Deep Ecology vision of transcending biological givens and recognizing interconnectedness of all species and therefore the blurring of the animal–human border. Thus, when he offers a revisionary Biblical story of origins, he says that when 'Jesus first called as his Apostles two fishermen', he did so in order 'to help conserve the Fish population' (2009: 234).

Debates in the public domain about euthanasia often revolve around the nature of 'life' in a comatose patient. Popular horror thrillers have an entire sub-genre devoted to the 'undead' zombies, so much so that commentators have seen the zombie figure as a response to the dehumanizing nature of contemporary global capitalism (Lauro and Embry 2008). Scholars and commentators tracing the histories of monstrosities (Cohen 1996, Nina Auerbach 1997, among others) have argued that freaks represent cultural anxieties about the nature of the human and the individual, troubling the 'conventional boundaries between male and female, sexed and sexless, animal and human, large and small, self and other' (Fiedler 1978: 24).

In each case the texts and their commentaries are concerned with a basic question: is the 'nature' of 'life' the same across its various 'expressions' in the form of bodies, anatomies and physiologies? Is any form of life unique, and truly autonomous? Do some forms – animal, mutant, disabled – have a *lesser* life?

In the twentieth and twenty-first centuries, the nature of the human has been the subject of debates within bioethics, especially over euthanasia, genetic engineering, prosthetic technologies and implants. These debates have also addressed not just the question of what it means to be human but also that of the very nature of life, thus including within its broad sweep the nature of all forms of life, including bacterial, plant and animal life. Thus, with xenotransplantation and chemical engineering of human bodies and minds, the nature of the human has run up against arguments about, for instance, the animal incorporated within/into the human. Debates about political rights have revolved around issues of 'biological citizenship' and 'biovalue'. These are clearly debates about the value of life and the methods – and methodologies – through which biovalue is computed in different life forms.

One of the most powerful arguments for critical posthumanism has emerged from within animal studies where this precise problem – what constitutes 'life' and 'normal life' – has been addressed. But first, a quick recap of the human within posthumanist thought.

The human in the critical posthumanist vision

- can no longer be separated from material (including organic – plants and animals – and inorganic), technological and informational networks; and
- its very consciousness depends upon these networks (of which it is not the dominating agent: it is not any more human + technological prosthesis or human + data flows but rather an inextricable interface in which the technological constitutes human identity); and
- it shares not only origins and evolutionary stages with other life forms but also mortality and vulnerability with them, even as all forms of life are embedded in power structures and discourses that produce their very materiality and meaning.

Human life is what is traversed by and embedded in flows of life that cut across species, life forms and inanimate things. If human evolution depends to a very large extent on its neighbouring species as well, then does it not follow that human life, or subjectivity, is inextricably linked to these other life forms?

Critical posthumanist thinking, this chapter demonstrates, has drawn both inspiration and theoretical rigour, but also its politics, from contemporary work in monster studies and animal studies.

Monster studies is the sustained examination of various cultural monsters – mythic beasts, monstrous races, vampires, hybrids and chimeras. Monster studies is concerned with the cultural representations and discourses through which particular forms of life are excluded as non-human, abhuman and inhuman. In animal studies, critics and commentators have noted that species differences and boundaries have been drawn up by humans through centuries of speciesist cultural representations so that the borders of the human might be sustained, even though contemporary research shows that these categories (non-human, human) are not really sustainable. Critical animal studies is a discipline in which the 'nature' of life has been fiercely debated from moral, ethical and legal standpoints. While the aim here is not to map the many layers of these two domains – monster studies and animal studies – the chapter does intend to show how particular strands of critiques in animal studies have enabled critical posthumanism to probe the boundaries of the human, the machine and the animal.

The critical posthumanist offers a critique of the traditional 'human' by noting how humans have consistently (i) defined themselves *against* the 'animal', the mutant/deformed/monstrous and the machine; (ii) marked the boundaries of the human by separating, through rigorous socialization, sanitization and coercion, particular characteristics of human life as merely 'animal' to be expelled, and the 'essential' human to be retained; and (iii) dominated, controlled (including their birth and breeding) and exterminated animal life. The human, the critical posthumanist proposes, is treated as the universal.

The critical posthumanist treats the human as a form of life that determines the categories to which other forms of life belong, or can be relegated. *Homo sapiens*, as the philosopher Giorgio Agamben put it, 'is not a species – it is a machine for producing the recognition of the human' (2004: 26). This human, Agamben notes, is deemed to be 'the articulation and conjunction of a body and a soul . . . of a natural (or animal) element and a supernatural or social or divine element' (16). From a very different theoretical standpoint, the postcolonial critic Gayatri Spivak exclaims:

The great doctrines of identity of the ethical universal, in terms of which liberalism thought out its ethical programmes, played history false, because the identity was disengaged in terms of who was and who was not human. That's why all of these projects, the justification of slavery, as well as the justification of Christianization, seemed to be alright; because, after all, these people had not graduated into humanhood, as it were. (Spivak, cited in Wolfe 2003: 7)

Both Agamben and Spivak are concerned with the issues Leslie Fiedler raised in his work on freaks: who *counts* as fully, properly, human? And what is *only*, or *merely*, an animal? These are the two framing questions that, within animal studies and bioethics, give the discourse of critical posthumanism its charge. Critical posthumanist studies is interested in the discourses and institutions through which this engineering of species differences, and the consequent oppression, exploitation, annihilation of species, has been made possible.

Critical posthumanism draws upon monster and animal studies for several reasons.

First: monster studies demonstrates how particular forms of life, such as the disabled, the insane or the differently embodied, that do not fit the norms of the 'human' are deemed monstrous and consigned to the categories of 'freaks', non-humans or the inhuman. Animal studies shows how the animal as a life form is the constant other to the human, and it is the animal that enables the construction of the human as a category – and critical posthumanism is interested in the forms of thought through which the human has been centred in history.

Second, and proceeding from the first: animal studies reveals the anthropocentrism that positions the animal as an oppositional and inferior other to the human while monster studies shows that the monster can be constructed as such because of a certain normative value attached to particular physiognomies, skin colour, shapes and behaviour.

Third: monster studies shows how the monster's body or face always means something other than itself – it becomes symbolic of something else

(Cohen 1996: 4). Thus, monster studies shows how some deformed babies or mutant animals were treated as bad omens, and 'abnormal' physiognomies as indicative of a moral malaise in those people.

Fourth: animal studies shows how the very term 'animal' homogenizes all non-human life forms.

Fifth: animal studies shows connections, networks and linkages across life forms, ecological systems, environments by demonstrating how life forms evolve together, embedded within relational structures.

Sixth: animal studies demonstrates how criteria like autonomy, rationality or sentience cannot be used as modes of separating species any more.

Seventh: monster studies and animal studies examine the representational modes in literature, the arts and media that have portrayed animals and non-human forms in certain ways for the institutionalization of species boundaries.

Eighth: monster studies shows how species boundaries and origin stories of animals, or other life forms, consign certain forms of life, and certain ethnic groups, to the abattoir, camps or death.

Ninth: monster studies, like animal studies, shows how cultures harbour certain anxieties about mixed and indeterminate forms of life and seek to invent categories into which these might be suitably (re)located.

Tenth: critical animal studies calls for a shift from the focus on killing of animals (their mortality at the hands of humans) to natality (the planned breeding of animals by humans), where economies, institutional mechanisms and ideologies clearly offer different ontologies for animals and humans (Pedersen 2011: 70).

This emphasis on the material and representational aspects of the human–non-human interaction (whether in abattoirs or laboratories), species boundaries and the 'question' of the animal (best exemplified in Wolfe's work in *Animal Rites* (2003) and *What is Posthumanism?* (2010), where he moves across literary texts, philosophical tracts, science writings and material practices) or monster is what marks both animal/monster studies and critical posthumanism, whose interdisciplinary nature itself marks the interrogation and crossing of boundaries.

★

By the late twentieth century in United States scientific culture, the boundary between human and animal is thoroughly breached. The last beachheads of uniqueness have been polluted, if not turned into amusement parks – language, tool use, social behavior, mental events. Nothing really convincingly settles the separation of human and animal. . . . Movements for animal rights are not irrational denials of human uniqueness; they are clear-sighted recognition of connection across the discredited breach of nature and culture.

(Haraway 1991a: 152)

Haraway's claim, made well before the emergence of animal studies as a discipline, and influenced by the work of biologists and animal ethologists like Jane Goodall and Barbara Smuts, calls for a serious reconsideration of the hierarchies of life that mankind has instituted. These hierarchies have been instrumental in establishing human life as 'unique', and are no longer borne out by studies of animal behaviour. Haraway's rigorous valorization of human-animal-machine hybrids (cyborgs) was a major political shift, for it called for a philosophical, ethical, legal examination of not only forms of life but also the systems of classification that ranked these 'forms' of life and then 'naturalized' the ranking. Haraway's work on cyborg cultures and techno-science also drew parallels with the institutionalization and marginalization of difference between species, life forms, genders and races. It has also been instrumental in re-examining epistemological biases and classificatory regimes. In the above paragraph cited from her cult text, 'A Cyborg Manifesto', Haraway summarizes in advance the posthumanist project: of interrogating the regimes of classification – including literary and discursive *representations* across genres and media, but also *material* conditions (laboratory life, industry, genetic testing) – that consign the animal to a lesser form of life (and discourses are, as we have seen after Karen Barad in the first chapter, material).

Species borders and our perceptions of (the materiality of) animal and non-human others are increasingly mediated by narratives and representations. In an argument loaded with important consequences for the ethics of representation and therefore of the way we humans intervene in the materiality of animal lives, Akira Lippit offers a different perspective on modernity. Lippit suggests that modernity is characterized by the near-disappearance of wildlife from human lives, and therefore from its vision *and* material experience. Wildlife and animals instead appear, Lippit suggests, 'in humanity's reflections on itself: in philosophy, psychoanalysis, and technological media such as the telephone, film, and radio' (2000: 3). This means there is a marked shift in our *experience* of animals: while once they were experienced first-hand (face-to-face), they can now only be experienced in the virtual spaces of representation, in print, photographs, or on screen (and now, in the immersive environs of virtual reality). For Lippit this shift in the experience of the animal has serious consequences for our understanding of the 'animal' itself. Lippit's analysis of the shift in the material interactions between animals and humans and the consequent changes in representational modes – which in turn affect the interactions – is an important one. It draws attention to the necessity of dealing with not just questions of cruelty to animals in abattoirs, circuses or laboratories, but also the *mediated representation* of the animal in narratives, literature and art. It offers us a way of seeing the philosophical and disciplinary foundations of critical posthumanism.

MONSTER THEORY: CULTURES OF OTHERNESS

Monsters, these studies show, are expressions of cultural anxieties about – and demonization of – forms of life as diverse as the black races, particular animals, mutant babies/animals, the impaired and the insane. Strange animals, different physiognomies or skin colour and different bodies were categorized as monsters because they seemed to be outside any category. The discourses of the monstrous in popular culture were concerned with what Jeffrey Jerome Cohen calls figures of 'ontological liminality' (1996: 6).

This ontological liminality is what characterizes Shakespeare's 'lascivious Moor' (Othello), Frankenstein's monster, Stoker's Dracula, Stevenson's Mr Hyde, humanoid robots like Marvin the Paranoid Android in Douglas Adams' *The Hitchhiker's Guide to the Galaxy*, the vampires of Octavia Butler and Anne Rice and cult series/films like *Blade* or *Underworld*, and the zombies of twentieth-century horror films. These are life forms that are *between* categories: human with animal/bestial features and behaviour (Mr Hyde), a huge hairy thing that approximates to the human (Frankenstein's creation), a human-like creature who sucks blood and lives for ever (Dracula), the undead (zombies), automata with the same kind of emotional responses as humans (Marvin). Life forms and bodies too distant from 'normal' humans – such as beasts – and too uncomfortably close – such as humanoid robots or creatures that exhibit human emotions and/or intelligence – are both equally monstrous in cultural representations of otherness. Relatedly, interspecies or 'trans-species democracy' (Chaney 2011) in comics – Spiderman, Batman, Krazy Kat, the cat and mice in Spiegelman's *Maus* – represent troubling questions about identity.

Forms and ways of human life that are different get subsumed into the category 'monstrous', and the differently formed/functional bodies as 'monstrosities'. Thus, the very idea of the monster allows the construction of difference. Monster studies here examines the structures of *exclusion* through which some races and bodies were marginalized and demonized as beastly (but not beasts). The Bible portrayed Canaanites, the aboriginal inhabitants of Canaan, as giants. Aboriginals – whether in the New World or Australia – were labelled as 'savages' by the European 'discoverers'. This label enabled domination and the grabbing of land from the native inhabitants. From the thirteenth century, monstrous races of being were thought to inhabit the peripheries of the earth. These beast-men were neither beasts nor men. Medieval travellers, basing their judgement on social customs, categorized races as monstrous, and this in turn helped them develop particular notions of humanity (Ramey 2008). John Mandeville's (fictitious) travelogue described people with the heads of dogs, one eye, and other such 'different' bodies. Many of these monstrous races in cultural accounts inhabited the African continent (Wittkower 1942). The blacks were considered morally monstrous (Neill 1989), and hypersexed. Hence Shakespeare's Othello, critics have noted, is consistently presented as 'monstrous' (Aubrey 1993) and a 'lascivious Moor'. Thomas More's representation of Richard III as a monster allowed him to depict the king's physical deformities as symptomatic of a moral deviance. This moral monstrous fitted in with the Christian world view in which sin resulted in deformity (Jewiss 2001). Mary Shelley's

Frankenstein gave the world its first sci-fictional monster, who demands that he be treated as a human, with Human Rights. Stevenson's Mr Hyde became the prototype of the moral monstrous, a man who becomes bestial, and the worst aspects of the human – which makes him akin to the 'animal' – are articulated incrementally so that, soon, there is nothing of the human left in him. Like More, Stevenson shows moral depravity as articulated in the form of twisted physiognomies and body structure. Bram Stoker's Dracula became the forerunner of the cultural icon, the vampire. In the twentieth century, the sustained representation of Jews as vermin, and therefore as an inferior form of life, in the Nazi state is what ultimately justified the Final Solution and the genocide.

Even this short inventory of cultural representations indicates how a form of life that was significantly different from the socially constructed, mythicized norm, and whose cultural practices were different, was excluded from the realm of the human. Humanity survives by constructing modes of exclusion, and the monster's ontological liminality enables domination, persecution, incarceration/containment, exhibition/display, genocide, displacement and elimination of certain forms of life. Monster studies maps these processes of categorization and exclusion.

Structures of exclusion and boundary marking, monster studies notes, involved criteria based on appearance or character. Cohen defines the monster thus: 'This refusal to participate in the classificatory "order of things" is true of monsters generally: they are disturbing hybrids whose externally incoherent bodies resist attempts to include them in any systematic structuration. And so the monster is dangerous, a form suspended between forms that threatens to smash distinctions' (6). Thus, strange beasts – chimeras, for example, or Grendel in the Old English epic, *Beowulf* – are monstrous because they do not fit into the classification of identifiable animals. But there are also humans whose physiognomies and bodies situate them outside the realm of the human. The 'incoherent bodies' (patched together from other bodies, as in the case of Frankenstein's creature; which doesn't die and decompose, as in Dracula; mixed, as in the case of the sphinx) constitute a humanoid monstrous.

However, monstrosity was also the morally different or disobedient character of humans. Humans who function on the level of sheer animality – as in Stevenson's Mr Hyde – are morally monstrous. Racial classifications, from the medieval to the present, have relied upon this mode of categorization of the moral monstrous. Corruption of any kind, moral, psychological, physical, was deemed monstrous. Hence madness was monstrous, according to medieval medical theories – but even well into the twentieth century – because it was the corruption of the processes of thought. Such ideas of corruption were of course gendered, with women being deemed mere 'matter' as opposed to the male 'mind', and seen as corrupting, or vulnerable to corruption. Questions of reproduction, of species, individuals and families, often revolve around the 'corruption' of women's bodies, as we see in numerous sci-fi films and popular fiction such as *Rosemary's Baby* or Doris Lessing's *The Fifth Child* in which *what* the woman gives birth to is a key thematic.[1] The woman's role in accommodating/housing a monster baby/creature, the woman as monstrous, and reproduction as monstrous all revolve around particular anxieties about the origins of species and individuals.

Monster theories and studies of the grotesque propose that monstrosities are made of 'something illegitimately *in* something else' (Harpham 1982: 11, emphasis in original). 'Co-presence . . . harbours the essence of the grotesque, the sense that things that should be kept apart are fused together', writes Harpham about the grotesque (11). This is true of the monstrous as well. Chimeras, especially in genetically modified creatures, are excellent examples of forms of life whose 'constitution' includes another gene, another species. As we shall see in the case of animal studies, commentators have noted that the human defines itself as such by denying the illegitimate animal within itself, by seeking an expulsion of the animal inside, as the presence of the animal makes the human monstrous (as in Mr Hyde).

Monster and grotesque studies illuminate the construction of species boundaries and the classificatory regimes that seek to separate out and displace the 'non-human'. Harpham notes that when we see new forms we first seek to compare them with what we are already familiar with. This is an effort to locate the creature/form as adjacent to a known category, till such time as we 'discover a proper place for the new thing, and we recognize it not only for what it is like but also for what it is, in itself' (Harpham 1982: 16). Thus, he notes, 'we have learnt to call mouse-birds bats and horse-men, centaurs' (16). It is in the interval between recognizing various constituent forms of the object and the clear sense of the dominant principle that defines the object that the grotesque exists. Thus, we recognize in Frankenstein's monster, Dracula, the mutant children in *Geek Love*, the mutants of *X-Men*, human and non-human characteristics. But we are not sure of the percentile of human features in any of them. Does the human feature serve as the dominant, defining characteristic of Wolverine or of the creature in *Frankenstein*? Till such time as we have a category for these others, we treat them as monstrous/monsters. We, of course, now have a label that categorizes many of these 'deviations': freaks and mutants. Monster studies suggests to us that the confusion (Harpham consistently plays on the subtext of the term: con-fusion) of species is what produces anxieties in humans because humanity exists in determining the limits of all species.

Species borders are also defined when cultures and races develop myths of origins. Geographical, genetic, cultural origins are central to ethnic, racial and species identities. The crisis of mutant babies works precisely on this theme. Children born to parents of different races were deemed to be monstrous in medieval Europe (articulated in tracts like Ambroise Paré's 1573 *Of Monsters and Prodigies*). St Augustine, meditating on the origins of monstrous races, writes:

It is asked whether we are to believe that certain monstrous races of men, spoken of in secular history, have sprung from Noah's sons, or rather, I should say, from that one man from whom they themselves were descended. . . . It ought not to seem absurd to us that as in individual races there are monstrous births, so in the whole race there are monstrous races. Wherefore, to conclude this question cautiously and guardedly, either these things which have been told of some races have no existence at all; or if they do exist, they are not human races; or if they are human, they are descended from Adam. (cited in Ramey 2008: 82)

Lynn Ramey's gloss on Augustine draws attention to the way origins are talked about:

If they even exist, which is in doubt, and if they are men (defined as rational and mortal), the monstrous races must be descended from Adam. Rationality is a clear component of humanness, but Augustine does not attempt to determine whether monstrous peoples are capable of reason; rational thinking is a test that will become central to later discussions of other races and their humanness. (82–3)

'Unnatural births' signify the monstrous, and creatures such as Victor Frankenstein's invention, born inside a laboratory, would readily classify as monstrous due to the process of his birth. The monsters of sci-fi are either from 'outside' the Earth or occupy spaces that are unknown and unknowable (the sci-fi film's theme of alien invasion by creatures from 'outside' fits into a tradition in which the monster has always occupied the regions beyond the map, or the peripheries of the known world: see Mittman 2006, Cohen 1996: 13–16). Creatures at a temporal distance, i.e., from the past – such as the Loch Ness monster or the yeti, but also revenants and ghosts – are also monstrous too for they do not belong to 'our time'. The spatial and temporal distancing of species is also infused with a different politics: that of ethnic identity. Cultures distrust people from a different spatial location, and hence ancestry debates, as Asa Mittman has demonstrated in the case of early Britain (2006: ch. 1), are often *origin* stories to establish the purity – and therefore boundaries – of a culture, or ethnic group. This is why cloned beings are referred to in popular accounts as monstrous: these are not born through acceptable 'natural' processes and do not carry a reliable origin story. The same is true for nomadic tribes, like the gypsies, migrants and refugees – people with origin stories and geographical origins that are different from those of the receiving societies.[2] Vampires present an apotheosis of this problematic origin story theme because they 'breed' through asexual reproduction: one becomes a vampire, enters the family or race of vampires when bitten by another (Nayar 2010: 66).

The ability of the monster to feel 'human' emotions is usually presented as a redeeming feature. Here, essentializing the human as one possessing certain kinds of emotions – a line of thought that comes in for interrogation in animal studies as well – is a cultural construction. Readings of the creature's remorse at the death of his maker Frankenstein therefore treat the monster as understanding the sanctity of life. This, when juxtaposed with the life-saving gesture of the replicant Batty in Ridley Scott's cult work *Blade Runner* (Deckard, out to end Batty's life, is saved from certain death when he loses his grip when dangling from a great height: Batty grabs Deckard's hand), suggests that monsters can be 'humanized' as well (Abbott 1993). Once again, such representations seek to define essential species characteristics, and hopefully speculate on the possibilities of monsters being 'humanized' through the acquisition of a moral outlook. In other cases the monstrous is one where the human abandons her/his 'essential' humanity and exhibits behaviour akin to animals, or automata. Thus when Connie in Marge Piercy's *Woman on the Edge of Time* discovers that she will be implanted with a device that will help the asylum doctors to manipulate her behaviour she thinks: 'she would be a walking monster with a little computer inside' (1976: 277). Connie and Skip, another inmate who has had the surgery and been implanted with controlling biochips, greet each other with 'hello monster', to show what they have 'evolved' into (279). Once again, autonomy and rationality are seen as essential human charac-teristics, and ones whose loss would shift the human closer to animals or automata: in short, monsters. In Kazuo Ishiguro's novel about cloning, *Never Let Me Go*, the artwork of students is taken away and put in a gallery so that it can be proved that clones who possess artistic abilities also possess souls (2005: 248, 255). Art, generosity and remorse are seen as humanizing the monsters in these cases.

Monster theory thus demonstrates the speciousness of species borders, the cultural construction of difference and the essentializing of identity in representations of hybrid creatures, deformed bodies and 'deviant' beings. Monster theory's major contribution to critical posthumanism is to point to the problematic of species identity by showing how various criteria – origin and birth, spatial location, 'essential' qualities, form, identifiable species categories – have been invoked to relegate particular forms of life to the realm of the monstrous, thereby ensuring a clear boundary for the human. It thus reveals the constructed nature of species boundaries when, by analys-ing the politics of monstrous discourses, it draws attention to the cross-over, the interspecies and the hybrid that very often share space, characteristics and genes with humans. This is also the territory that animal studies maps for the ways and processes in which the human/animal boundaries are constructed.

ANIMAL NATURE, HUMAN NATURE

Within animal studies, the debates about the human/non-human have been multi-layered. A short inventory of the realms within which 'animality' has been sought and questioned would include:

- the ability of animals to experience pain and suffering;
- animal consciousness;

- animals' sense of their own mortality (as opposed to 'mere' death);[3]
- altruism, responsibility and other such ethical 'qualities' in animals;
- communications.

Vegans ask whether we would eat a cow if we could consider that the cow *thinks* like us, humans. The point is, they argue, we have specific assumptions as to what 'to think' means. How and what the cow's thinking processes are will not be deemed to be 'thoughts', and this allows us to consume the cow. This is anthropocentrism, of course, and explains why cannibalism is such a taboo: one cannot eat a life form that is deemed to think exactly like us (Fudge 2002: 14). This problem of consuming a life form that thinks like us humans is resolved in Atwood's *Oryx and Crake*. Jimmy encounters lab-grown chickens. This is the description of the animal: 'A large bulb-like object . . . with stippled whitish-yellow skin . . . with thick fleshy tubes'. These are specialized 'chicken parts', not chickens, just chicken breasts in one, drumsticks on another. So the horrified Jimmy asks 'what's it thinking?' And he is informed, 'they'd removed all the brain functions that had nothing to do with digestion, assimilation, and growth' (2004: 237–8). So whether the 'animals' think becomes an irrelevant question.

It is the human's definition of the human's autonomy, thought processes and rationality that constitutes the central problematic for animal studies.

The uniqueness of human life, it has been argued throughout history, has to do with qualities such as the human's autonomy, rationality and ability to reason, and communication (language), and since they do not possess *these* qualities, animals are not 'equal to' humans. But, as Patrick Fuery and Nick Mansfield point out, it is the human who has determined which qualities *count as human* (cited in Castricano 2008: 6). Further, it is the human cognition of what the animal (or human) *is* that determines who 'possesses' or 'deserves' rights.[4] This means, further, that what distinguishes the human from the animal is that the former has appropriated the right to grant rights to itself. It allocates to itself, or invents, the forms of classification and categorization through which the animal other is consigned to the *animal* or non-human species. Thus we might be willing to extend some rights to, say, apes and chimps because they are 'almost like humans', even if considerably 'lower' in the degree of human-like qualities. As Wolfe would put it, 'it's not humans versus great apes, it's humans and great apes – the "like us" crowd – versus everyone else' (2003: 192).

Philosophers critiquing humanism have pointed out that it is human cognition of what the animal is that matters: we do not at any point want to deal with a situation in which *the animal might know us in ways we do not understand* (Stanley Cavell refers to the 'sceptical terror' of the human when faced with this question of the animal's other-understanding, or an animal-understanding, of the human – cited in Wolfe 2003: 4).

In other words, the circularity of the argument in favour of ranking the human above the animal lies in the fact that humans evaluate life forms by deploying a set of criteria of qualities: these count as 'human' qualities, and these others are 'animal' qualities. But the very ranking of qualities as human and animal is the task of the human species; the animals have no means of establishing the superiority of their qualities. This argument ignores the socialization processes that instil these qualities, preferring, instead, to see them as 'natural' to the human life form. Particular qualities are developed over years of socialization and are then treated as natural to the human life form, and distinctive, by implication, from animal life.

Cultural historians note that the categorization of animals and their incorporation into capitalist exchange in contemporary culture (by way of commodification as meat, for products such as leather, as pets or for sport) has resulted in the suffering of animals. Tracing the genealogy of this exploitation, Bruce Boehrer writes:

> more species and breeds of animals became available in Europe during the period from 1400 to 1600 than ever before; they became available in greater numbers, over a wider geographical range, than ever before; and they were put to a broader variety of uses than ever before. As a result, animals in the Renaissance begin to assume the status of mass commodities. (cited in Vint 2010: 32)

Coterminous with this process is a socialization of *Homo sapiens* which, the philosopher Giorgio Agamben argues, is a process through which the human expels the animal or non-human within, so that the 'pure' human emerges (Agamben 2004: 15–16). Agamben echoes Walter Benjamin who wrote years before posthumanism appeared on the philosophical scene: 'The horror that stirs deep in man is an obscure awareness that in him something lives so akin to the animal that it might be recognized' (cited in Fudge 2002: 6). This process of socializing the animal out of the human, or domesticating the wildness within man, is exemplified in Margaret Atwood's *Oryx and Crake*. Atwood shows how the 'Crakers', a group of genetically modified humans who survive the plague that wipes out the rest of mankind, have been 'tamed', with the 'sense' of racism, sexuality, hierarchy all erased (2004: 358). Atwood's novel, as Hannes Bergthaller has argued, suggests how ecocide on Earth was the result of humanity's biology. Crake's modification of the humans, as described above, plays out the 'pastoral fantasy of humanism – he has employed the tools of genetic engineering in order to breed the wildness out of man, creating a species of human beings that will be congenitally unable to soil the planetary *oikos*' (2010: 735). The project here is to separate, through technology and socialization, those hormone-driven, animal features within man that have resulted in the human species being non-sustainable. The species boundaries here are clearly to be reconsidered.

From a different domain, the animal–human interaction has been examined for the way animals affect humans. (In a later chapter I shall explicitly address the question of symbiotic relations between and across species.) In Atwood's *The Year of the Flood*, Adam One offers a posthumanist vision of this cross-species dependency: 'Where would we be without the Flora that populate the intestinal tract, or the Bacteria that defend against hostile invaders? We teem with multitudes, my Friends – with the myriad forms of Life that creep about under our feet, and – I may add – under our toenails' (2009: 192). This is very close to Alphonso Lingis' exposition of the interaction quoted in chapter 2.

Erica Fudge argues that pets humanize us, and we treat them as individuals rather than as animals. Fudge's argument is worth citing at some length for she draws attention, like the sci-fi and fantasy authors discussed above, to the species-crossing involved in caring for pets:

The pet crosses over species boundaries. It is an animal – it cannot speak – but it is also an ideal human – it says what we want it to say. It is only when the pet displays its animal nature – when it pees on the carpet, brings in a half-dead sparrow, destroys the furniture – that we lose the tranquillity of the relation. Then, and only then, do we really confront the existence of something beyond our control in our home. (2002: 33)

Agamben, Benjamin and Fudge are all, in different ways, speaking of the *recognition* by humans of species difference and their institutionalized negotiations with these other species. To expel the animal, to care for an animal, and to suppress the animal means assuming we can identify species borders. When animals and other forms cross these species borders – and one cannot deny there is a not insignificant disquiet in us when we see animals talking in anthropomorphic films and 'animation' – the classifier-human is disturbed.[5]

These arguments are important for posthumanist thinking, for they point to the institutionalization of species differences through social and so-called 'civilizational' processes. What is also crucial here is that Agamben draws connections between mechanisms of species differentiation (between animal and human) and racism. Agamben writes: the 'anthropological machine' of humans 'functions by . . . isolating the non-human within the human'. The human is defined as such by drawing 'figures of an animal in human form': 'the slave, the barbarian, and the foreigner' (2004: 37). Our task is to examine the production of such 'extreme' (38) figures of the human and the inhuman/animal in slaughterhouses, genocides and concentration camps. This echoes Derrida's comparison in the powerful passage cited as the third epigraph to this chapter, and draws attention to the institutions of speciesism and racism.[6]

Other commentators have argued that a shared finitude (mortality) characterizes both humans and animals. Hence, argues Jacques Derrida, the very idea of 'animal life' is constituted by a 'heterogeneous multiplicity' of entities and a 'multiplicity of organization of relations among realms that are more and more difficult to dissociate by means of the figures of the organic and inorganic, of life and/or death' (2002: 399). Recent studies, Matthew Calarco notes, also show that supposedly unique human features like altruism exist among animals as well, and therefore there is no real break between human and animals in terms of cognition and morality (2008a: 62).

The evolution of consciousness and the forms of meaning-making, cognitive sciences tell us today, are not immanent to the living system. The system depends on the environment – which includes non-human forms of life – in order to develop modes of meaning-making. In critical theory, Donna Haraway's recent work, in biology the work of Lynn Margulis, and in cognitive sciences and neurobiology the work of Humberto Maturana and Francisco Varela seems to indicate that human consciousness evolves due to its embeddedness within a system that is open to the surroundings.

In the matter of language, philosophers right from René Descartes have argued that the ability to communicate in language is a mark of the human. Beings with interior life use language to express that life. Animal training experiments through the twentieth century indicate that animals like chimpanzees, orang-utans and gorillas can be trained to use sign language, thus suggesting how animals might possess an interior life after all. However, what is troubling about the issue of language is, yet again, the anthropocentrism that makes the question of language central to species identity. The question has in some cases been turned right around. Erica Fudge cites a moderator on a chat on AOL about Koko the gorilla being trained to recognize sign language. Discussing the acquisition of language, the moderator asks: ' "I've heard people say she's not really communicating – I think she's smarter than we are – after all, how many of us can speak Gorilla!" ' Fudge comments:

This inversion of the original question, in which 'can animals learn to speak human language?' becomes 'can humans learn to speak animal language?', pulls out from under us the notion of our inbuilt superiority that persists in much of the language research. Why is it that our language is primary? Why not attempt communication in the other direction? If we are so superior, surely we should be able to speak ape? (2002: 127–8)

Consequent to researches in cognitive sciences and communication studies, the uniqueness of language as a human trait has been questioned by Noam Chomsky, Donna Haraway and others (Wolfe 2010: ch. 2). Relatedly, the late twentieth century also demolished the idea that autistic individuals do not have a subject inside them because they lack language as we understand it. Because rationality and subjectivity are seen as embedded in language, those with language 'problems' are treated as 'not subjects' – a theme that has been severely critiqued within animal studies, autism studies and cognitive studies. This means language is not a marker of the pure human and its alleged lack does not make the animal a lower subject or a non-subject.

Animal studies scholars demonstrate how a supposedly key feature of the human – sentience or subjectivity – is common among animals as well.

Tom Regan, ever since his *The Case for Animal Rights* (1983), has argued that animals are the same as human beings in being 'subjects-of-a-life' (his term), with personal preferences, being self-aware, with memory, the ability to initiate action in pursuit of their desires and goals, with a sense of autonomy, a sense of the future and an emotional life. And because animals demonstrate subject-like traits, they should be given the same moral consideration as humans. Proceeding along this line of thought, it would then follow that the very concept of subjectivity and the subject implies *human* subjectivity and the *human* subject.

The debate about the unique subjectivity of humans which animates the posthumanist critique also revolves around the question of personhood. Is a dog a person? While self-reflexivity, intelligence or consciousness, the way we humans understand these, might not be available to or present in animals, the issue is whether these determine 'personhood'. Would it be possible, asks David Sztybel (2008), to see suffering as an index of personhood? Sztybel argues that intelligence cannot be seen as an index of personhood because that in itself is an anthropocentric notion, for humans define what we understand as 'intelligence' in the first place. He further proposes that if we experienced an animal's pain, we would think of it as a 'personal' experience. Our experience would be generically identical with the animal's. The animal's own experience would be personal, and hence the animal might be considered a person (248). We no more wonder whether, as Derrida puts it, 'what [we] call animal could *look at* [us] and *address* [us] from down there, from a wholly other origin' (2002: 382).[7] The undecidability of what the animal sees ensures that we ought to understand the limits of human knowing.

THE HUMANIMAL

In Italo Calvino's *Mr. Palomar*, the protagonist Palomar speculates about animal being. Observing that the blackbird's behaviour replicates the behaviour of Palomar and his wife, he thinks of how the 'discrepancy between human behavior and the rest of the universe has always been a source of anguish. The equal whistle of man and blackbird now seems to him a bridge thrown over the abyss' (1983: 27). Calvino here locates the human as one of several animals where species differences are, at best, specious.

Contributing in a major way to critical posthumanist thinking, animal studies shows overlaps and continuities, even when there are differences, across species, and thus refuses the animal–human binary as an untenable, anthropocentric one.

Animal studies, especially in philosophy, has been interested in exploring the history of the human–animal distinction, to see how institutions, social and cultural practices, texts (of many kinds) have reinforced this distinction – what Cary Wolfe would identify as the discourse of speciesism and its institutionalization (2003) – and naturalized it. It is this genealogical study of the construction of the human–animal divide that has most directly influenced the posthumanist. The divide, according to animal studies, is founded upon ways of perceiving animal and other non-human life forms. Thus animal studies is interested in both the *representations* of animals within human forms of expression (literature, films, discursive writings, science writing) and the *materiality* of animals (animals as labour, as experimental subjects in laboratories, as meat for consumption).

Critical posthumanism is concerned not with questions of animal rights as much as with the issue of species borders, of the supposed 'uniqueness' of humans and the relations between and across species. This involves an exploration of the ways in which humans have perceived and represented other non-human species, ways that have then codified species differences, ignored similarities and established human dominance, and which critical posthumanism seeks to overturn.

Popular culture has also contributed to the ways in which we perceive animals. Metaphors, argues anthropologist Annabelle Sabloff, indicate the ways in which we think of animals. In the domain of the domestic, we see them as members of the family; in the domain of agriculture or industry, they are objects/artefacts to be exploited and used for production and profit; and in animal rights domains, they are citizens. Sabloff is gesturing at the many ways in which humans look at and therefore relate to animals, even as the animals themselves disappear into a language. All animals become, in this reading, objects of human perception, where the metaphor becomes a human way of dealing with animals (cited in Fudge 2002).

In the now cult film *Babe* (1995), which inspired many, including James Cromwell who played the role of Farmer Arthur Hoggett in the film, to take up vegetarianism and veganism, pigs are given humanoid characteristics: speech, desires, beliefs, preferences and emotions. The animals were also shown as being 'able' to suffer, which thus situated them closer to humans. While the anthropocentrism of the film cannot be denied, what is important to take away from it is that it is possible to *see* animals differently. Children's books now read as classics, including *Charlotte's Web* and *The Wind in the Willows*, also use anthropomorphic representations of animals. In science fiction, numerous authors have probed the problematic (and programmatic, since they are meant to reinforce the hierarchies of human over animal life) distinction between animal, human and machine. Sentience, for instance, treated as a crucial element of human nature, has been the stuff of sci-fi dreams and nightmares for a long time now. While this is not the space to elaborate a genealogy of sentience as a literary theme, a few examples from contemporary pop culture are in order.

Sci-fi asks: what does it mean to be 'truly' human, or 'merely' machine or animal? It is the genre that most often raises what Jacques Derrida in his 1991 essay 'Eating Well' would call the 'question of the animal'. The genre has often cast numerous animals – and aliens served up in forms that humans might re-cognize as animals – alongside humans in order to explore the (supposed) animal–human boundaries. In H. G. Wells' classic *The Island of Dr Moreau* (1896), Moreau seeks to make animals more like humans, and claims that, theoretically, it should be possible to educate a pig. What Wells seeks to demonstrate is the proximity of species: the animal-men in his novel are frightening monstrosities because they reveal not the separation between species, but their *kinship*. Wells therefore shows how vivisection of animals by humans is horrific because it refuses to see this kinship. In fiction that deals with Artificial Intelligence and advanced computers (in, say, William Gibson), we see sentience, self-awareness and desire as attributes of non-humans as well, specifically machines, which (who?) evolve into higher forms of conscious 'beings'. While Gibson's fiction is not engaged with animals, it does worry about the status of an authentically sentient being, if we see consciousness as the epiphenomenon arising out of a network and a system in which the being is embedded. This line of thought extended means that we see the interconnectedness of all sentient beings because we cannot, from a tenable moral position, claim hierarchic superiority over other sentient beings. These novelists make a case for a mutual dependency of humans and machines.

But this is not the only kind of 'rehumanization' of the human that sci-fi foregrounds. In other kinds of sci-fi and fantasy fiction, we see the theme of 'related' species. Anne Rice's vampire fiction (*Interview with a Vampire* and others), to take a prominent example, depicted vampires constituting families and social structures akin to – pun intended – humans, thereby suggesting a 'domestication' of the vampire. This domestication-of-the-vampire theme is replicated in recent pop culture, notably in Stephenie Meyer's *Twilight* saga (Nayar 2010). Octavia Butler makes a strong case for various species co-evolving, drawing upon each other's specific traits. In her last novel, *Fledgling* (2005), Butler proposes that vampires are a distinct 'cousin' – as she calls it – species to the humans, but have co-evolved with the humans. This converts the vampire – traditionally a monstrous other to the human – into something 'connected' to the human species. As the novel proceeds, Butler even proposes that the humans bitten by vampires do not become vampires themselves. Instead they become 'symbionts': dependent upon the vampires, but gaining longevity and greater powers of healing as a result of the connectedness.

Derrida himself in his later writings has proposed that philosophical work must be about 'tracing such a line, between the human *in general* and the animal *in general*', 'casting doubt on all responsibility, every ethics, every decision, and so on' (2003: 128, emphasis in original) of this human–animal boundary.

The lead in examining the history of this institution of speciesism has come from literary and cultural studies scholars. In the last two decades, researchers focusing on the human–animal relations and on the representation of animals in Europe since early modern times have worked to reveal the mechanisms through which the 'practical and political mystery of separation [of animals and man]' (as Agamben phrased it) has been achieved (2004: 16).[8]

Humanity, as these arguments and studies show, occasionally acknowledges its kinship with animals but simultaneously also sees the human domination of animals as 'natural' because the animals are mere objects. As Erica Fudge puts it: 'to have an understanding of a shared origin, and shared capacity, but also, and simultaneously, to believe in the human right to dominion', is the paradox of the human–animal relation (2002: 21). Fudge argues, following Marc Shell, that when humans speak of their pets they are not speaking of animals as animals; they are speaking of them as pets first. This signifies a whole new way of 'looking at' animals (32). Further, the ownership and care of a pet makes us more human. That is, it is the way we treat animals that reveals the extent of our humanity (32).

There is yet another kind of linkage of species that scholars in animal studies now forward. Species borders are drawn based on the assumption that humans have a higher degree of autonomy, intelligence and rationality which supposedly separates them from animals. However, as Paolo Cavalieri points out, this cannot be a measure of species differentiation. If we take functional autonomy, reasoning and intelligence as markers of a 'person', then, Cavalieri argues, we have to accept that all human beings are not equally 'persons':

It is not true that all human beings possess the attributes that allegedly mark the difference between us and the other animals. It is undeniable that there exist within our species individuals who, on account of structural problems due to genetic or developmental anomalies, or of contingent problems due to diseases or accidents, will never acquire, or have forever lost, the characteristics – autonomy, rationality, self-consciousness, and the like – that we consider as typically human. (2001: 76)

Thus, 'there are members of our species – the brain-damaged, the severely intellectually disabled, the anencephalics, the irreversibly comatose, the senile – who, while being human in the biological sense, are not human in the philosophical sense' (2001: 76). Cavalieri's point is one that autistic animal trainer Temple Grandin has emphasized about her own life. Grandin, who designs special cattle handling systems – which keep the animals calm – for slaughterhouses, writes:

My life as a person with autism is like being another species: part human and part animal. Autistic emotion may be more like an animal's. Fear is the dominant emotion in both autistic people and animals such as deer, cattle, and horses, etc. My emotions are simple and straightforward like an animal's, my emotions are not deep-seated. They may be intense while I am experiencing them but they will subside like an afternoon thunderstorm. (2006: 184)

The urgent need therefore, given the demolition of the uniqueness argument (human as unique), writes Matthew Calarco, is to develop 'an alternative ontology of animal life in which the animal–human distinction is called into question' (2008: 141). This means that we accept that the animal confronts us with the same ethical force as any human. This ethical dimension of the 'question of the animal' is related not only to the ontology of the animal but also to larger issues of rights and racisms.

SPECIESISM

Thus far, as we have seen, animal studies has explored the ways in which the animal's ontology has been circumscribed within the definitions and defining characteristics evolved by humans. Looking at, observing, recording animals, the human species has consistently determined what it is to be animal. Writing about this tendency, John Berger states: 'Animals are always the observed . . . They are the objects of our ever-extending knowledge. What we know about them is an index of our power, and thus an index of what separates us from them' (cited in Rohman 2009: 64).

A critique of this separation of species by one of the species on Earth is animal studies' final contribution to critical posthumanist thought. But before we move on to this critique a word about biologists' attempts to undo species identity is in order.

Biologists are certain of a 'species identity' for most life forms on Earth. Yet animal-to-human and human-to-animal cross-overs and mixing to produce chimeras – indicating species-blurring – are now common. For example, transgenic rabbits (Eduardo Kac's fluorescent Alba), human kidneys in mice or transgenic primates in laboratories suggest human attempts to effect species-blurring. As early as the 1960s scientists were speaking of such species mixing (see Krimsky 1982), and now such chimeric creatures that blur the border between human and non-human species are very much a reality.

Speciesism positions the human as the dominant species that then controls, domesticates, oppresses, exploits, guards and pets non-human, animal species. Speciesism is a discourse and a mode of cultural representation – in popular culture, but also in science writing, the law, rights campaigns, conservation movements – through which this exploitation is naturalized and made possible. Critical posthumanism calls for an undoing of these discourses by pointing to species-crossing, hybridity, mutual dependency and co-evolution.

Central to the critique of speciesism and the informing anthropocentrism of humanism that separates humans from non-humans is the 'justice' argument made by animal liberation and bioethicist scholars like Peter Singer. Singer, the pioneer of animal rights studies, argues that a 'speciesism' has marked the human–animal relationship. Singer goes further and makes a comparison of this relationship with racism which, he suggests, is also a kind of speciesism. Singer writes:

the appropriate response to those who claim to have found evidence of genetically based differences in ability between the races or sexes is not to stick to the belief that the genetic explanation must be wrong, whatever evidence to the contrary may turn up; instead we should make it quite clear that the claim to equality does not depend on intelligence, moral capacity, physical strength, or similar matters of fact. Equality is a moral ideal, not a simple assertion of fact. There is no logically compelling reason for assuming that a factual difference in ability between two people justifies any difference in the amount of consideration we give to satisfying their needs and interests. The principle of equality of human beings is not a description of an alleged actual equality among humans: it is a prescription of how we should treat humans. (cited in Castricano 2008: 8–9)

And later Singer draws the parallels between racist Europeans who believed that, unlike them, the Africans did not feel pain and speciesists who believe that animal pain is far less intense than human pain (cited in Castricano 2008: 8–9).

Singer here is criticizing speciesism that produces and reinforces differences among species but also makes a significant move. Singer argues that biological or genetic difference cannot be the yardstick for differential treatment of species. What is also striking in Singer's stance is the link he forges between speciesism directed against animal species and racism directed by Europeans against 'lesser' races – where the latter was founded on myths and theories about the immunity to pain among, say, the Africans.

Singer's emphasis on equal treatment of different species is an important moral position within animal studies, and one which enables the critical posthumanist to extend in another direction. Singer's moral ideal argument calls for equal *consideration* across species, even if there are differences. One could say that this is less a question of the fact of difference than a question of *responding* to that difference with empathy. New cultural studies and theory, which draws upon animal studies' arguments such as the above, therefore emphasizes the human–animal relationship as one based on empathy and connectedness (Castricano 2008: 5). It is this emphasis that has a direct route into critical posthumanism.

What animal studies do is to point to the constructed nature of the 'animal'. That is, it treats the 'animal' as a category or a definition that has been constructed by the humans, and which has been naturalized through centuries of representations which in turn have naturalized particular kinds of exploitative material interactions of human and animal. Through this construction, a relation and comparison of human and animal is also naturalized, erasing the constructed nature of the two categories.

Yet the erasure of categories and the human-induced species-crossing itself suggests a kind of speciesist discourse because it reinstates the *authority* of the humans to control species-crossing. Culturally, such cross-overs attract opprobrium for the usual reason: mankind playing God, disturbing the 'true' order of nature, disrespecting 'essential' species traits, among others. But they also attract notoriety and anxiety because such creatures become unclassifiable as human or non-human. The human 'authority' to impose classifications and attribute 'essential' species traits is also part of the politics of such species-mixing. More importantly, as Robert and Baylis argue, it is the uncertainty of our human moral obligation to creatures whose genetic code is partly human that leads to an implicit critique of human-engineered species-mixing (2003: 9).

Artists advocating species exchange, border crossing, animal rights and worrying about what it is to *be* an animal have also contributed to rethinking the question of species (Baker 2003). However, as the critical animal studies scholar Helena Pedersen points out, the importance attached to boundary dissolution between animals and humans ignores the fact that the relations between animals and humans are never symmetrical. Adapting the work of Crist (2004) and Weisberg (2009), Pedersen argues that border dissolution itself suggests the human urge to 'be a part of an expanded context and community of life forms', indicative of an 'ecological colonialism'. For many species, she notes, where suffering has come from others, it would be essential to protect 'their subject boundaries from uninvited intervention' (2011: 72). In other words, the posthuman impulse to cross species borders might itself be read as a traditional human colonizing impulse, with the other species not necessarily keen on such border infiltration. Like Pedersen, Zipporah Weisberg criticizes Haraway's argument about species border-crossing, because Haraway ignores, according to Weisberg, the unequal and instrumental nature of the relations between human and non-human species (2009: 29).

To summarize, animal studies suggests that we rethink the categories of 'animal' and 'human' and recognize the anthropocentric construction of these categories. It interrogates the foundations of the criteria used to evaluate essential 'humanness' and 'animality'. It demonstrates how notions of care, pets, stewardship (by humans of animals, embodied in the zoo), superiority and even animal rights are anthropocentric in their assumptions. It proposes that speciesism is a form of racism in which some forms of life are consigned to the margins to be exploited, brutalized, ignored or eliminated. Giorgio Agamben summarizes it this way: 'The Jew is the non-man produced within man, the comatose person is the animal separated from within the human body itself' (2004: 37). Animal studies emphasizes that species borders are constructed but permeable. It insists that there need to be other ways of looking at and responding to animal life: empathy is here a key element. It is also wary of human attempts to break species boundaries because, as noted immediately above, such attempts recall the human race's colonization of other species.

Animal studies contributes to critical posthumanist thought by suggesting that species borders are not valid, that different forms of life must be seen as different but not inferior, that all forms of life are interconnected, that life forms evolve in cooperation not competition alone. A pithy summary of critical posthumanist thought that draws the animal into debates about the human is available from philosopher Matthew Calarco:

The posthumanist critique of humanism is to be understood . . . as a critical investigation of human subjectivity, of the material . . . forces at work in the formation of human subjects . . . [it shows how] the presubjective conditions that gave rise to human subjectivity . . . cannot easily be restricted to human beings . . . the subjective being of many non-human animals too is constituted by differential structures of exposure that render standard accounts of the human–animal distinction suspect . . . what we encounter . . . [is] complex. (2008: 89)

5 Life Itself: The View from Disability Studies and Bioethics

In Kazuo Ishiguro's *Never Let Me Go*, the artwork created by the individuals – these are clones, created for the explicit purpose of becoming 'donors', to donate their organs to those in need, and eventually 'complete', i.e., die when all their crucial organs have been harvested – in Hailsham, the school for clones, is collected for a mysterious gallery by a 'Madame'. Years later, the clones Tommy and Kathy turn up at the house of the Madame to find out why she collected those paintings, and what she did with them. The Madame and her friend Emily, who was a teacher at Hailsham, tell the two clones that they took away the students' art because they thought it would 'reveal' their 'inner selves', their '*souls*' (2005: 248, emphasis in original). Their art, therefore, was an index of the humanity of the individuals in Hailsham: 'we did it to *prove you had souls at all*' (255, emphasis in original). Ishiguro's novel asks: what does it mean to be human? Is a clone, derived from human DNA, a human, a person? What exactly is the soul that is taken to be the determinant of all things human? These are bioethical questions. Bioethics is the domain from which sustained interrogations of contemporary life-changing, life-creating and life-merging technologies have emerged. It is in bioethics that the boundaries of life and death, of 'complete individuals' and 'unfinished' individuals (such as those who are differently abled) and therefore of 'persons' and 'non-persons' are explored.

To take cultural representations of a different kind, think of Long John Silver, Captain Hook, Shakespeare's Richard III and Lear, Hawthorne's Chillingworth, Firdous Kanga's famous autobiography (*Heaven on Wheels*), Herman Melville's maniacal, one-legged Captain Ahab, D.H. Lawrence's Clifford Chatterley, villains with prosthetic devices or with particular disorders (albinism in Dan Brown's hugely successful *The Da Vinci Code*, the giant resistant to pain in Stieg Larsson's *Millennium* trilogy), where varying kinds of impairments in individuals position them in different ways vis-à-vis society.[1] Impairment and disability become markers of difference with the affected individuals always the Other to 'normal' human beings. They are unfinished and 'disabled' *persons*. In numerous films – most famously in Clint Eastwood's award-winning *Million Dollar Baby* (2004) – such individuals believe themselves to be better off dead rather than living with permanent disability that limits them as individuals.

In both cases – cloning and impairment/disability – what emerges is an issue that we have already examined from a different perspective in the animal studies chapter: the construction of boundaries between human and non-human, or rather, 'normal' human and Other 'human'. Monsters, beggars, madmen, freaks, mutants, animals and the differently abled have all been culturally represented as the radical, evil, repulsive Other to the human – they exist on the other side of the border. It is this issue of boundary-marking and personhood that brings disability studies and bioethics into the ambit of critical posthumanism.[2]

Critical posthumanism has already been defined as a philosophical approach that involves a rethinking of the very idea of subjectivity because it sees human subjectivity as an assemblage, co-evolving with machines and animals. It argues for a multispecies citizenship of humans, in which the human is a life form with trans-species dependency, affinity and linkages. It therefore calls for a more inclusive definition of life, and a greater moral–ethical response, and responsibility, to non-human life forms in the age of species-blurring and species mixing. Posthumanism interrogates the hierarchic ordering, exploitation and eradication of life forms. Normative subjectivity, which defined and categorized life forms into 'animal', 'plant' and 'human', is now under scrutiny for its exclusivism, and it is this that more than anything else marks critical posthumanism. It also entails an ethics and a *politics* of response and responsibility toward all forms of life, toward difference, as already noted in the preceding chapters.

Disability studies, which interrogates existing normative standards of what counts as the 'complete' human, contributes in significant ways to critical posthumanist thought. It calls for a shift from purely biomedical notions of disability to a social constructionist view in which the impaired body and the environment and social order are in a dynamic relation and the hierarchic ordering of the 'normal' body is seen as an unethical social construction that denies different bodies subjectivity and equal citizenship rights.

Bioethics itself, in the age of increasingly networked bodies, xenotransplantation, cloning and other new scientific and social conditions, has become more complicated where the boundedness of the human, the 'status' of life and living (whether in people in persistent vegetative states, foetuses or intelligent 'machines') are all under dispute. Bodies and personalities – enhanced, modified, networked – are all *different* and the very idea of a 'person', the subject of philosophical and political debates on Human Rights, demands overhauling. In the age of biobanks, 'genetic citizenship' (Kerr 2003) and 'tissue economies' (Waldby and Mitchell 2007) when human biomaterials circulate in the capitalist market exchanges – legally and illegally, the latter in the form of organ trade – governance and surveillance of humans (Gottweis 2008) for their genetic materials calls for new legislation and a new bioethics. New conceptualizations of the body and its sociality, transformed radically through transplantation, veer between the hybrid body as a threat to species integrity and the monstrous and 'different', but essentially accept it as 'denatured' (Sharp 2006).

Like critical posthumanism's emphasis on the networked and co-evolved nature of human life and consciousness, disability studies since the 1990s has veered away from an emphasis on the subject-body to one on the subject-body *in relation/networked with* settings, technology and other bodies, and toward the systems and environments in which bodies live and act.

DISABILITY STUDIES AND THE NORMS OF THE 'HUMAN'

In 1968 Erving Goffman's work *Stigma* argued that the stigmatized were those who had a physical impairment, or were members of particular communities (homosexuals, Jews, religious minorities), and who were treated by the rest of the society as 'not quite human' just because they deviated from 'anticipated norms'. Goffman was one of the first to point to disability or disfigurement as a *social* condition that was treated as a deviance from a norm. The establishment of norms for what constitutes the complete, perfect or acceptable human is also found in contemporary disability studies which foregrounds disability as a social rather than a medical issue.

As in the case of animal studies and critiques of liberal humanism, disability studies examines the construction of the human in biomedical, ethical and other discourses. Disability studies shows how 'disability' is produced within discourses that build on preconceived notions of normal bodies. These discourses cut across institutions, the state, welfare organizations and individuals, and fix particular kinds of identities on 'different' bodies.[3] Disability studies critics argue that the 'standard' or 'normal' human body is essentially a corporeal ideal, and very few bodies actually attain this ideal.

Contemporary identities – masculine, feminine, white, black – are built around particular hegemonic norms. For instance, masculinity is associated with men who are strong, aggressive and independent (Connell 1987). Thomas Gerschick and Adam Miller write that the 'body is a central foundation of how men define themselves and how they are defined by others' (2008: 3). These are *cultural* values eddying around bodies. Therefore, men with impairment experience what Robert Murphy refers to as 'embattled identities' (cited in Gerschick and Miller 2008: 4). 'Embattled identities' are, in other words, the result of some individuals and their bodies not fitting the established (hegemonic) *norms of the prevalent age/culture*.

In an early essay, activist and critic Paul Hunt argued that there is a great deal of emphasis on conformity, and society sets up 'rigid standards of what is right and proper', and the 'disabled person's "strangeness" can manifest and symbolize all differences between human beings' ([1966] 2008: 29–30). Hunt focuses on the dignity of persons with impairments and the stringent measures of classification that reduce them to non-persons lacking all dignity and identity. Differences, Hunt suggests, are less important than commonalities. In critical race studies and feminist critiques of liberal humanism, as we have already noted (chapter 1), it is the construction and policing of differences between humans that constitutes the etiology of racisms. Hunt's comments add one more layer to the critique of the politics of difference.

Autonomy, Environment and the Body

Disability studies rejects the purely medical sense of disability for its emphasis on limitations on physical activity and efficiency. Due to biomedical preoccupation with limitations and inabilities, no attention is paid to the 'possibilities of modifying the environment . . . or alternating the expectation that all men and women are required to possess a full range of physical, mental, and emotional capacities to qualify for membership in the human community' (Hahn 2008: 59–60). To assume that disability arises only from physical flaws in a person is to ignore the defects in an 'unadaptive environment' (60). Therefore it is necessary to locate the physically different body in its environment and ask whether the structured social environment can adapt to the needs of this different body. Disability therefore is not immanent in the impaired body but is the result of an interaction with an environment that prevents it (the body) from engaging in a full range of tasks and actions. There exists, in other words, a 'disabling environment' (64). Impairment, when it faces a disabling environment, becomes 'disability' (Thomas [2004] 2008: 383), disability being 'an emergent property' of the 'interplay between the biological reality of physiological impairment, structural conditioning (i.e., enablements/constraints), and socio-cultural interaction/elaboration' (Simon Williams, cited in Thomas [2004] 2008: 387; see also Vehmas 2008). Clearly, disability here is a 'cultural interpretation of human variation rather than an inherent inferiority' (Garland-Thomson 2008: 197).

With this an important shift has been made, and one crucial for rethinking the human–environment/system relation that critical posthumanism is interested in. The subject-body is no more the 'damaged' or partial human. Disability is the unresponsive *environment* in which this subject-body finds it impossible to work or live to the full extent of its needs and aspirations. Disability studies here, as Hahn defines it, is primarily interested in the *mutual connectedness of body and environment*.

Another reading of the cultural history of disability, with reference to the American context, sees the change in representations of the disabled body as linked to the capitalist economy emerging in the nineteenth century: the disabled body is not a productive member of the workforce or the nation in this capitalist economy.[4]

The shift also entails recasting the individualist modes of seeing disability when it treats the impaired and the 'able' body as both enmeshed in an environment which is inherently unfair to people with variant bodies and physiologies. Therefore, critics like Mike Oliver (2008) argue that liberal humanism's valorization of the autonomous human subject foregrounds independence as the determining characteristic of the individual. This, in Oliver's reading, enacts two essentialisms:

- it ignores the mutual dependency of all human beings in which even self-care is contingent upon social structures, inter-human relations and environs in which one can take care of the self;
- it constructs the impaired body as dependent upon the state or organizations because, it is believed, the functional limitations of this body prevent it from fully caring for the self.

The criticism of the impaired body's supposed dependency in this reading is an important one for it asks: what are the norms through which the functionality of the body is evaluated?

Objectification and Normalization

In popular culture, objectifications of disability are legion. Dennis Hopper seeks to wreak vengeance upon the city after he loses his hand while on duty as a cop in the 1994 hit *Speed*. Disabled villains with prostheses figure in the cult Bruce Lee film *Enter the Dragon*, James Bond flicks like *Goldfinger*, thrillers like *I Know What You Did Last Summer* and the Harrison Ford-starrer *Fugitive*. Each of them seems to suggest the individual's predilection for evil acts is somehow connected to his deformity or disability.[5]

As in the case of monsters and animals, impaired bodies are objectified, rendered 'objects rather than subjects' (Shakespeare [1994] 2008: 196). The object becomes a screen onto which all anxieties and fears of the community are projected. In an argument that echoes Leslie Fiedler's about 'freaks', Shakespeare suggests that the presence of disabled people serves an important function: they facilitate able-bodied people to feel good about themselves (197), and a disabled body reminds them of their own vulnerability (209). If animals and monsters are invariably reduced to matter and bodies, so are disabled people whose *bodies* are seen as ugly, threatening and constraining/impaired. Such strange, anomalous bodies must therefore be restrained, labelled and controlled. Shakespeare argues that disability is seen as a state between animality and humanity, a border or liminal condition that is inherently uncategorizable. People with restricted growth could be children or adults, mental illness was treated with incarceration, the eighteenth century wondered whether deaf people were fully human, and deformed babies were portents of disaster right from early modern times in Europe (203–6).

This objectification means an impaired body is reduced to its impairment: impairment is the individual's primary identity. All social roles are determined by this view of the individual as a 'disabled' individual and nothing more in the culture of 'physicalism' (Corker 2008: 70). Impairment achieves, in Rosemary Garland-Thomson's words, 'the determining force of a master status' (Brueggemann et al. 2008: 182) because 'strangers do not let us forget that their perception of us is dominated by the ways in which we are different' (Keith 2008: 29).

The human body of a particular type, shape and functionality has been seen as natural and normal. The impaired body, therefore, is abnormal, deficient and unusual. This results in a discourse of normalization in which deviant and deficient bodies have to be 'corrected' and brought in line with 'normal' bodies. Objectification was very often a process through which the disabled body was spectacularized, as in the case of the Elephant Man in Victorian England. The disabled body was a freak body, and was put on show for people to come and marvel at.[6]

This objectification – which also consigned 'blacks' and 'coloureds', along with the 'disabled', to the domain of the useless body (Lennard Davis, cited in Mitchell and Snyder 2006: 125) – has often produced three key stereotypes of the disabled: the disabled as evil, the disabled as disgruntled (due to their impairment) and the disabled as vengeful (Longmore [1985] 1997). This stereotyping enabled restrictive and containment policies toward the disabled, Longmore argues. It is also important to note that such representations almost always showed the disabled as solitary, painfully isolated individuals: there was little or no attempt to present the social conditions of their disability, conditions that dehumanized them and forced them into the seclusion of their rooms, homes, prisons or hospitals.

Resisting the objectification–normalization structures of the social order isn't easy for the impaired body. However, cultural representations of such a resistance are visible in fictional figures like Melville's Ahab in his classic *Moby-Dick*. Driven, monomaniacal and tempestuous, Ahab hates being a disabled captain. Yet, as we see the novel's plot progressing, we understand that Ahab controls everything on the ship. Ahab is an embodiment of the 'reformulation' pattern of the disabled individual's coping with hegemonic views of the male or human body. Thomas Gerschick and Adam Miller (2008) suggest that some individuals cope with disability and its lack of fit with hegemonic bodily and other norms through a process of reformulation wherein the disabled acts *through* others. Rather than see themselves as dependent on others, these individuals see themselves as controlling their carers, employees and friends. The dominant standards of what the complete man should be are reformulated here. Thus Ahab

is the sole dominant authority on the ship. He reformulates the model
of the fit, able-bodied and authoritarian captain when, despite his impairment, he manages to ensure his authority over all the others on the ship.
What is significant is that this reformulation in Ahab's case relies on
others (including prosthetic devices), but it is not seen by him as reliance.
Reformulation, then, (i) recasts the impaired body in a different relationship with its environment, and (ii) rejects established hegemonic roles for
the body.

Cyborged Bodies

In James Cameron's *Avatar* it is a cyborged soldier, Jake Sully, who eventually becomes the hero of the alien species, in contrast to the so-called 'full'
humans who are keener on destroying them. Lincoln Rhyme, the detective-
protagonist of Jeffrey Deaver's thrillers like *The Bone Collector*, is a cyborg:
quadriplegic and able to move only two fingers but bestowed with superior
intellect, Rhyme solves crimes while sitting networked in his bed. Disability
here is often presented as an opportunity to continue to experience life
through prosthetic technologies.

Disability studies calls attention to discourses of deviance and normalcy
that relegate the impaired body to the realm of the monstrous. It argues
that the 'normal' body is itself the consequence of a set of discourses and
has always been enmeshed with prosthetic technologies, institutions and
networks. That is, disability studies proposes that we see so-called 'normal'
bodies as always already networked and co-evolving with technology. There
is no 'natural' body in this interpretation, one which holds much value for
posthumanist thought (Moser [2000] 2008).

When Melville shows Ahab as a monomaniacal, irritable and unpleasant
captain (he is described at one point as 'desperate, moody and savage'), he
also attributes this to the loss of his limb to the whale. Thus Melville writes
that Ahab's foul temper had its origins when 'sharp, shooting pains in his
bleeding stump' started after his encounter with the whale. But Melville
also presents Ahab as a cyborged body, dependent upon a whole set of
apparatuses to help him navigate ship and shore: a banister that he grips,
the prosthetic leg, a winch hook and specially designed saddle to lift him
into the ship, extra sheathing for the boat's bottom, among others. Thus,
even though Ahab is a captive to his impaired body – for which Melville
provides an allegoric parallel, by showing how Ahab is captive to his whale
obsession – he is presented as a cyborged being determined to transform
his 'odd' embodiment into a weapon of vengeance (Mitchell and Snyder
2000: 137).

The prosthesis itself, writes David Wills, is about 'measuring the distance
– that of the necessary separation and unavoidable complication between
animate and inanimate form, between natural and artificial' (1995: 40).
Later he adds: 'There never was any idea of the human constituted without

reference to prosthetic articulations, relations to supposed othernesses; what seem to be the possibilities of subsequent prosthetic attachments – principles of nonintegrity, detachability, and replacement – are in fact the constituting principles of the human mechanism' (71). This argument has important consequences for how we view (i) disabled bodies with prostheses, but also (ii) able bodies that use devices and tools.

Bodies working in conjunction with tools and devices are not always 'impaired'. Instead bodies augment themselves through technological devices into and with which they are, in the twenty-first century, more or less consistently connected/embedded. Thus, it is not that there is a body and *then* there is the prosthesis, even for 'normal' bodies. Bodies are bodies+machines where the body evolves in conjunction with assorted tools. All 'natural' and 'normal' bodies are always bodies+machines. This means we need to see bodies as networked, hybrids or congeries in which the subjectivity of the individual is constituted through and within the network, or the connection s/he has with machines and tools. 'Ability' for the 'normal' body is the consequence not of innate features of the body but of the normalized negotiations the body has, right from childhood and over the years of human evolution, with tools. Networks are in place for certain kinds of bodies to tap into and connect with – and this is what en-*ables* these bodies. In other words, disability studies shows how the 'able' body is one that has had a different kind of relation and evolution with socially constructed and facilitated networks and tools: ability is not immanent to the body.

Extending this argument, it could be said that the disabled body is one for which no networks exist. These are bodies that do not fit into available systems and institutionally created structures (the width of passageways in buses or stores, for example). It is not immanent to the body that it cannot deal with the structure: the structure does not accommodate different bodies. Here, too, bodies co-evolve with structures, but for the impaired, this evolution takes a different route. If, in the case of 'able' bodies, the bodies converge with the structures and networks, the differently shaped bodies do not. 'Assistive devices', as the special structures are called, are treated as 'add-ons' to the impaired body, whereas the devices used by so-called 'normal' bodies are not seen as assistive but as extensions that augment the already able body, when in fact these extensions constitute the very 'ability' and subjectivity of the 'normal' body as well. However, for bodies with different orders of functionality these devices offer opportunities to create new identities through technology.

Thus:

- all bodies, irrespective of abilities, are cyborged bodies because their abilities and subjectivities are the effect of a convergence and co-evolution with devices and institutionally facilitated networks: all bodies are hybrid;

- it is not a subject (human individual) + object (device) model that works any more within disability studies: it shows how the very subjectivity of the subject is always already the effect of interactions with 'objects', and thus the organic/inorganic, human/non-human boundaries break down.

Disability studies in this interpretation of cyborged bodies draws attention to *relations* (human–non-human, subject–object) that constitute subjectivity and ability. Just as critical posthumanism emphasizes the co-evolution of the human with animal and other forms of life, disability studies proposes that the human subject, even the 'able' human subject, comes into existence only in relation with other non-human 'actors' and objects.

To summarize, then, disability studies contributes to critical posthumanist thought in several important ways.

Disability studies traces the construction of norms of difference through which physical bodies are classified as deviant, disabled and dependent and therefore separate from 'normal' humans – foregrounding the classificatory regimes through which a form of racism is founded on the body's abilities, functions and shape.[7] These classificatory regimes and border-conditions masquerade as 'objective' or scientific in their evaluation of disability but actually reflect the biases and moral evaluations – reflected in cultural representations of deformed villains or diseased and damaged 'sinners' – of the social order.[8] Disability studies demonstrates how this 'difference' then becomes the marker and determinant of welfare and interventions but also of segregation, attitudes of pity and revulsion and Othering.

It argues that notions of autonomy and independence have become established as the characteristics of the human in a culture of individualism, and therefore, in its corollary, construct the impaired body as dependent and helpless. Simultaneously it argues a case for non-uniform subjects and actors who do not fit the norm (Moser [2000] 2008: 313). The diversity of species must also be seen within the different abilities, bodies and physiologies of the impaired as well. Able and 'normal' human bodies are constructed through their contrast with deviant, deformed and disabled bodies – therefore disability becomes central to the very idea of a 'normal' human. 'Able' bodies are not 'natural' but the effect of evolution with devices, and the 'natural' body is one that has a particular relation with the devices and environment – a relation that works differently for impaired bodies. This argument in disability studies demolishes the myth of the natural body + extensible prosthesis by showing how the prosthesis – any tool – has always been a part of the making of human ability and subjectivity.

Disability studies underscores how the history of negative imagery about disability and impairment has often portrayed the disabled as non-human. Finally, it emphasizes the close link between bodies and environments, and argues that the body, whether 'normal' or 'different', needs to be located in environments and the latter evaluated for its ability to adapt to the needs of the impaired individual.

BIOETHICS AND PERSONHOOD

In vitro fertilization, cloning, artificial ventilators and organ transplants in clinical medicine have changed the ways in which we perceive life. These have altered significantly the relationships between parents and children, especially when the children are not genetically related to the parents. Technologies have called into question the very definition of life when the patient is kept alive by assorted machines. 'Bioethics' is the set of ethical issues that arise from health care, clinical medicine and biomedical sciences. It extends the older 'medical ethics' paradigm (which focused on patient–doctor relationships) by examining 'the value of life, what it is to be a person, the significance of being human' (Kuhse and Singer 2001: 4).

In the film *Gattaca*, Jerome Morrow is a genetic miracle, but one whose potential has been curtailed due to his disability. The film shows him as suicidal. But the film also shows Jerome as embodying the burdens of genetic choice: 'he suffered under a different burden: the burden of perfection', says the voiceover when Vincent meets Jerome. This perfection-as-burden raises a concern of the bioethics of genetic engineering and posthumanism (I shall return to *Gattaca* later in the chapter). Does germ-line engineering and genetic choice in reproductive technologies inspire/cause parents to burden their offspring with their ambitions and choices? Do parents have the right to modify their genes so that any children they might have excel in ways and domains the parents themselves couldn't? Jerome's complaint when he wins the silver medal voices this concern through the 'victim', the enhanced progeny: 'Jerome Morrow was never meant to be one step down on the podium'. The dilemma, as Colin Gavaghan notes (2009), is that we assume the child is burdened with the dreams of his parents because the parents chose a certain genetic profile *for* him. But then, Gavaghan notes, children cannot determine the choices made by their parents anyway. Would it be better that the child was not born at all? That is, would it be better to have no existence than a posthuman existence? Relatedly, the film also provokes a reaction against genetic choice by raising the bogey of genetic determinism in its representation of the 'in-valids', those whose genetic profiles are not quite the best for the society. This also assumes that one's genotype is one's destiny: it determines one's personhood.

For critical posthumanism, bioethics is a key discipline because it

- examines the boundaries of life and death in its debates over the persistent vegetative state and euthanasia;
- examines the nature of 'personhood' – whether it is centred in the genes, nurture or the environment, whether it is ethical to programme a machine so that it mimics human emotions and psychology, and whether such a machine would then be a 'person';

- examines the dilemma of the moral enhancement of humans so that they are morally more human, if biologically less so;
- ponders over the ethics of genetic choice and germ-line engineering.

Personhood

The term 'person' is used to indicate both the biological organism belonging to our own species (*Homo sapiens*) and individuals and creatures whose mental life approximates to that of 'normal', adult human beings (Tooley 2001: 117). It also includes the belief systems, memories, attitudes that constitute the 'personality' of the individual – all of which reside in the upper half of the brain, while the life processes, including respiration, are controlled by the lower half. Thus, the question to be asked is: if the upper half of the brain is destroyed, would the individual organism, minus the beliefs, specific memories and attitudes, still be a 'person' just because the bodily functions continue and it nominally therefore constitutes a 'body' akin to all *Homo sapiens* bodies? If technology allows a rewiring of the upper brain to put in additional, or different, memories and attitudes, would it mean we have a new 'person'? This last is of course the stuff of sci-fi in which humans are rewired to become 'someone else'.

In Marge Piercy's *Woman on the Edge of Time*, Connie Ramos is admitted to a psychiatric facility where they will rewire her brain because her attitudes and behaviour are anti-social (she beats up a pimp who had beaten up her pregnant niece). Through specific surgical procedures the hospital seeks to control her behaviour: a neurotransmitter would be implanted in her brain. Connie visualizes this scenario: 'Tomorrow they were going to stick a machine in her brain. She was the experiment. They would rape her body, her brain, her self . . . She would be their experimental monster . . . Their tool' ([1976] 1983: 273). She is a 'socially disorganized individual' (as the medical report, the final chapter of the novel, puts it) who needs to be adjusted in her biological brain so that she becomes a different *person*. The purpose of the experiments, Sybil – another patient – tells her, is 'to turn [them] into machines so we obey them [the doctors]' (193). The normally wild, uncontrollable Alice, after the implant, is literally stopped in her fury and when asked how she is responds quite docilely with 'I feel good. I feel so good' (196). The bioethical perspective on this tale would be: does the reconfiguring of the mind of an individual of this recognizably *Homo sapiens* species constitute the creation of a *new* person? As Jeff McMahan puts it in his essay on brain death and bioethics, 'in cases involving radical amnesia and personality change, most versions imply that one would cease to exist and be replaced in one's body by a different *person*' (2001: 257, emphasis in original). Alice, therefore, is a new *person*.

Piercy's novel documents the destruction of a person, and the creation of a new one. But does the medical intervention into her biological brain and the resultant changes in her mind/soul constitute the 'killing' of her personhood? Piercy seems to suggest that normative standards that prescribe certain kinds of behaviour among particular classes – Connie is Mexican, ill-educated and working-class – and proscribe some others are essentially technologies of oppression, control and regimentation that, in the name of 'rational' behaviour, destroy 'persons' who are different or who do not fit the taxon.

But what constitutes a 'full' person? Does mere consciousness or a capacity for rational thought make a person? If that is the case, consciousness is what even Connie or Alice in Piercy's novel possess. But their consciousness of themselves (self-consciousness) is often at odds with what the society demands of them. Does consciousness also imply a moral agency, wherein a being/individual utilizes her or his consciousness in agreement with social norms? That is, it is not enough to say an individual is a person if s/he possesses certain capacities (rationality, self-consciousness): the individual needs to *exercise these capacities to qualify as a 'person'*. The key point here is of norms and socially acceptable utilization of faculties and capacities by individuals that qualify them as persons. Piercy's critique in the novel focuses primarily on this issue: is it ethical to 'bind' a person's capacities to a set of social norms? Would it be possible, she wonders, for society to accept a different 'person', since all persons cannot possess the same capacities or even want to exercise the capacities in the same way. It is also underscored throughout the novel that Connie has not had the opportunities or material resources to utilize her capacities. So then, does personhood depend only on the individual's capacities, or does a society or culture have the responsibility of providing the structures in which these capacities might be fully exercised?

Utopian fiction often focuses on alternative forms of behaviour among humans so that the social order itself can be changed. But, as we see in the case of realist utopian fiction (Octavia Butler), there is an awareness of and alertness to the possibilities of the moral enhancement of humans also being commercialized and exploited for reinforcing power relations in the social order. Thus, in Piercy, does Connie's vision – imagining – of a different world where there are more equitable gender roles classify her as 'mad', or simply utopian? If utopia, as Ruth Levitas defines it, is the 'imaginary reconstitution of the world' (n.d.), then is Connie's imagining a marker of advanced thinking or of derangement? Does the ability or potential to plot and imagine a future constitute personhood (Tooley 2001: 121–2)?

Piercy's novel, which shows depersonalization of a 'person', also raises fundamental ethical and moral concerns. Alice, reduced to a very quiet individual after the implant, is more or less a shadow of her earlier self. Her higher intellectual faculties and attitudes – anger at the doctors, for example – have been erased. As a moral agent, she is now a perfect fit into the social order. By limiting the psychological abilities of this individual, the doctors reduce her 'personhood', in one sense. 'We can electrically trigger almost every mood and emotion – the fight-or-flight reaction, euphoria, calm, pleasure, pain, terror! . . . we can control Alice's violent attacks and maintain her in a balanced mental state', the doctor proudly announces in Piercy's novel ([1976] 1983: 196). The 'zoo', as another doctor calls it (197), would be a place of placid, harmless animals. It is the expulsion of the animality – violence, uncontrolled frenzies, anger, non-cooperation (as the doctors define it) – from their inmates that the doctors seek. As noted in the preceding chapter, humans who function on the level of sheer animality – called 'irrational behaviour' – are treated as monsters that need to be reined in. Alice becomes, in short, something akin to a pet animal which, as Erica Fudge puts it in her study of animals cited earlier, 'is an animal – it cannot speak – but it is also an ideal human – it says what we want it to say' (2002: 33). It is the morality of this 'domestication' that bioethics, such as is expressed implicitly in Piercy's novel, questions, for it has to do with the 'conversion' of individual people with socially unacceptable traits – characterized as 'animal behaviour' even in humans – into different 'persons'. If animal studies showed critical posthumanism the modes through which humans deal with animals, bioethics offers the emergent discipline a critique of how societies and the technocultures of medicine and science deal with the 'problematic' person: one whose behaviour, personality, capacities and consciousness do not function within 'acceptable' parameters. Once again, critical posthumanism, via bioethics, meditates upon borders: of persons and non-persons.

At this point, it is necessary to ask critical posthumanism's key question of bioethics: what is a person and what is personhood?

Bioethics, which discusses the ethical issues around corporeality, bodies and embodiment within medicine, psychiatry and other such domains, explores whether cyborged bodies, foetuses, individuals in persistent vegetative states are persons. Personhood may be defined here as *an individual who is a moral agent*. A moral agent is *a being who is able to make moral judgements about moral matters and is able to act on those judgements*.

Let us take a few examples here. In Ridley Scott's classic film *Blade Runner*, the android, toward the end of the film, reaches out a hand and thus saves the life of Harrison Ford. In the *Terminator* series, we see a progressive humanization of the killer machine when it/he begins to care for the child. Now these two cyborgs are not from the human gene pool, nor do they possess the same psychological features as the vast majority of the human species. But the third requirement, as Stephen Coleman and Richard Hanley define it, for being a member of the species *Homo sapiens*, is that they have to be individuals with a moral standing (2009: 45). An individual who can take moral responsibility for her/his action is a moral agent and a person.[9] In *Blade Runner* and *Terminator*, the robots that become humanized need to be treated as persons because they are not working according to a pre-recorded programming but of their own will. Thus, they take moral responsibility for their actions. One important clue to this shift toward the moral agent end of the spectrum is the increasing emotionalism of the robots/cyborgs. From being unfeeling machines, we see these evolving into creatures who think (according to their programming) and feel (beyond their programming). They become moral agents when, like Frankenstein's monster, they emote and their engagements with the world and community are also determined by their emotions. Further, these cyborgs begin to think about themselves and their programming – and this suggests the arrival of self-consciousness, a characteristic of the human person.

In terms of bioethics, such as the ones implicitly discussed in films like *Blade Runner* or *I, Robot*, we have to conclude – and this is crucial for posthumanist thought – that 'the morally important categories of moral agents and persons are not necessarily exclusively populated by members of the species *Homo sapiens*' (Coleman and Hanley 2009: 53). The cyborg Yod in Marge Piercy's *He, She and It* (1991) is an excellent example of this posthumanist bioethics. While his emotions are programmed into him, the cyborg begins to reason about his existence. A debate erupts in the community about the 'personhood' of Yod. Paralleling this story of Yod's is the Golem of an earlier era. This Golem, Joseph, falls in love with his maker's daughter, Chava, and eventually is returned to the dust, perhaps for daring to hope for a full citizenship and its associated advantages like marriage and family. In both cases, Yod and the Golem illustrate the posthumanist bioethics position: humans alone cannot claim monopoly over emotions, self-consciousness or selflessness. Yod blows himself up in Piercy's novel as an act of sacrifice that saves his human beloved (Shira) but also as an ethical stance against further cyborg-manufacture. Yod therefore is a moral agent and thus a *person*. Genetic codes or programming do not determine personhood. Yod is programmed to protect Shira and her child, Ari (408), but not to protest or support human causes. Yet the assertion of agency – in his act of self-sacrifice (a hint about this agency is given to us when Yod is described as an extremely considerate lover) – moves him beyond a program or robotic machinery into the realm of the person.

Critical posthumanism, while supportive of the genetic choices in reproductive technologies, does not consider an individual to be merely the sum total of the genetically programmed features – the environment, nurture and forms of socialization contribute equally to the 'making' of an individual. When interrogated by the corporate officers, Yod's response is an assertion of agency: 'I'm not programmed to answer questions I don't choose to answer' (390). This choice and Yod's growth into a thinking–feeling person, Piercy shows, are not programmed, or programmable: they are emergent properties that are the consequence of Yod's interactions with his environment and of extended interaction with the human species that enables him to acquire the features and characteristics of the humans. Hence

Malkah's insistence – when the corporate establishment describes Yod as a 'property of the town' – that Yod 'is not the property of anyone . . . but . . . a citizen of the town' (392). The contradiction between programming and Yod's emergent properties is best captured toward the end of the novel. Shira is trying to persuade Yod that he does not have to commit suicide – even if he is *programmed* to die protecting her – for her sake. Yod replies: 'I don't want to be a conscious weapon. A weapon that's conscious is a contradiction because I develop attachments, ethics, desires. I don't want to be a tool of destruction. I judge myself for killing, yet my programming takes over in danger' (410). Yet, even at the moment Yod steps out on his suicide mission, he has taken decisions he is not programmed to, based on 'attachments, ethics, desires': he blows up the laboratory. Yod's final message to Shira is partly his programming speaking and partly the consciousness he has become/acquired:

I have died and taken with me Avram, my creator . . . I want there to be no more weapons like me. A weapon should not be conscious . . . I die knowing I destroy the capacity to replicate me . . . I can't permit him to continue experimenting with beings who are fully conscious . . . Whatever may happen . . . I have done one good thing with my death. I have made sure there will be no others like me. (415–16)

No programming limits the possibilities of consciousness, Yod suggests. If consciousness has been programmed into Yod, it evolves and grows based on its 'socialization' (the term Piercy uses throughout the novel to describe Yod's interactions with humans). And this socialization is what makes Yod take an ethical stance, completely at odds with his programming that can only allow him to die defending Shira. And Shira thinks about Yod's death: 'he died convinced he had accomplished a goal that made his death palatable to him. Thus he had salvaged something for himself out of Avram's fatal orders' (428). The 'himself' is the assertion of a personhood Yod was not designed/programmed for.

In the dystopian film about genetic engineering, *Gattaca*, the entire efforts of Vincent and Jerome are directed at genetic impersonation. Vincent's genetic code consigns him to menial labour in the world of *Gattaca*, while Jerome, with his perfect genetic code, cannot fulfil his potential because an accident has left him disabled. Although Vincent is not Jerome's clone, his masquerade in and through Jerome's genetic code suggests that he is, indeed, 'derived' from Jerome, at least for the sake of the fraud he seeks to perpetuate. Jackie Stacey's queer reading of the film proposes that *Gattaca* calls into question the 'fantasy of masculinity' itself as the performance of masculinity is 'disavow[ed] by locating [the characters] firmly within a eugenic aesthetic associated with dangerous delusions of totalitarianism and fascism' (2005: 1861). While Stacey's interpretation does identify a central problematic of the film, it excludes from its ambit the larger bioethical issues it throws up. The 'eugenic aesthetic' is not exclusively a highly visible spectacle of masculine or feminine identity in this, a dystopian vision of the future. It is an aesthetic that spectacularizes the identity of the human in which – and here Stacey is right in juxtaposing the two – image and informatics (the genetic code) contribute to the idea of a *perfect* human. 'Perfect' persons here are a congeries of software (which programs the DNA people want), wetware (the DNA itself) and hardware (the material body put through its regimen and striving for physical perfection). The eugenic aesthetic induces humans to attain the perfection available only in fantasies – picture-perfect bodies, excellent skills – where the line between cyborgs and humans blurs. If cyborgs, as *Blade Runner* and Piercy's novels suggest, can approximate to humans, then humans can, theoretically at least, begin to appropriate the surreal perfection of artworks, models or computer-generated 'perfect' bodies. *Gattaca* is therefore not simply the fantasy of masculinity playing itself out within a eugenic aesthetic but a larger fantasy of border-crossing humans. The masquerade is of one human impersonating another, but it is also of a physically perfect human impersonating a genetically perfect one, resulting in a constant dynamic between identity (the genetic code) and identification (the impersonation).

In the age of surveillance, as David Lyon proposes (2009), the ID card is not about identity but about the verifiability of that identity – the person who checks the card is verifying that you are who you say you are: and the card pronounces this – in what is essentially a process of *identification*. In *Gattaca* there is a genetic identity for one individual but this 'works' only when *identified* through scanners and such in the body of another. It is, of course, no longer the photograph that validates identity but the genetic print, and in *Gattaca* it is the genetic print that is forged. But what the film suggests in its theme of masquerade is the identification of a genetic code irrespective of the body in which it 'resides' and which it supposedly 'forms' or constitutes. Jerome validates Vincent and vice versa through the switching of genetic materials. We are looking at a structure of repetition here where human repeats clone repeats human in an endless dynamic of identity and identification that blurs the species boundaries (if we assume the clone to be a different species, or a sub-species within the human one).

Much of the (posthuman) bioethical debate around personhood revolves around origin questions. Now the Golem, as Elaine Graham informs us (2002), can emerge from the mother's womb or from the earth, and so is at once human and posthuman. The Golem and cyborg Yod in Piercy's *He, She, and It* (1991) begin to exhibit human-like traits: loyalty, courage, moral agency and love. Clones, that are 'born' in laboratories, complicate the origin story as well. As for developing human traits, this applies to the clones in *Never Let Me Go* as well. Golems and clones, these novels suggest, are like humans, and yet not quite – perhaps they lack souls, as the 'guardians' at Hailsham seem to wonder. Thus, and to extend the argument, if one species – cyborgs – can exhibit and develop characteristics of another (human), then it raises a significant question of a critical posthumanist variety: is species membership a precondition for becoming moral agents? Can there be humans whose species membership is not entirely in the human gene pool, and are not born in the 'natural' way, and are therefore *akin* to Golems or clones? Are there humans who are variant models, and therefore whose 'personhood' is more complicated?

Doris Lessing complicates these questions of biological, human and other origins, leading – as noted above – to questions of personhood and identity, when she creates in Ben (*The Fifth Child*, 1988) a figure who/that is human and not quite, but one who understands basic human conditions and behaviour directed at him. He understands rejection, and he understands affection. He demonstrates loyalty, but one which is *not* predicated upon kinship. Clones remind us of the future of the human race, but Ben reminds us of the *past* of the human race in an instance of atavism. He is not, let us be clear, genetically engineered. He is more like an accident. The issue is whether Ben is a person, with moral agency. Lessing offers us a posthuman vision. Ben represents a 'species Gothic'. The Gothic too, as we know, is characterized by a 'fearful sense of inheritance' (Baldick 1992: xix). The past is a 'site of terror' (Spooner 2006: 18). Harriet's mode of addressing the uncanny that is Ben – or rather, her perception of Ben – is to locate Ben, and his horror, in the human race's past. The 'resolution' of the uncanny as a return to the race's past offers Lessing the chance to articulate a whole new vision, as we shall see.

In most popular cultural forms dealing with the gynaecological Gothic, Andrew Scahill (2010) notes, the pregnant woman feels herself invaded, and at the mercy of the unborn child. (Lucy Fischer, 1992, points out that in the gynaecological Gothic the mother has an antagonistic relationship with the foetus inside her.) The (human) mother herself is made monstrous by the horrific (alien?) secret within her. Harriet's fifth pregnancy proceeds badly. She believes she is being 'poisoned' by the foetus inside her (Lessing [1988] 2001: 41). She feels an 'imperative' beat inside her and 'hard' movements (45). Harriet cannot believe that 'such a tiny creature could be showing such fearful strength' (49–50), and as a result she is in constant pain. Harriet begins to imagine that what she is carrying is a chimera, 'pathetic botched creatures', hybrids and deformed creatures (52). This supposedly unindividuated monstrous is beginning to show signs of something alien inside her.

This marks the uncanny extimate relationship of mother and foetus in Harriet's case. The extimate, writes Mladen Dolar, is 'located where the most intimate interiority coincides with the exterior, provoking horror and anxiety . . . [It is] simultaneously the intimate kernel and the foreign body' (1991: 6). Whatever is growing inside her, is connected to her and is feeding off her, is at once the extreme of intimate interiority and yet external to Harriet. The extimate and its uncanny is an anterior moment to the theme of the alien, as we shall see.

Though there is absolutely no suggestion anywhere in the novel that her pregnancy is the unexpected result of any scientific experiment, Lessing refers us to a quasi-scientific *explanation* for the creature in Harriet's womb. This move is a crucial one for it suggests that hybrid creatures, or hybridization, cannot be controlled by science (Squier 1998). Lessing uses 'foetus' and 'creature' alternately from this point, suggesting an uncertainty over the identity. Harriet screams out to the doctor that what is inside her is '*absolutely* different' (59, emphasis in original), as her stomach 'heav[es] and seeth[es]' ([1988] 2001: 59). This heaving seething foetus *inside* is the Thing: unnameable, defying description.

The parturition Gothic has its climactic moment in the childbirth when whatever is inside Harriet's womb emerges as a recognizably *individuated* individual. When Ben emerges into the world he is 11 pounds in weight, does not look like a baby, is 'heavy-shouldered' with a weirdly shaped head, yellow hair, thick heavy hands, green-yellow eyes, like 'lumps of soapstone' (60). Yet Lessing ensures that the physiognomy and anatomy are not the truly horrific things about Ben. The parturition Gothic can only achieve its most intense horror in the mother–baby *relationship* at the moment of birth, i.e., the moments after the *separation* of the two bodies. Lessing's narrative acquires its searing intensity not because of Ben's obvious physical difference but in his parents', especially his mother's, reaction to him: 'He opened his eyes and looked straight up into his mother's face. She [Harriet] had been waiting to exchange looks with this creature . . . but there was no recognition there . . . her heart contracted with pity . . . poor little beast, his mother disliking him so much' (60). Acceptance, recognition and the forging of a relationship is what the parturition Gothic of Lessing subverts to generate horror. Ben is not a person because he does not physiologically, physiognomically, resemble a human person, even though his origins are like those of all humans. But, as I shall argue, even this origin story of Ben is complicated.

Ben as a foetus, we have seen, blurs the individuated/unindividuated distinction. Inside Harriet, even though a foetus still connected to the mother, he is distinctive and works as an *alien* presence, at least in Harriet's perception. Once outside, as a separate entity, Harriet feels pity for him *because* she is his mother. Thus, when Ben ought to be unindividuated (inside), he appears as an alien – Harriet does *not*, at any point in this pregnancy, think of what is inside her as a part of herself, as her child. Once out in the world, Harriet feels pity, recognizes him as *her* child. What had seemed alien when inside is now, ironically, identified as her child, even though his physiognomy situates Ben outside the 'normal' child category. This is where Lessing begins to foreground the non-human nature of Ben.

The Thing, Ben, is variously described as 'alien', 'Neanderthal' (65), a 'changeling' (72) and a troll or goblin. From the misfit in the womb, the mother–child relationship and the family, Ben does not fit the human family now. The novel has already anticipated the 'species Gothic' in these descriptions. This species Gothic is the space of the uncanny, in the way people perceive Ben, but also uncanny for Ben's horrific antiquity. He seems to contain within him, partake of, a different and ancient species. Ben is not a person, he lacks personhood.

In the London clinic Harriet asks: 'how do we know what kinds of people – races, I mean – creatures different from us, have lived on this planet?' Ben is then described as a 'throwback' (127). If the Gothic traditionally dwells on the arcane and the atavistic (ancient evil, spirits, the undead), as does the uncanny, then in Lessing's novel what we see is a species Gothic in which another race has *returned* in the form of Ben. Ben's was a race, Harriet believes, 'that reached its apex thousands and thousands of years before humanity, whatever that meant, took this stage . . . perhaps [they] had left their seeds in the human matrix, here and there. To appear again, as Ben had' (156).[10]

Ben is familiar and yet strange. When compared with other humans, the difference is startling, of course. Ben evokes dread as the uncanny 'human' (or humanoid), at once strange and familiar. His strangeness Harriet now attributes to his 'ancient' seed. Like the spectres that people stories of the Gothic and the uncanny, Ben, in Harriet's view, is the expression of an ancient form, the embodiment of a gene long thought dead. He is, in one sense, the return of the repressed gene. At this point Lessing's story folds the gynaecological Gothic, with its emphasis on the uncanny's extimate (in the form of the mother's relationship with the foetus), and the consequent maternal and familial Gothic into a species Gothic. The horror of Ben-as-Thing is now recalibrated as Ben-as-return-of-the-past-species. He represents here the radical disruption of the evolutionary scheme because he *is* the human race's past.

The posthuman Gothic in *The Fifth Child* and its horrors here are not about Ben, but in our perceptions and (intolerant) treatment of whatever is different. The posthuman Gothic offers a critique of what we see as horror by suggesting a different way of tackling difference (Ben appears both to belong and not to belong to the human species).

Lessing's is a posthuman vision in which a human can be at once human and not-quite-human, being, in point of fact, an ancient form predating the *Homo sapiens* (Ben squats like an animal throughout). Beginning with the question of the 'alien' foetus and its maternal Gothic, with its theme of individuation and broken placental economy, she moves on to locate the Thing in a species frame, to suggest to us that alterity and fusion are both essential to survive as a race/species. Ben represents not just a throwback but alterity, one which is 'inside' the human (literally, since he is born of human parents). That is, Ben is the Thing within the human, within us. We are Other. Ben is not an alien because he represents our own ancient roots and genetic traces. Ben recalls for us our ancestry. Lessing's might be read as a critique of a plain evolutionary scheme in which the past is a 'foreign' country when, ironically, the past continues within us as a genetic trace. The horror therefore is not in Ben, but in how we, as humans, see our own past as a radical Other, in our intolerance for this Other and, finally, in our refusal to recognize the Other-which-is-us. Norah Campbell and Mike Saren argue that such an atavism is a posthuman vision:

But by exhibiting atavistic traits of the evolutionary past and future, such figures confuse the linear progress of evolution, and instead argue that past, present and future are humanist responses to disorder. In a posthuman imaginary, all three 'stages' coexist. Proto-atavism is the argument that multiple paradigms of life exist on the peripheries of humanist life. Ancient and future evolutionary traits exist in the *present* – both in the aesthetic imagination and in everyday life. This has one important consequence; it shows us how (human) life may not be a singular progression but a cacophony of coexisting, interacting states of past, present *and* future existences with no recourse to a single, reassuring Origin. (2010: 169–70, emphasis in original)

By complicating Ben's origins in both human and some unidentifiable non-human, or early human, moment, Lessing offers us a *multispecies being*. The novel concludes with this question of acknowledging difference, even if it is of a different, or multiple, species. Harriet insists 'I want it *said*. I want it recognized' (Lessing [1988] 2001: 127, emphasis in original), indicating that the unnameable Thing must be recognized and identified: the alien other she has birthed and cared for is an interspecies, born of human parents but with the attributes of a different species. 'Recognition' here is about the respect for a different species. Throughout Ben's life in the Lovatt household, he stands and sits apart from the rest of the family: 'He sat apart from the others, always apart; and, as always, his eyes were on others' faces, observing' (156). Clare Hanson argues that 'Ben himself is a stranger or alien about whom she [Harriet] speculates with detachment' (2007: 175). I would like to reverse this argument: it could also be Ben seeking recognition from the others, to be identified and identify with somebody of his own kind. This reading of Ben's supposed 'detachment' is invited by the conclusion to the novel itself.

The novel's last line is in fact a plea for the recognition of whatever/ whoever Ben is. Lessing writes that Harriet expects, when she puts on the TV, that 'she would see Ben, standing rather apart from the crowd, staring at the camera with his goblin eyes, or searching the faces for another of his own kind' ([1988] 2001: 159). What Ben seeks is recognition and respect, a reciprocity of gaze that would give him his affiliation, since his filiation-based identity has given him nothing. Posthumanism as envisaged by Donna Haraway, among others, is a conscious effort to move beyond species boundary with/as response to, recognition of and respect for the Other. 'Species' in its etymology ('respecere'), Donna Haraway notes, is related to 'respect', 'response' as well as 'to see' ('specere'). 'To respond', she writes, '[is] to respect' (2008: 23). Cary Wolfe points to a 'wet' version of posthumanism in which 'a blind person and a guide dog form a third, prosthetic kind whose experience of the world cannot be well explained by reference to the traditional human vs animal' (www.carywolfe.com/post_about.html).[11] Lessing's novel concludes with this question of acknowledging difference, even if it is of a different species. The human, Lessing's novel suggests, might be characterized by the ability and desire to accommodate, or even incorporate, difference.

Lessing's *The Fifth Child* takes recourse to the uncanny and the Gothic in order to articulate a wholly new vision of what it means to be human. To be human is to be able to recognize difference, to understand the companionate nature of all species. If the past survives in us in Ben-like ways, then how do we perceive and treat the Other as different from us?

Enhancement Bioethics and Moral Posthumanism

Bioethical debates about human enhancement revolve around individual enhancement through genetic, surgical or chemical interventions. The debates have also addressed the threat to individual liberty (to enhance oneself) from community controls over genetic manipulation, especially preimplantation genetic testing (wherein embryos are tested and selected for specific genetic traits before in vitro implantation – see Ford 2009). Nanotechnology and nanomedicine, poised to revolutionize both medicine and ethics, generate heated debates. Robert Freitas speaks of pharmacytes (that deliver drugs at cellular levels), respirocytes (that carry oxygen) and surgical nanorobots in what has been called a 'nanomedical utopia' (O'Mathúna 2009: 131).

Ethicists disagree over what kind of interventions constitute *treatment*, and which ones approximate to *enhancement*. When Sabin and Daniels first postulated the idea of 'medical necessity' in their 1994 essay (in which they discussed conditions like shyness and unhappiness and explored the dilemmas of medical insurance for treating such conditions), they inaugurated the treatment–enhancement distinction. Subsequently, the treatment-advocates argue that the 'legitimate goals of medicine are to treat or prevent disease and restore people to normal health, while medicine should not be used to enhance or improve people beyond the normal' (O'Mathúna 2009: 134). However, some interventions, such as vaccination, are both treatment and enhancement because they improve the body's 'natural' immune systems (Bostrom and Roache 2007: 121). Cosmetic surgery, which is treated as being outside the strict definition of 'health care', is championed by some as enabling the individual to 'feel better' about himself or herself (for a quick account of the problems with cosmetic surgery as enhancement, see Mary Devereaux 2008: as she puts it, 'Talk of *medical* enhancement thus obscures the fact that the dimension along which things are enhanced is not medical' – 169, emphasis in original).

Enhancement could be improvements of physical appearance/characteristics (speed, strength), cognitive abilities (memory, reasoning), affect (emotion, motivation), immunity, longevity (Buchanan 2011: 25). Posthumanists such as John Harris (2007) advocate the right to enhance humans so that *better* humans can be created. Now this involves biological enhancement but something else as well – and this concerns bioethics. As was noted in chapter 2, if there is really a *biological* basis for empathy – the mirror neuron theory propounded by Christian Keysers and others – then it should be feasible to intervene in ways that enhance the mirror neuron activity in the brain. Is it ethical to engineer humans with greater capacities for compassion, sacrifice and selflessness?[12] More complications arise when we consider that evaluation of 'essential' human capacities cannot be the same for all races and ethnicities. Likewise, as Prograis and Pellegrino point out, medical ethics also needs to consider the experience – of sickness and health – of, say, African Americans to account for transracial disparities, and ponder over the social effects of the 'likely unequal and racially disparate access to and possession of bioenhancement' (2007: 12–14).

Moral transhumanism, as this branch of transhumanism is called, seeks the moral improvement of humans.[13] This means, as commentators have argued, that individuals might not be humans in the biological sense but are human (or more human, and humane) in the moral sense (Persson and Savulescu 2010). Moral enhancements by biomedical means would involve cognitive enhancements that could help us become more virtuous, wherever virtuous behaviour depends on cognition, while they might make us less vicious or more virtuous by increasing our sympathy or moral imagination (Buchanan 2011: 75–6). Technological interventions that produce moral agents with a greater sense of altruism, compassion and fair play, and which help them to focus on greater sociality and collective concerns, become, therefore, the parallel to the humanization of robots and cyborgs that we examined in the preceding section. Allan Buchanan calls for moral enhancements when we start thinking of innovation in connection with justice, proposing, as an example, that cognitive enhancements that might help people with lower intelligence might prove in the long run cheaper than educational improvements (247).

If human beings are characterized as possessing a moral agency as well as 'dignity' (where dignity implies a sense of self-worth but also a right to be treated with a minimum degree of respect by the world), do posthumans also possess a certain kind of dignity? Does the cyborg in *He, She and It*, and *I, Robot*, or *Blade Runner* possess dignity, or understand it when it doesn't? Or is dignity, as Francis Fukuyama seems to suggest in *Our Posthuman Futures*, a human trait alone (149)?

Enhancement bioethics here focuses on those qualities associated with humans and which would construct posthumans whose species membership is not always restricted to *Homo sapiens*. This approximates to the critical posthumanist view in which the borders of the human with machines and other life forms are blurred. But, more than anything else, the bioethical issue here is of the improvement of the human species through biomedical interventions in the agreed-upon 'essential' qualities of being human. We see an instance of this bioethical concern in Octavia Butler's fiction.

In her *Parable of the Sower* (1993) (set sometime between 2024 and 2027), Octavia Butler presents Lauren Olamina, an African American teenager who suffers from a 'hyperempathy syndrome'. Olamina can literally feel the pains and pleasures of other people. This is the effect, perhaps, of a 'smart pill' her mother took (the mother dies in childbirth) that would give her a baby with advanced consciousness. Butler of course converts this 'advancement' into an affliction as Olamina is trapped inside a ghetto where there is no pleasure and only pain – and Olamina has to experience the pain of all the suffering others. Butler seems to suggest that the advanced human being could be more compassionate, but she also locates this advanced human person within a context. It cannot, Butler proposes, be entirely genetically determined that a select few can become 'empaths' in a world given over wholly to suffering and pain. Once again, personhood and advanced humans are embedded in social and cultural environments. Olamina's emerging philosophy of change while on the one hand rooted in her biological characteristic (increased empathy), on the other, gestures at an advancement in the social order and human ways of thinking. Butler's critique of hierarchies – something she does in all her fiction – is visible in Olamina's theories of the collective (Scott 2010). But that is not my point here. What I want to emphasize is that Butler is proposing a bio-medically induced *embodied advancement in human values, qualities and virtues* – most notably to feel, literally, the pain of others. Whether this psychosomatic condition can be the foundation for a new human(e) intersubjectivity is Butler's larger concern. In fact, as one commentator reads it, Butler sees Olamina's hyperempathy as 'a way out of a dystopian future' (Bollinger 2007: 344). Olamina puts it this way:

If hyperempathy syndrome were a more common complaint, people couldn't do such things. They could kill if they had to, and bear the pain of it or be destroyed by it. But if everyone could feel everyone else's pain, who would torture? Who would cause anyone unnecessary pain? . . . A biological conscience is better than no conscience at all. (Butler [1993] 1995: 102)

This is a bioethical argument for moral posthumanism in which the enhanced humans might be the solution to the world's problems, in Butler's view (which Bollinger endorses in her reading, 2007: 345).

Adjacent to, but not strictly connected with, the debates about enhancement is the question of cloning. In Ishiguro's novel *Never Let Me Go* (2005), the clones serve a utilitarian purpose: they are reservoirs of organs for humans to harvest when needed (in Atwood's *Oryx and Crake*, special animals are bred – pigoons – with extra kidneys and livers which could then be harvested – 2004: 25–6). They give up their organs, and then they die. But the novel also asks: what is the bioethical view of creating clones and denying them personhood? As this chapter's opening noted, the artwork of the clones in Hailsham is supposed to indicate their humanness, their 'soul'. This attribute/attribution of a soul is the bioethical theme of the novel. The clones who wish to defer their 'donations', as Kathy and Tommy discover, do not have their wishes fulfilled: they have no agency over their own bodies. Their sexual but non-reproductive bodies are instruments of humanity. While some humans are exceedingly uncomfortable about the existence of clones – Emily at the school is one of them – they cannot, or do not, question their utility. Bioethics here comes up short against human utilitarianism. The making of 'new' humans or enhanced humans but without Human Rights is a bioethical problem – one that Ishiguro's novel foregrounds.

One final dimension of disability, bioethics and posthumanism needs to be addressed. Do disabled individuals have the right to *not* enhance themselves? One commentator writes: 'If it is widely accepted that we have the right to control how our bodies are changed both in the positive sense (using available tools for self-transformation) and in the negative sense of being free to not change, then it becomes harder to argue for a compulsory change' (Sandberg 2001, cited in Bradshaw and Ter Muelen 2010: 672). Disability studies calls for treating the disabled body as one variant within the human species. Therefore the above argument against enhancement might be read as a statement against the standardization of bodies, whereby the disabled are refused the freedom to be different. Posthumanism of the enhancement kind, in such cases, is seen as a coercive mode of homogenization. This is where the moral strand of enhancement technologies begins to acquire significance. Heather Bradshaw and Ruud Ter Muelen isolate, in the context of disability, what they term 'morphological freedom'. The disabled have a right to say 'no' to enhancement technologies and to retain their morphologically different bodies. They identify two responsibilities: the disadvantage responsibility and the non-abandonment responsibility. The first is one where 'society has no further obligation to "cure," enhance, or encourage self-enhancement for those disadvantaged by freely chosen morphologies' (2010: 680). The second is one where 'we do retain a strong obligation to continue with enhancement research for the benefit of others with the same disadvantage who, voluntarily, do not choose to retain it' (680). In both cases the emphasis is on the individual choice, whether to stay disabled or to enhance oneself. Bioethics here returns us to the question of agency – which, as noted above, was also a theme in Ishiguro's novel – of the different body.

Both disability studies and bioethics contribute to critical posthumanism by unravelling the politics of 'normal' bodies, by showing the constructedness of the human/non-human boundaries and by suggesting that bodies, able or not, live in conjunction with the environment, and that bodies can inhabit multispecies identity and citizenship. Ideals of bodily shapes and functions become hegemonic and refuse the right to be different, note both.

Both emphasize cooperation, sharing and mutuality as opposed to competition and difference as the (necessary) markers of the human-to-come, or, if we accept Lessing's thesis in *The Fifth Child*, the human that we were.

More than anything else, both disability studies and bioethics foreground alterity and difference as integral to our very conceptualization of our-selves as human. In feminist philosopher Rosalyn Diprose's words, which seem to point to a critical posthumanist stance, 'it is the other's alterity that makes me think, rather than ideas I live from and that seem to make me what I am' (2002: 141).

6 Posthuman Visions: Toward Companion Species

Human beings fear difference . . . Oankali crave difference.
(Butler 1988a: 186)

Life forms with multispecies identity, or whose identity is often liminal and blurred, abound these days: vampires, werewolves, shapeshifters, zombies, living machines, chimeras – *Blade, Buffy the Vampire Slayer, Fledgling, Underworld, Van Helsing, Twilight, Pride and Prejudice and the Zombies* . . . Humans also 'house', within their own bodies, other species (*Alien, Spawn*, Stephen King's *Dreamcatcher*) and are modified in the process of this relationship with an alien other within (Octavia Butler's *Clay's Ark*). The 'elemental' of Alan Moore's *Saga of the Swamp Thing* (1987) is a dead human (Alec Holland), pumped full of a 'biorestorative' chemical when alive, who comes back to 'life' when his memories merge with the plant life in the swamp. In Le Guin's 'Vaster than Empires and More Slow' (1987) Osden points out that the plants on the planet World 4470 are all connected and think together, transmitting their thoughts and feelings across the entire planet. Harfex muses: 'It isn't thinking . . . it's merely a network of processes. The branches, the epiphytic growths, the roots with those nodal junctures between individuals: they must all be capable of transmitting electrochemical impulses. There are no individual plants then, properly speaking . . . That all the biosphere of a planet should be one network of communications, sensitive, irrational, immortal, isolated' (1987: 122). The indigenous life form on the planet, the Spackle, in Patrick Ness' multi-award-winning young adult trilogy *Chaos Walking* (*The Knife of Never Letting Go*, 2008; *The Ask and the Answer*, 2009; *Monsters of Men*, 2010) are connected to the land, and communicate with each other through this connection. As Ben explains it: 'The Spackle speak the voice of this planet. They live within it . . . That's the secret of this planet . . . Communication, real and open, so we can finally understand each other' (2010: 452). The Mayor elaborates: 'This planet is information. All the time, never-ceasing. Information it wants to give you, information it wants to take from you to share with everyone else' (463). In *Avatar* too the life forms, Na'vi, on the planet Pandora seem to communicate with the planet. In each case the texts seem to talk of connections, networks and information-exchange that sustain life, where the planet and its various life forms are part of the great network, with no hierarchy (or minimal hierarchy).

Humans apparently share the planet, and body fluids, with many life forms like these. We are not alone even within our own skins. Then we also have a strange relationship with prosthetic devices and animals, even though we evolve with the dog in the house, and adapt our bodies to the device we wear or carry.

Critical posthumanism sees the human as co-evolving with, symbiotic with, sharing an ontology and a teleology with other species. Interconnections, intersections, mergers and acquisitions with other genes, life forms and species mark the human's existence on Earth. We are what/who we are because we are also Other. We are companion species with numerous other species, most of which we are unaware of. Posthumanism argues a case for companion species, for multispecies citizenship and what I shall call a species cosmopolitanism.[1]

The rejection of binaries is also the rejection of any kind of autonomous subjectivity. Authors like Butler and Le Guin seem to see empathy and connection – with all forms of life, the ecosystem and the mineral world – as the next (necessary) stage of human evolution. If mirror neuron activity is indeed the foundation for empathy (see the work of Keysers and others on mirror neurons) then it suggests that, through brain activity, imitation and empathy, we are connected to others. Each of us then has a *social* brain since our very consciousness learns from others' actions. This empathy that Butler and Le Guin propose, and neurobiologists are in the process of unravelling, suggests a rejection of autonomous subjectivity in favour of an intersubjective condition, a communitarianism that I am calling species cosmopolitanism. It retains alterity but also connectivity in what Lauren Bollinger calls a 'placental economy' (2007).

This chapter brings together the threads of the earlier ones through a reading of the works of Octavia Butler, mainly her last novel, *Fledgling* (2005), the now-cult vampire text *Twilight*, as well as Anne Rice's vampire fiction. Butler's continued interest in symbiogenesis (theorized by Bollinger) climaxes with *Fledgling* in which species politics is less about alien invasions (her theme in *Xenogenesis*) than about the co-evolution of species. This posthumanist *biology* foregrounds the potentiality and constitutive co-dependency of biology and rejects the valorization of the autonomous subject of traditional humanism. By demonstrating how Shori, the modified specimen of the vampire species Ina, and her human symbionts and Ina are all mutually dependent, Butler suggests that autonomy and sovereignty are not only overrated but illogical. The new biology encourages, indeed demands, multispecies citizenship. In *Twilight*, as in Butler (but far less effectively), Meyer suggests species transformation and species mixing when her vampires shed their vampiric tastes, behaviour and predispositions and train themselves to become humanized.

Fiction such as Butler's moves toward a species cosmopolitanism via configurations of biology and new modes of biological citizenship. The preliminary stage is a posthuman biology in which authors like Butler present a new theory of origins and move toward the idea of species domestication and deracination. This domestication marks the moment when a new kind of posthuman*ist* biology becomes visible. Individuals are now trained to deal with their new biology, but also to acquire a biological citizenship in more than one species through memory acts and a newly instilled sense of the ethical.

POSTHUMAN BIOLOGY

For critical posthumanism, changes in biology constitute a crucial anterior moment in a larger transformation of the human, or any other species for that matter. Posthuman biology 'focuses on alternative ways to think about life in an age when technology creates new paradigms of life' (Campbell and Saren 2010: 172). 'Technology' here might be taken to mean the genetic experiments of the Oankalis in *Xenogenesis* and the Ina experiments in *Fledgling*. Posthuman biology prepares the species – vampire, animal, human, Oankali – for a new way of life itself. It involves deracination, the acknowledgement of symbiogenesis (species origins that are multiple, diverse and 'impure'). Deracination is the losing, conscious and voluntary in many cases, of species characteristics so that cohabitation with other species is possible. It is the absorption of other-species characteristics as well. Contemporary vampire fiction clearly makes this a key theme.

Symbiogenesis

Firmly committed to the companion species ideal, Octavia Butler's fiction constantly returns to the theme of co-evolution. She proposes alternative stories of evolution in which co-optation and cooperation triumph over competition in the production of new species. Butler's *Xenogenesis* trilogy maps a near-apocalypse scenario where Earth is all but destroyed. The survival of the last few humans is possible only through their genetic merger with the alien species, Oankali. Butler, in Cathy Peppers' prescient reading (1995), appropriates the Biblical, the socio-biological, the paleoanthropological origin stories of humankind and the narrative of the African diaspora to fashion a new origin story that refuses primacy to any of the four in what Peppers calls a 'dialogic' origin story. In this new origin story biology plays a significant role.

Posthuman symbiogenesis is explained by Nikanj in Butler's *Adulthood Rites*:

Examine Tino. Inside him, so many different things are working together to keep him alive. Inside his cells, mitochondria, a previously independent form of life, have found a haven and trade their ability to synthesize proteins and metabolize fats for room to live and reproduce. We're in his cells too now, and the cells have accepted us . . . Even before we arrived, they had bacteria living in their intestines and protecting them from other bacteria that would hurt or kill them. They could not exist without symbiotic relationships with other creatures. Yet such relationships frighten them . . . I think we're as much symbionts as their mitochondria were originally. They could not have evolved into what they are without mitochondria. (1988b: 182–3)

This is practically a paraphrase of Lynn Margulis, Scott Gilbert and other theorists of evolutionary biology (see chapter 2).[2] Margulis and Sagan write in *Microcosmos* of the genetic mixing that enables evolution: 'a second evolutionary dynamic is a sort of natural genetic engineering . . . Prokaryotes routinely and rapidly transfer bits of genetic material to other individuals' (cited in Clarke 2008: 172). What Nikanj is telling Lilith is that all biology is multispecies, symbiotic and mutually dependent. The Oankali, as they inform Lilith, have a 'long, multispecies . . . history' (Butler 1988a: 61). One of the meanings of the very name 'Oankali' is 'gene traders'.[3] As Jhdaya, one of the Oankali, explains to Lilith:

We trade the essence of ourselves. Our genetic material for yours . . . We're not hierarchical, you see . . . But we are powerfully acquisitive. We acquire new life – seek it, investigate it, manipulate it, sort it, use it. We carry the drive to do this in a minuscule cell within a cell, a tiny organelle within every cell of our bodies . . . One of the meanings of Oankali is gene trader. Another is that organelle – the essence of ourselves, the origin of ourselves. (39)

If the Oankali have evolved through strategic genetic mixing, the vampire species Ina in Butler's *Fledgling* seeks a new origin. In order for the Ina's origin story to reflect the symbiogenesis, Butler starts afresh, as already noted. She does this by rendering Lilith, like much of humanity, and Shori the vampire, into bare life, or *zoē*. Theirs is life 'stripped of its historically specific form', as Ziarek puts it in a gloss on Agamben's idea (2008: 96), because they have lost their writing, their history, their memories and their skills when the Oankali find them (*Xenogenesis*) and when Shori is rescued by Wright (*Fledgling*). The cancer in Lilith is something that draws Oankali attention – in addition, of course, to the fact that human genes are what the Oankali crave. Shori is an amnesiac with no memory of her inherited identity: 'there was nothing in my world but hunger and pain, no other people, no other time, no other feelings' (Butler 2005: 1). Injured and hungry, Shori kills: 'I discovered that I was strong. . . . I seized the animal. It fought me, tore at me, struggled to escape, but I had it' (2). Shori is beginning to discover her-self, primarily as a body, focusing on her injuries, physical prowess and hunger, more animal than human (Smith 2007: 388). With species memory lost as a result of trauma, she can only speculate on her connections with other people: 'it felt like something I would want – living together with other people instead of wandering alone' (Butler 2005:

5). Shori is some-*body* whose primal instincts are in place, but very little of anything else, even though she does understand human speech (7–8). It is this primordial, primeval – biological – self that marks the start of the origin story in *Fledgling*.

In *Xenogenesis*, *Clay's Ark* (1984), *Fledgling* and other works, Butler foregrounds biology as the preliminary moment to a new route of multispecies evolution. The Oankali, intrigued by a human disease, cancer, appropriate and genetically engineer it so as to help the regrowth of lost limbs and produce shape-changer children. In *Clay's Ark* infected humans become leaner, stronger, faster; their senses sharpen and they age more slowly. Shori becomes sunlight-tolerant because her vampire genes have been modified due to the miscegenation with human DNA.

Butler's cyborg origin story in *Fledgling* works by erasing 'culture' in favour of 'nature', where biology and not history – or, if one were to be truly accurate, a history of her biology – is the determinant of all things. Butler foregrounds Shori's biological citizenship as *zoē*: a vampire-animal. Her biological citizenship is grounded in her genes, and her responses at the beginning of the tale are the nearest we can think of to embodied memory. When Shori kills Hugh Tang, the man who comes looking for her, she has fulfilled a promise built into her body, but not her conscious self. Her behaviour then – for which she feels a sense of shame (2005: 66–7) and the other Ina castigate her later in the text (75) – is pure *zoē*. Later, animalizing tropes are used to describe Shori by her detractors ('goddamn mongrel cub', 173; 'clever dog', 238), even as she hopes she won't be treated as an animal (239). This animal in her and the animal powers that constitute her Ina body – which is material–discursive since the materiality of her body and her recognition of its biovalue as 'animal' are produced through the inter-actions of apparatuses such as Ina experiments and internalized discourses of animality – are what she has to subjugate and harness.

Here we perceive a state in which nothing but an unexceptional biological state exists, minus personal–cultural memory, minus history and minus affiliations or identity. Butler calls attention to Shori's biology so that the next step can be taken: a recalibration of 'biovalue'. Understanding one's self in biological terms, the properties of life – from the mere 'living' to the reproductive/regenerative – are enmeshed within the systems of global financial, and therefore political, exchanges so that specific characteristics of particular species, races or ethnic groups acquire particular values (Rose and Novas 2005, Sundar Rajan 2006). Bodies, in Butler, Le Guin and all the posthumanist authors, are at the centre of all social change and new citizenship projects.[4]

Lilith and Shori start off as merely biological *zoē*, as mere bodies – nothing more. With the representation of *zoē*, Butler calls attention to biology *as techn*ē: the tools Shori and Lilith fall back on are *biological* states – hunger, smell, mobility, strength – and not culturally acquired/inherited ones (although the Butler vision of these as merely biological is itself a discourse that constructs boundaries between the biological and the political). Butler foregrounds Shori's biological citizenship as *zoē*, a vampire-animal, and Lilith's as potential mother. Their biological citizenship is grounded in their (modified) genes.

In Shori's case, her acquisition of a new biovalue, and insertion into a new biological citizenship as a vampire–human hybrid, demand, first, a domestication and deracination of her vampire characteristics and a careful amplification of her human ones. Posthuman biology reorders the very nature of Shori's or Lilith's biology as species-specific or unique since whatever is unique has to be eroded. Lilith, for instance, is very clear that, with their modified biology, the course of a new human evolution can avoid the disturbing events of the 'original' one (Peppers 1995: 57–8). Posthuman biology enables a wholly new narrative – at least in memory – of origins. Paul Titus exclaims that the humans would have to go back to the Stone Age, where Lilith has to live 'like a cavewoman'; men will 'drag [her] around, put [her] in a harem, beat the shit out of [her]' (Butler 1988a: 92). Lilith rejects this anxiety: 'we don't have to go back to the Stone Age', she says (90). She stops eating meat and the Oankali discourage hunting. Together, these choices alter the Stone Age moment of human evolution. With their new biovalues the older scheme and path of human evolution can be avoided, suggests Butler. This too is suggestive of a deracination.[5]

Domestication–Deracination

Domestication is essentially species mixing and the making of interspecies communities where the biology of all species is suitably modified to enable cohabitation and survival. In *Xenogenesis*, aliens and humans cohabit and make communities. In *Fledgling*, vampires and humans cohabit. Contemporary vampire fiction, as noted above, foregrounds the possibility, or necessity, of vampires adapting to human forms of sociality and life.[6] Thus the solitary vampire figure of the nineteenth and early twentieth centuries makes way for Anne Rice's covens of vampires and Stephenie Meyer's families of vampires. The vampire creates families through non-traditional means, of course, with the mixing of blood marking the making of blood-relations. With Anne Rice's *Interview with the Vampire* (1976), the nuclear family of vampires became a commonplace theme (Benefiel 2004). This vampire family becomes in some sense a mirror image of the 'standard' human family as well, despite their other predilections.

The theme of vampire families also shows the sociability and socialization of vampires. We are told that other vampires who do not locate themselves in a family structure, or 'belong', such as James the tracker in *Twilight*, are seen as aberrations. Edward explains: 'Most won't settle in any one place. Only those like us, who've given up hunting you people [humans] . . . can live together with humans for any length of time' (Meyer 2005: 290). Edward's character also suggests a human/non-human linkage here, a model of mutual racial coexistence but one based on a *denial* of the vampire's true nature.

Much of Anne Rice's recent work focuses on love rather than killing, and her vampires are keen on *not* being monsters (Rout 2003). In Meyer's vampires we see a similar desire – of not being true to their vampiric identity and seeking a whole new way of life, changes in attitudes and emotional intelligence. In *Twilight*, Edward, repentant at hurting Isabella, seeks to win her over and to create a vampire family built on love rather than anything else. Carlisle, despite being a vampire, works in the life-saving profession of medicine. The Cullens, to adopt Rout's terminology, have developed a 'moral code' that allows them to coexist with human beings. This marks the domestication of the vampire who, having given up the thirst for human blood, can live with and replicates the family structures of humans.

In his first 'version' Carlisle, having become a vampire, 'strayed as far away as he could from the human populace . . . wandered by night, sought the loneliest places, loathing himself' (Meyer 2005: 337). Later, having discovered that he could prey on animals instead of humans, he realizes that 'he could exist without being a demon' (337).[7] 'He found himself again', writes Meyer (337). But what exactly is this 'himself'? I propose that the vampiric masculinity and solitariness of the monster are erased in favour of a return to the identity of a harmless human. The route to this humanization of the vampire, in Carlisle's case but also in the case of Rosalie, Emmett, Alice, Jasper, Esme and, of course, Edward, is the family.

The domesticated vampire family is also distinguished by their clothing, looks and manners. Take the following description of the 'regular' vampires who arrive when the Cullens are playing baseball:

As they approached, I could see how different they were from the Cullens. Their walk was catlike, a gait that seemed constantly on the edge of shifting into a crouch. They dressed in the ordinary gear of backpackers: jeans and casual button-down shirts in heavy, weatherproof fabrics. The clothes were frayed, though, with wear, and they were barefoot. Both men had cropped hair, but the woman's brilliant orange hair was filled with leaves and debris from the woods . . . Her [Victoria's] posture was distinctly feline . . . [Laurent's] eyes moved appreciatively over Carlisle's refined appearance. (376–8)

Meyer clearly aligns the new vampires with animals and the Cullens with urbane lifestyles and a more socially acceptable appearance.

Vampires blur family lines, mix races (Winnubst 2003). In Meyer's saga this 'mixing' becomes a code for interracial coexistence. The vampire can coexist, as we have seen, with humans. The Edward–Isabella 'connection' initiates a new 'line' as well. The 'family' now includes individuals from different racial and ethnic backgrounds. If Kal-El (a.k.a. Superman) can 'fit' into the human race, and if superheroes can coexist with humans, then vampires, Rice's and Meyer's work proposes, can also contribute to the society/race as professionals (Carlisle as the eminent doctor), and even miscegenate with humans. In Anne Rice's *Merrick* (2000), we have witches and vampires with African American antecedents. Merrick mourns how the later generation tried hard to disown this genealogy: 'they wanted to get their hands on anything that said they were colored and tear it up' (27). By showing how the vampire humanizes with 'vegetarianism', lifestyle choices and family-belonging, Meyer casts the vampire as a member of a different species whose difference need not be feared: they can be educated and reformed. If, as the epigraph from Butler suggests, humans are scared of difference, posthumanist visions show us how we incorporate difference within ourselves.

The vampire both 'promises and threatens racial and sexual mixing' (as Donna Haraway put it, 1997: 214), but also species mixing. Contemporary vampire fiction makes moves toward multiracial origins, multiracial families and questions, in some very literal themes, the origins of blood- and family lines. Isabella's fantasies of life with Edward can be read as a coded fantasy of multiracial relations, and thus subvert the very idea of racial and species purity.

It is a step toward the posthumanist species cosmopolitanism.

Shori biologically embodies an intraspecies alterity (the Other to, and therefore different from, Ina) and an interspecies alterity (a vampire and thus the Other to humans). Lilith, like Shori, is exiled from home and is outside to Oankali but is also estranged from her fellow humans as well. Eventually, however, we see both Lilith and Shori acquiring a new 'biovalue' because they are caught in this bind of being doubly Other.

A pure state of *zoē* cannot exist where the body is unmarked by technology (Esposito 2008: 15). In Shori *zoē* is presented as a condition in which she does not *remember* her cultural *technē*. Her *zoē* is consequent upon her ignorance about her biology that has already been traversed by technology: genetic engineering. Butler suggests a *zoē* that is primordial only in the sense that Shori relies on her *biological* memory of hunting. The transition from *zoē* to *bíos* involves a complicated traversal through specific practices and discourses (such as those of care) that render Shori a hybrid. In the case of Lilith and the other humans in *Xenogenesis*, they are prevented from using any remnants of their cultural memories – Lilith, for example, is denied paper to write on.

In Butler's posthumanism each species needs to lose its sense of exclusivity and acquire a sense of merger and mutuality. If posthumanism is about a whole new *bíos*, the 'improper' of *zoē* must be excluded, a process that demands a certain technology (Campbell 2011: 32–4). Posthuman biology entails not only the acquisition of a new/renewed body, as in the case of figures like Shori and Lilith, but also an entire process of socialization in which the individual 'body' learns its new uses and responsibilities. Humans need to come to terms with the animal (as in Butler's *Clay's Ark*) and the Oankali (as in *Xenogenesis*) in them. The Oankali have to *learn* to understand the human need for autonomy. Vampires have to acquire human traits of community even as they 'domesticate' their vampire behaviour (*Fledgling*). In Shori's case, this means the animal-vampire – the alleged improper – in her biology must be subsumed to the human. But it also means that the humans with whom the vampires will cohabit, and whose body fluids and genetic material the Oankali will absorb and/or modify, will lose some of their humanness.

Indeed, vampires began, suggests Rice, when some humans desired to leave the human race. Louis in *Interview with the Vampire* says: 'it was detachment that made this possible, a sublime loneliness with which Lestat and I moved through the world of mortal men' ([1976] 2010: 38). Once bitten by the vampire, the 'victim' begins to lose her/his sense of family and home and begins to see her/him-self more attached to the species of vampires. This might be interpreted as a deracination of the human, a slide away from the human toward the vampire species. The bite is a ruptured border, the flow of blood marks the loosening of familial and species ties – both materially and discursively, when the freshly minted vampires begin to 'see' and articulate different species borders vis-à-vis vampires and humans – and a forging of new relations and identities.

Humans move closer to other species as well, as Butler suggests from very early in her oeuvre. In the *Patternist* series (*Patternmaster*, 1976; *Mind of My Mind*, 1977; *Survivor; Wild Seed*, 1980; *Clay's Ark*, 1984) Butler anticipated several of the posthuman themes of *Xenogenesis* and *Fledgling*.[8] The 4,000-year-old Nubian, Doro, breeds humans and modifies them into a new species. In *Wild Seed* he seeks Anyanwu, a 300-year-old Igbo priestess with shape-shifting powers, so that they can combine their genetic materials for this purpose. The humans that will result, says Doro, will be a 'strong new people' ([1980] 2007: 19). They will be psychically sensitive human beings bred for their telepathy, telekinesis, psychometry and regenerative healing powers. Shori is prefigured in Mary, Doro's daughter and the subject of *Mind of My Mind*. Mary is described as a symbiont and has, after her transition, become the originator of a new race: in control of six telepaths with whom she is linked through telepathy. Mary is described in the novel in terms we have come to recognize as central to the posthumanist vision: 'a symbiont, a being living in partnership with her people. She gave them unity, they fed her, and both thrived. She was not a parasite' ([1977] 2007: 448). Butler emphasizes connections not sovereignty, species mixing rather than species autonomy, here already. We do not recognize the protagonists here as human in the conventional sense, being bred for specific powers and functions. The loss of humanity, in Butler's view, enables the humans to survive through greater cooperation, skills, longevity and healing abilities. For humanity to survive, it must *become posthuman with other species*. Thus, when Lilith in *Dawn* asks what the 'constructs' (born of humans and

Oankali) will look like, she is told: 'Different . . . Not quite like you. A little like us' (1988a: 40).

Rather than filiation with families and species, Butler, Rice and Meyer propose a conscious effort at affiliation of a different kind: cross-species relationships initiated through conscious, agential acts, or imposed, or through necessity. In the case of Edward and others in *Twilight*, their slide toward the human is both by choice and by necessity, since they wish to live in human communities and pass off as humans. Shori, unlike the interviewer or Louis in *Interview with the Vampire*, has little choice in her species-crossing, since she has been genetically altered by her elder generation. Mary and the other symbionts are reared to be a different species in Butler's *Patternist* series.

Posthuman biology in Butler's characters, as in Rice and Meyer, is altered so that traditional evolutionary explanations for biological traits are called into question. *Xenogenesis* contains a fine example of deracination through modified biology. Lilith is informed that it is her body's tendency toward cancer that attracts the Oankali. Now cancer is not always an invasive condition. As Cathy Peppers notes, one cannot use traditional imagery of 'foreign' or 'alien' invasion to describe this disease since it is very often the cells of the body, on their own, that rage out of control (1995: 52). In chapter 2, we noted how new models of immunity have demonstrated the falsehood of the belief that no entity originating in the organism will trigger an immune reaction and that every 'foreign' entity will trigger an immune reaction. The body betrays itself, human biology fights itself. In Butler, the human race is also condemned because their biology is prone, internally and with little external stimulus, to destroy itself. Deracination involves the *loss* of such potentially lethal biological traits and the development of post-human biology through intervention. We could even go as far as saying that Lilith's cancer is a mark of her 'bare life' (*zoë*), a biology doomed to self-destruction, and what the Oankali do is to offer a posthuman biology that would be closer to *bíos*. It is with the exclusion, instigated and imposed by the alien Oankali, of the 'improper' elements of what in human *discourse* is flawed (*material*) biology – cancer – that humanity can survive. The Oankali material–discursive construction of cancer as life-saving marks a posthumanism.

Butler, always concerned with the loss of species specificity, adopts a different scheme in *Fledgling*, in her theme of deracination and species-blurring in which 'growing up' means an exclusion of the 'improper', or whatever feature can prove a hindrance in species mixing. This process of exclusion is achieved through a cultural apparatus, or a *dispositif*, which Foucault saw as an ensemble of law, administrative measures, scientific notions and philosophical ideas that sought to regulate populations. The *dispositif* is a process of individuation within a social apparatus with its isolation, realignment and reorganization of relations in which the subject is formed (Deleuze, cited in Campbell 2011: 45; see also Agamben 2009: 11).

Dispositifs allow the division of a living being into two natures of different qualities, with one subjugated by the other (Campbell 2011: 69). If the human emerges as a result of the expulsion of the animal within (Agamben 2004: 15–16), the cultural apparatus needs to enable this expulsion or separation of a living being into two: the animal and the human 'person'. It must induce, in Shori's case, a 'domestication' of the vampire. Shori must be deracinated and expel the Ina qualities in her.

Shori's posthuman biology is the 'naturalization' of a new, hybrid biology. Her identity as an Ina is uncertain because her altered biology – genetics constitutes a *dispositif*, with all the attendant relations and tensions of various 'actors' in the Ina scientific network – sets her outside the species border. Further, the 'human' in her genes must necessarily modify her 'natural' Ina traits: a process that requires tutoring. 'Posthuman biology' here is a site of acculturation where Shori's negotiations with her biology and its implications, her ideas about life and her biovalue are enacted, and *her biology becomes 'naturalized' into doing things that are neither entirely Ina nor fully human*. It is a step toward a more communally productive use of her altered biological state in which she will eventually become a biological citizen of a wholly different kind. Ina *dispositifs* organize Shori's political subjectivity when they engineer her genes but also instil histories, memories and habits. The route from bare life to political life, in other words, lies via this *dispositif*, of which we can isolate two specific forms.

Pedagogy

Sarah Outterson has argued that Butler's characters always have to *learn* something (2008: 433). Shori's main task is to acquire knowledge of herself, her identity, her identification (with other vampires) and her integration into the Ina community. Her more formal 'education' begins with Wright helping her surf the internet for vampire information (Butler 2005: 30), which she dismisses as 'worthless stuff' (30). Now, if Shori is unaware of what she is, how is she in any position to dismiss the information she gleans off the www as 'worthless'? Despite this inexplicable logic, one could make the argument that it is her species memory that kicks in when she reads about vampires, a memory that causes her to evaluate what she reads. It is Wright, a human, who first instructs her about sources she might access for reliable information (30–1) and the human myths around vampires (59–60).

Shori's informal education at Ina hands begins when Iosif tells her that they 'have very little in common with the vampire creatures Bram Stoker described in *Dracula*' (63). In the course of a disquisition Iosif teaches her modes of social engineering the humans:

Let them see that you trust them and let them solve their own problems, make their own decisions. Do that and they will willingly commit their lives to you.

Bully them, control them out of fear and malice or just for your own convenience, and after a while, you'll have to spend all your time thinking for them, controlling them, stifling their resentment. (73)

This is remarkably similar to *Parable of the Sower* in which Lauren is told: 'It's better to teach people than to scare them, Lauren. If you scare them and nothing happens, they lose their fear, and you lose some of your authority with them. It's harder to scare them a second time, harder to teach them, harder to win back their trust. Best to begin by teaching' (1993: 58).

In *Fledgling*, Preston reassures Shori that her behaviour is truly that of an Ina (2005: 152–3), and Brook instructs her on how Ina–human relations work and how she needs to touch her human symbionts more: 'we protect and feed you, and you protect and feed us. That's the way an Ina-and-symbiont household works . . . I think it will work that way with you' (177). Other modes of instruction include Shori's reading of Ina history (187–90, 195, 231), Brook's recounting of Ina history (129–32), and Daniel Gordon's detailing to Shori the ways of the Council of Judgment (220–3). The Ina also warn her to control her temper (239) and help her 'relearn the things . . . [she] should know about . . . [herself and her] people' (277). This is a pedagogy that 'domesticates' the Ina qualities of Shori in order to make her biological nature better suited to living with humans.

Put together, these pedagogic modes not only tell Shori what she does not know of her, and Ina, history but also instruct her in forms of behaviour, social engineering and her own abilities. These might be seen as processes of Ina socialization but also as instructions on interspecies interaction. The *dispositifs* of education are crucial elements in the reconfiguration of the new social order in Butler.

This interspecies interaction is not, in Butler, restricted to humans or vampires. In *Xenogenesis* Butler shows how the Oankali wishes to learn everything about humans. As she puts it in *Dawn*: 'It needed less sleep than she did, and when she was not asleep, it expected her to be learning or teaching. It wanted not only language, but culture, biology, history, her own life story . . . Whatever she knew, it expected to learn' (1988a: 59). Lilith is assigned the task of teaching the other humans just awakened to a new life with the Oankali: 'To teach, to give comfort, to feed and clothe, to guide them through and interpret what will be, for them, a new and frightening world. To parent' (110). Indeed, the acquisition of knowledge is essential to survival itself. Kahguyaht tells Lilith that the alien Oankali have 'learned' to eat Earth food 'by studying teachers to whom it isn't poison. By studying your people, Lilith. Your bodies' (48).

Pedagogy is not only central to survival, it is also the most important element in the evolution of a new species and a species cosmopolitanism. Pedagogy, as seen in the *Xenogenesis* books, demands the 'violation' of body boundaries (Outterson 2008: 446–7), and thus constitutes a step along the merger of species. The exchange and merger of genes and learning is what keeps the Oankali going, as Nikanj tells Lilith: 'We are as committed to the trade as your body is to breathing. We were overdue for it when we found you. Now it will be done – to the rebirth of your people and mine' (Butler 1988a: 41). This suggests that the networking of genetic material across species and time is what enables evolution. Evolution therefore is not about competition but cooperation and co-optation: 'There is evidence to show that we are recombined from powerful bacterial communities with a multi-billion year history. We are part of an intricate network that comes from the original bacterial takeover of the earth' (Margulis and Sagan, cited in Clarke 2008: 173).

The 'evidence' of linkage and intersection that Margulis and Sagan offer is precisely what Butler will take up when deploying her theme of memory citizenship.

Memory Citizenship as Multispecies Citizenship

The humans need to lose their species-specific memories, the Oankali believe. When Lilith asks them if they have left any of the ruins of cities behind, the Oankali inform her that they have been destroyed:

'You'll begin again. We'll put you in areas that are clean of radio-activity and history. You will become something other than you were.'
  'And you think destroying what was left of our cultures will make us better?'
  'No. Only different.' (1988a: 32)

A memory citizenship is essential, but this cannot be species-specific, nor restricted to one's immediate genealogy. A careful recall, mediated by the Oankali, reveals a problematic and messy inheritance.

Throughout *Xenogenesis*, genetics and memory are intertwined. But even a memory citizenship has to be grounded in biology, according to the Oankali. When Lilith pleads that she be given some writing tools, the request is refused. Instead, Nikanj offers to modify her body so that she can learn and retain her learning in her body better: 'I must make small changes – a few small changes. I must help you reach your memories as you need them' (73). The Oankali carry within them memories of all their previous forms, of the genetic material they had incorporated. In fact, what sets the Oankali apart from humans is their eidetic memory, as opposed to the 'plodding slowness and haphazard' memory Lilith sees in herself (59). Humans need prosthetic devices to aid memory, the Oankali store it in their bodies (hence Nikanj's offer to change the biology of Lilith's body so that it can remember, without prosthetic aids like writing). Humans remember only their immediate and Oankali wish to change that. As Bruce Clarke puts it, 'human status is defined precisely by its defects of memory – *its selective obliviousness to its environment and its history*' (2008: 177, emphasis added). In other words, *what the humans need to remember is an entangled history of companion species*, of cooperation and co-optation rather than of competition. What it has to perform is a memory citizenship where recalling this entangled history will position Lilith and other humans as multispecies citizens, not just 'human' or 'alien'.[9]

Remembering, in the case of Shori, Lilith and Dana (in Butler's *Kindred*, 1979), is also the memory of pain. Their memories of origins are essentially memories of loss: Dana recounts the loss of her arm and her psychological damage; Shori recalls, vaguely, that she had suffered; Lilith is woken from sleep with memories of a destroyed life/world and herself feeling strange in her body. Indeed, all their memories of their origins seem to be narratives of wounds, damages and loss. That all women – and African American women, it must be noted – protagonists wake to such memories of pain and loss is significant. Ashraf Rushdy in a perceptive reading of *Kindred* has proposed that 'remembering' and 'dismembering' seem to go together in the novel, as in other novels about slavery (1993: 138). Recalling, painfully, the past – very often a slave past – is also a way of comprehending the present and creating a 'historically defined self' (139). In Butler, memory works to enable protagonists like Shori or Lilith to find a *different* history of their own self, but also to see human history as one of self-destructive pride and arrogance (as Lilith does in *Xenogenesis*). The memory citizenship of each of these women involves redrawing the narrative of their origins.

The theme of memory citizenship is intensified in a different direction in *Fledgling*. Shori seeks to understand her Ina identity through acts of mourning her dead Ina relations. Posthuman biology here works as the site of memory retrieval – of both individual and species memory. Acts of memory are central to the *dispositif* through which Shori tries to find her biological ancestry and cultural inheritance.

She discovers that she has absolutely no memories of her family. When she is told of her human mother and the Ina family, Shori thinks 'I shut my eyes and tried to find something of this woman in my memory . . . But there was nothing. All of my life had been erased . . . what should have been a familiar, welcoming place and finding absolutely nothing, emptiness, space' (Butler 2005: 133). At the Council, Shori screams at the Silks: 'My family is gone! . . . My memory of them is gone. I can't even mourn them properly because for me, they never really lived. Now I have begun to relearn who I am, to rebuild my life, and my enemies are still killing my people' (265). Shori's conscious, i.e., recent, *memories can now only be of a family where she has co-evolved with humans: it is not an Ina-specific memory at all*. 'My family' makes minor theoretical and rhetorical sense here for Shori. 'My people' here are humans and Shori tied to each other. She has had to invent a new ontology for herself – one that cannot separate her Ina being from the human elements inside her.

Yet Shori consistently mourns the family she has no memory of. Performances of memory, Michael Rothberg and Yasmin Yildiz argue, are 'acts of citizenship'. These acts emerge from the people, regardless of their formal citizenship status (2011: 34). When Shori mourns her dead family, she mourns with the *Ina* who have lost their relations. Shori's acts of mourning situate her as an Ina citizen through this act of memorialization. If, as Rothberg and Yildiz suggest, 'identity-based understandings of collective work in the form of ethnic property' (36) influence the work of memory, then Ina collective memory would automatically exclude all other species from the work of mourning. Shori's peculiar status as Ina and not-all-Ina means that she can demonstrate her ethnic- and species-affiliation only through acts of memory. Her biological citizenship can move into the category of *bíos* only when she participates in acts of memory citizenship as Ina even when these memories are *learnt* and are of a companion species: vampires *becoming with* humans.

Shori has no embodied memories of family, mothers or community, but having 'learnt' her species identity, and the Ina ethics of care, she goes on to perform these acts of care and mourning. *Bíos* is the climactic moment of acceptance when the other Ina perceive her mourning. Shori's outburst about her inability to mourn is construed as a performance of the *act* of mourning by the Ina. Thus Shori's acts of memory citizenship are only performed as the inability to mourn her Ina relations of whom she has no memory. The admission of the need to mourn is also implicitly accepted as an act of memory citizenship which then changes the status of her biological citizenship *as* an Ina. The biology which determines Shori's Ina citizenship is modified through pedagogy and memory citizenship. While her amnesia erases her memories of the Ina-lineage, the newly learnt memories are – like Lilith's on being 'awakened' in *Dawn* – of species mixing and cooperation. What Shori is given is information about a posthuman genealogy.

In the latter sections of the novel, Shori's future mates become the matter of considerable speculation. It is implied that she must choose with care and with responsibility to the gene line she carries. Thus Daniel suggests Joel Harrison as a possible mate for Shori because Joel would later help Shori manage the 'business affairs of . . . [her] families' (Butler 2005: 152). Having been privileged with a biological citizenship unique to her, Shori now needs to see how best this citizenship can be extended to other Ina, even as she has to remember that she is responsible for her human symbionts as well in a burden of multispecies responsibility. The future of the Ina and human community that she 'carries' inside her is a project of biological citizenship in itself: this would be her great biovalue, whose true nature comes home to her through the *dispositifs* of Ina instruction. This is biovalue that is added to due to her learnt memories of her multispecies origins and citizenship.

Pedagogy is enabled, in Shori's case, by her amnesia. This narrative strategy allows Butler to offer her, and us, Ina history. First Iosif (67–8) and then Brook (129–32) give her short accounts of Ina pasts. This includes, significantly, a history of their persecution – as 'foreigners' – at the hands of humans (130). This chronicle of species extermination leads later in the novel to the larger political theme of species co-evolution and cooperation. Ina continue to be attacked by humans and by those Ina who favour genetic purity. It is precisely this pattern of violence that Butler suggests might end if species learn to co-evolve and respect / respond to each other. Lilith, for instance, is told by the Oankali that humanity has tried to wipe itself out. Butler seems to suggest that humanity does not need alien invasions for its destruction: it is perfectly capable of doing this to itself. But Butler's optimism here also offers as a solution: humanity can survive if it is modified through genetic interventions, which the Oankali can perhaps offer. As mentioned before, the human race can survive if it becomes a little less human.

Memories that are revealed to Shori, Lilith and others in Butler's novels are facilitators of a multispecies citizenship and of a more problematic history and kinship than they could otherwise have known.[10] As memories are implanted – whether through pedagogy or through genetic–neurological–chemical alterations of organic material in Ina or humans – they are made aware of their belonging to more than one species. The implantation of memory in their biology prepares them for their posthuman life thereafter. This biology, with the implanted memories of joint histories, messy origins and multispecies citizenship, constitutes a posthuman*ist* biology.

POSTHUMANIST BIOLOGY

Posthumanist biology, as Butler sees it, is a condition in which the new biology, drawing upon a multispecies origin and development, generates positive biological features that enhance corporeal and *moral* qualities of the species. As noted above, (biologically) implanted memories of their multi-species origins and entangled histories reconstruct the past, present and future for Ina, Lilith and other humans and any other species. But here in this section I want to focus on another theme that proceeds from the earlier one of memory citizenship.

This theme is common to Butler's *Xenogenesis* as well as *Fledgling* and occurs in different forms in the *Parable* texts (1993 and 1998). In *Fledgling*, Butler presents Shori as the starting point – a fledgeling – for a whole new species. In *Xenogenesis* it is Lilith and her 'brood'. All of these are members of a particular species (vampires and humans, respectively) with DNA and learning from other species. Posthuman*ist* biology with such a multispecies genetic make-up is the creation of a new biovalue for Shori, a biovalue where her special qualities as Ina and her 'human' advantages are together turned to the service of both species. Posthumanist biology is the effective transcendence of the dual-species biology in Shori, whereby she represents a new biological citizenship of an imminent species (one discerns a tilt toward the modified *human*, though the human remains at the forefront of Butler's imagination).

The new biological citizenship for Shori, Lilith and others relies on a posthumanist biology and has two distinct components: the new biology and its ethics of care and the making of a companion species within each of them.

Empathy, the Ethics of Care and Moral Transhumanism

'If we found the people who had murdered both my male and my female families, I wanted to kill them, had to kill them. How else could I keep my new family safe?' asks Shori (Butler 2005: 105). Here Shori displays her animal–vampire predilection for violence but also something more/different: her animal prowess is to be harnessed for the safety of her human dependants. This is the subjugation of her animal role to a different condition: care. It marks the emergence of a new subjectivity when Shori is able to make this split (Ina–animal versus human) within herself. She even displays a moral code that seems to suggest an entirely different subject inside her when, for instance, she has to steal food (122). At one point Wright, talking to another human, Brook, describes the genetically modified Shori thus: 'she's shown herself to be a weirdly ethical little thing most of the time' (162). Brook offers Wright the following insight: 'they're [Ina] not human . . . they don't care about white or black' (162). All this seems to indicate recognition of Shori's Ina (i.e., species) ethics, despite her hybrid biology.

Shori recalls fragments of her Ina identity when she recognizes the need for 'fresh human blood' and 'fresh meat for healing injuries and illnesses, for sustaining growth spurts, and for carrying a child' (19). Beside these instances of species memory that foreground her vampire nature, Shori also retrieves other memories that will eventually determine the emergence of an ethical, full-fledged vampire–human hybrid. That is, it is the *memory* of her *multispecies* origin and citizenship that enables Shori to function as a vampire–human *hybrid* with an ethics of care toward *both* species. Memory citizenship of this kind leads to the arrival of a moral posthuman.

Very early, in a surprising act of memory retrieval and subliminal socialization, Shori understands what she can do to Wright, her human companion: 'I understood – or perhaps remembered – that people could be weakened by blood loss. If I made Wright weak, he might get hurt. When I thought about it, I knew I would want more blood . . . I realized that to avoid hurting Wright, to avoid hurting anyone, I would have to find several people to take blood from' (15). It is Iosif who points to the remnants of Ina morality that Shori carries as a species memory: 'You've forgotten who and what you are, but you still have at least some of the morality you were taught' (66). This 'morality' is the ethics of care that *Ina* display toward their human symbionts, and care is the marker of Shori's emergent subjectivity as well.

An early moment in this emergent subjectivity of Shori's occurs when she recognizes that she had killed and eaten a fellow Ina and she is 'shamed' (65). It is her vampire-animal self, so to speak, that had killed and eaten the man who had come looking for her. With the dawn of a new subjectivity and her species-memory Shori recognizes the horrific nature of her deed. Shori has learnt the extent of her powers and she must now harness them effectively – a process that is also a part of her 'learning'. Iosif and the other elder Ina also teach her the limits and extent of Ina powers. The acquisition of the knowledge of power, Lauren Lacey rightly argues, helps Shori to understand how power operates and what 'impedes' her power (2008: 380). Therefore what Iosif teaches her is the power of social engineering, the manipulation of humans and Ina, for the greater good of both species.

For Shori it becomes a matter of pride that she safeguards other Ina and her human symbionts: 'I worry that I won't always know how to take care of you' (Butler 2005: 123). It is the ethics of care that distinguishes Shori – and inflects her urgent need to learn – from all others. When the expected attack materializes, Shori is at the forefront of the community's defence (166–76). The *dispositif* of care – the morality Iosif emphasizes – constitutes the expulsion of the animal-vampire in Shori and a perceptible shift toward the human, enabled and empowered by her new biology but also through the *dispositifs* that have *trained* her to utilize her vampire–human characteristics better.

Founded in a new genetic structure, Shori and the community-to-come (from her) are embodied in her revitalized biology. Preston declares at the Council meeting: 'Shori Matthew is as Ina as the rest of us. In addition, she carries the potentially life-saving human DNA that has darkened her skin and given her something we've sought for generations' (272). It is a hybridity much sought after wherein she remains resolutely Ina but with additives that make her more *useful* to both Ina and human. Her learned memories ensure that she is caring toward both the species of which she is a citizen.

Hybrid Shori is more than just an advancement over existing models of both, the vampire and the human. She embodies a posthumanist biology in which technological interventions into biology have effected changes not only in the body but also at the level of the mind, attitude and behaviour. Ina biology, modified in Shori, results in not only a special organic ability but also a whole new ethics of care. Biological citizenship has moved from the animal-vampire *zoē* state she begins with to the *bíos* of responsibility, new and renewed abilities, and a sense of her own hybrid state, a biology no longer species-specific or species-limited.

The climactic articulation of a posthumanist biology is the companion species 'condition' embodied in Shori. In Butler's *Parables*, Olamina's hyperempathy syndrome – indirectly the result of a medical experiment in which her mother's addiction to a particular drug resulted in Olamina's condition – makes her an entirely new human: one who 'relates' in completely different ways to the sufferings of other humans. She has become a morally augmented human by accident, just as Shori is a morally augmented vampire by intention. Olamina's moral augmentation is not, I hasten to add, one which gives her a greater degree of compassion. In fact it is primarily a condition that forces her to shut herself away from the pain of others, to avoid scenes and situations where the pain of others might impinge upon her. However, I would still consider this an inaugural moment in the moral augmentation of humans for reasons I outline below.

Butler, interested in reinventing human and race/species history, does present Shori as an anterior moment to a new race. In similar fashion, I suggest, Olamina with her hyperempathy, but also her 'earthseed' philosophy of interconnectedness, represents a new origin: if her qualities might be harnessed for future generations. If Olamina is at the moment simply morally augmented by accident, surely it is not impossible to imagine this characteristic becoming transmissible? Moral transhumanism, as one branch of transhumanism is called, seeks the moral improvement of humans. Individuals like Shori may not be humans in the biological sense but are human (or more human, and humane) in the moral sense (Persson and Savulescu 2010). A hyperempath like Olamina in Octavia Butler's *Parables* series is more human than others due to her increased sensitivity to the pain of others. Genetically modified humans in *Oryx and Crake* (Atwood 2004) do not 'register skin colour', do not possess a sense of hierarchy or family trees (358–9) – or anything that might lead to battles for domination and open up spaces for discrimination and exclusion based on the valoriza-tion of particular characteristics (face, skin colour, anatomy, intelligence, abilities, lineage). They also cannot make jokes because for jokes, Crake tells Jimmy, you need a certain 'malice' (359). Technological interventions that produce moral agents with a greater sense of altruism, compassion and fair play, and which help them to focus on greater sociality and collective con-cerns, become, therefore, the parallel to the humanization of robots and cyborgs.

In Butler's *Clay's Ark* (1984), while humans begin to acquire animal traits (as Sherryl Vint 2005 points out, the human subjectivity in the novel is constituted alongside animal subjectivity and Butler's characters literally exemplify a 'becoming-animal' condition), they fight to retain their 'human-ity'. As Meda tells Blake: 'we're changed, but we have ethics. We aren't animals' ([1984] 1996: 39). And the entire community of the infected seeks isolation in a bid to prevent an epidemic. This responsibility toward their species is treated as a sign of their humanity: 'We're trying to preserve humanity . . . We are. Our own humanity and everyone else's because we let people alone. We isolate ourselves as much as we can, and the people outside can stay alive and healthy – most of them' (84). What is also impor-tant to note is that the microbe even prevents humans from choosing to destroy themselves. In other words, humans survive because the microbe forces them to survive. Further, criminals stop being criminals once they have been infected. Whether this constitutes a moral advancement of the human species through a reformatting of the species' genetic make-up is a point Butler asks us to consider. As Olamina puts it in *Parable of the Sower* (and I have cited this before, in chapter 5):

If hyperempathy syndrome were a more common complaint, people couldn't do such things. They could kill if they had to, and bear the pain of it or be destroyed by it. But if everyone could feel everyone else's pain, who would torture? Who would cause anyone unnecessary pain? . . . A biological conscience is better than no conscience at all. ([1993] 1995: 102)

Lilith, Shori, Osden and others have now acquired a new biological citizenship. By demonstrating an amplified and enhanced moral dimension, and response-ibility toward other species, they begin to acquire a *bíos*. This *bíos* is marked by a species cosmopolitanism.

COMPANION SPECIES

Donna Haraway asks:

Who are my kin in this odd world of promising monsters, vampires, surrogates, living tools, and aliens? How are natural kinds identified in the realms of techno-science? What kinds of crossings and offspring count as legitimate and illegitimate, to whom and at what cost? Who are my familiars, my siblings, and what kind of livable world are we trying to build? (1997: 52)

Haraway's questions, concerning the ontological status of any species, inter-species relations and connections, are also questions *Fledgling* throws up.

Iosif tells Shori, even before she has met the extended community of vampires: 'We are another species . . . We evolved right here on Earth alongside humanity as a cousin species like the chimpanzee' (Butler 2005: 67). For Shori to understand that she is a member of an old species but also an advancement, she must put into effect the education and information she has acquired from Wright, Iosif and others.

Shori, incorporating within herself the vampire and the human, demon-strating greater respect and care for the human, treats the humans as her family but, more importantly, as a fellow-species with which she herself is inextricably linked. If posthumanism is marked, as Cary Wolfe suggests, by a 'challenge [to] the ontological and ethical divide between humans and non-humans' (2010: 62), then Shori represents an apotheosis of the post-humanist vision. This posthumanist vision calls for recognizing a 'constitutive codependency' with other forms of life and 'evolutionary history' as a history of the co-evolution of species in which communications and events across life forms constitute the life form (2010: xxv–xxvi, 10).

Shori has overcome her animal-vampire origins by co-evolving with human features. Drawing upon such adjacent ontologies (human and Ina), Shori begins to develop her subjectivity in conjunction with humans first (Wright and Theodora). It is Wright, Theodora and their relations with Shori that constitutes Shori's new subjectivity. The material conditions of her subjectivity are human and it is her exposure to Wright and his *response* to her that *makes* her. (But would this be possible if Shori didn't suffer from amnesia? Would her new subjectivity be possible if she had remained within the Ina community?) By giving Shori a new origin story, Butler manages to suggest a whole new ontology and a posthuman teleology. The human disrupts the vampire and the animal in her: Shori first learns to care, consciously, after she meets Wright. Ina and humans, *after* Shori, will have a wholly different relationship: they become companion species. Shori embodies this companion species ideal in that her very ontology is of a posthuman that has emerged out of the human–vampire intersection. If, as Matthew Calarco proposes in his *Zoographies*, the 'presubjective conditions that give rise to human subjectivity cannot be easily restricted to human beings' (2008b: 89), then, in Butler's novel, vampire subjectivity cannot be restricted to vampires alone either. When Butler rewrites origin stories, she makes sure we see how entangled origins can be: humans cross-bred with Oankali, and vampires with human genes. What Shori is (or Lilith and any of the 'wakened' humans in *Xenogenesis*) is dependent not on any pure biological state but on what each of them has absorbed by way of genes.

Butler's continued interest in symbiogenesis (Bollinger 2007) climaxes with *Fledgling* in which her concerns are with the co-evolution of species rather than invasions from outside (her theme in *Xenogenesis*). This posthumanist biology foregrounds the potentiality and constitutive co-dependency of biology and rejects the valorization of the autonomous subject of traditional humanism. Butler suggests that autonomy is overrated. The new biology encourages, indeed demands, multispecies citizenship.

The origin story here is neither the postmodern rejection of all origins nor the essentialist desire to claim a gender, species or racial identity, but a 'dialogue' between the two (as Cathy Peppers suggests about *Xenogenesis* – 1995: 59–60). This 'dialogue' is what I have examined as the pedagogic and other *dispositifs* in *Fledgling*. The origins of a Shori are trans-species: her education teaches her that both humans and vampires are her 'kin'. Shori marks the anterior moment of a whole new community of the future. *Fledgling* forwards the utopian idea that vampiric and human agency, working together, with shared biologies, can induce change (Brox 2008), a theme that extends Butler's earlier work in *Xenogenesis* where she holds out a promise of species transformation through merger (Goss and Riquelme 2007: 436). It suggests the emergence of a whole new hybrid species, but one in which competition is scarce and, instead, cooperation is common. The Ina, for instance, do not suffer sexual jealousies, and promiscuity is not frowned upon, irrespective of the gender, and they can have sex with both men and women (Butler 2005: 85). The Ina can flourish because they merge with the humans and the humans acquire new biological qualities – quicker healing, longevity – through a merger with Ina biology, thus embodying a companion species role for both. In *Xenogenesis* the Oankali had corrected human defects, slowed ageing processes and strengthened resistance.

There are two routes to this coming community: through a process of immunization and through a certain potentiality of Shori's biological citizenship.

Immunity

Timothy Campbell, appropriating Esposito, proposes that community emerges in a state of emergency (2011: 102). One must, however, see qualified life (*bíos*) as life embedded in a community that has *acquired* a form of immunity, whose efficacy is tested only in times of emergencies.

Shori's role as the most important care-taker of both fellow Ina and humanity emerges in moments of crisis. Genetically modified sunlight-immune Shori is the only one on guard in the daylight attack on the Ina (Butler 2005: 166–76). She demonstrates several things about hybridity. First, she has benefited from technological interventions that her elder Ina conducted. Second, she is 'naturally' or biologically gifted enough – her 'natural' gifts are the result of genetic experiments – to lead Ina. Third, she has acquired other crucial skills, such as the sense of morality, intelligent virtue and an ethics of care through both species memory and rigorous pedagogy.

Alice, an Ina, tells Shori that 'female Ina families passed for human for thousands of years by marrying male symbionts and organizing their communities to look like human villages' (234). What we are looking at here is not mere 'domestication' but a social process through which a community is constructed – by 'passing' (the vampire passing as a human) and deracination. Yet this community of vampires and human symbionts are not exactly companion species. For that to happen, it requires genetic engineering that results in an Ina like Shori. In order for Shori to be the next stage of Ina evolution, she must develop an immune system that offers sun-protection. But this is only a literal interpretation of the idea of 'immunity'. Butler's novel suggests a more politically nuanced sense of 'immunity' as well when she maps the rise of a *bíos* in Shori.

Bíos is formed by excluding the 'improper' (Agamben 2004), by declaring some forms of life to be 'improper' or barely living (*zoē*). The *dispositifs* examined earlier work at two levels. One, they enable Shori to expel the animal-vampire in her – subjugate it, in Esposito's terms, to the human – and enhance the human. Second, they also separate her from the rest of the Ina community as somebody like them, and not like them. The *dispositif* not only separates the person from her/his biological material, it also functions in ways that mean that the person both belongs and does not belong to a plurality, a community (Campbell 2011: 78). Shori's immunity locates her outside the vampire-*zoē* paradigm and closer to the human one. But Butler's biopolitics of the posthuman here leads her to suggest that this shift away from *zoē* toward *bíos* is not one in which Shori becomes merely less Ina and more human. The *dispositifs* (which include her new biology) ensure that she *co-evolves*, as a species variant, with humans, and toward a new community.

A community always fears the loss of its borders (Esposito 2010: 8). In order to protect this community, one might have to sacrifice one's life and surrender one's immunity to it. When this obligation toward the community is erased, it results in the immunity paradigm, and the individual, freed of the responsibility toward the community, is rendered immune (5). Therefore, Shori is biologically and otherwise immune to the demands of her community, being committed to *more than one species*. Shori must develop an immunity to the very condition of being Ina because her community now – and in the future – is inseparable, ontologically, from the human species.

Esposito argues that in order for life to preserve itself, to actualize its immunitary potential and to prevent its 'natural dynamics' designed for self-destruction, life must 'tear itself away from nature'. That is, for life to continue on its 'natural' course, it must step outside nature and acquire, through artificial means, some additional immunity (2008: 58–9). The Ina can continue only if their 'natural' sensitivity to sunlight is altered in the form of Shori's advanced, induced immunity. Ina can stay Ina only when injected with human immunity to sunlight: as embodied in Shori.

A similar tension of immunity and community is put in place for the humans. Wright experiences a shock when he realizes that a role-reversal has taken place: he discovers that all human symbionts are named after their Ina 'partners' – he is 'sym Shori', for example (Butler 2005: 255). The human develops a biological and social immunity: all human symbionts reduce their responsibilities toward their human species and are 'bounded' (Butler's term) to Ina. When Shori learns to care, when she understands that she has to utilize her special qualities as an immune Ina, she *subordinates* these to the needs of her community which now includes humans. She at once seeks and does not seek immunity from her relations with the community, even though – and this is important – she does not have a species memory of such a subordination. She is committed to being Ina and yet – as she demonstrates at the Council meeting – she seeks immunity from being committed *only* to Ina.

What we see emerging in Shori is a consciously crafted, self-reflexive and determinate posthuman. She opts for the role of protector as a vampire–human *hybrid*, using her biological immunity to further the cause of the companion species to come.

Potentiality

Bíos here is the emergence of a biological *potentiality* wherein a companion species of humanoid vampires, or vampiric humans, is possible. Shori is the first member of this new community with her genetically determined biological citizenship, and represents the conscious effort of a species to evolve differently by *responding* to human traits and qualities, and erasing some of their own 'natural' ones. (Shori is a version of Lilith in *Xenogenesis*, a work in which Butler undertakes what critics like Michele Osherow (2000) have identified as feminist revisionary mythmaking.) She marks a departure from traditional Ina identity, moving closer to a *bíos* that is a hybrid, one that co-evolves with, and is dependent upon, the human as well.

The posthumanist *bíos* of Shori now is also one where there are biological bases for affection, emotional attachments and dependencies. *Contra* traditional vampire tales where the vampire bite 'converts' the human, Butler shows how, in posthumanist biology, the bite instils affection and attachment across the species boundary. Despite the troubling biological essentialism this entails, it still remains an interesting move in which biological citizenship across species is both possible and desirable. If even consciousness has biological origins and foundations (as the work of Humberto Maturana and Francisco Varela demonstrates – see Hayles 1999, Wolfe 2010), then, Butler calls upon us to ponder, could we envisage an emotional bond across species facilitated by genetics? Relatedly, posthumanist biology could also be the means through which the 'perfectibility' of humankind could include enhanced empathy and compassion, as more recent posthumanists have suggested. In Persson and Savulescu's view, a being can belong to more than one species, and biological 'enhancement', theoretically speaking, could make beings more human in the moral sense even if they cease to be human in the biological sense, thus becoming truly posthumans (668). Throughout the latter parts of the novel, there are references to Shori mating and the children she *will* bear and rear. The coming community that Shori, of multi-species origin, embodies is the *potential* Shori carries in her to produce a whole new species.

Agamben sees the coming community as always in the process of coming, or one whose potential has not been realized fully yet. It offers a non-identity which is 'neither particular nor universal' (1993: 10). It offers also an 'indifference' to common forms of belonging: it is neither singular in its identity nor universal. Shori, neither singular nor universal, at once Ina and human, neither Ina nor human, is a fledgeling, the anterior moment of this coming community whose potential, as vampire–human hybrids and companion species with constitutive codependency, is yet to be fully grasped. The genetic engineering projects that produced Shori and altered her gene line are essentially therefore projects of biological citizenship. But, more importantly, this biological citizenship must be enacted through conscious acts of *memory*. Therefore, biological citizenship of the *zoē* kind modulates into *bíos* only when Shori *performs* a species memory that she has acquired not through her genetic predispositions or her biology but through the *dispositifs* that render her a self-conscious vampire–human hybrid with respect for both species.

Part of her new biological citizenship as a hybrid means that Shori would, like the Ina, reject any kind of race- or species-based discrimination. No racism exists among the Ina: 'The Ina weren't racists . . . Human racism meant nothing to the Ina because the human races meant nothing to them. They looked for congenial human symbionts wherever they happened to be, without regard for anything but personal appeal' (148).

This rejection of one kind of biological racism – we can think of it as epidermal, based on skin colour – of the variety practised by humans ensures that Ina constitute a post-racial world. (The human attacker is the one who calls Shori a 'dirty little nigger bitch': 173.) Shori, the Ina hope, with her dark skin approximating to the African American, will not only be post-racial but also post-species and the inaugural moment of a whole generation: 'Ina families all over the world were happy about my family's success with genetic engineering. They hoped to use the same methods to enable their future generations to function during the day' (133). It is, ultimately, biological citizenship in a new species that the Ina seek – but one in which the species distinctions are utilized and optimized for the future species. *Fledgling* is thus an origin tale of a new biological citizenship with a posthuman*ist* biology.

Fledgling prepares us for the critical posthumanist position this book has been working toward by foregrounding a new ethics of difference, co-evolution and hybridity. Butler demolishes the myth of sovereign species identity – whether of vampires or of humans. All species, she proposes in her posthumanist texts, are interspecies. The 'matter' that constitutes a body – whether vampire or human – is the result of boundary-making within discourses and apparatuses of science, religion and cultural practices. Care, community-feeling and genetic engineering are material–discursive practices that, in Butler's vision, with their intra-action (and I am reverting to Karen Barad's arguments first cited in chapter 1 here), also produce a whole new idea, and substance, of the species. The intra-actions of multiple discourses and apparatuses, instead of initiating self-identical identities (human, vampire, animal) and species boundaries, might also produce productive cross-overs with a greater sense of responsibility to all forms of life. New life forms and their 'matter' emerge, *Fledgling* suggests, not *within* a species border but without (I use the term to mean both 'outside' and 'absence') it.

Conclusion: Posthumanism as Species Cosmopolitanism

The preceding chapters, climaxing with a reading of Octavia Butler's *Fledgling*, traced the rise of a posthumanist politics grounded in the biological citizenship projects of genetic modifications, compounded by the ethical considerations of individual responsibility toward the companion species ontology of the hybrid. The human is made of difference, its evolution is marked by the negotiation and internalization of different species, organelles, forms of life and consciousness. This alternative view of biology – like Le Guin's view of a genderless world in *The Left Hand of Darkness* (1969) – marks the beginnings of a self-conscious species cosmopolitanism.

Posthumanism at the end of *Fledgling* was marked by the politics of Ina bodies modified by technology to produce a trans-species Shori. While the biological determinism and essentialism remain a matter of some concern in her work, Octavia Butler takes care to suggest that Shori's acquisition of knowledge about her own biological–genetic history might make her a more inclusivist individual, whose origins in companion species might prevent her from xeno- or species-phobia.

Butler does seem to suggest that posthuman configurations of biological citizenship are the solution to inherent 'contradictions' of species ('Contradiction' is the Oankali term in *Xenogenesis* to describe what they see as the two dominant features of humanity: intelligence and hierarchical thinking; see Tucker 2007). The vampires in her work, feared and reviled in human myth, are less hierarchic, less jealous and non-racist. Human and vampire species had had their species boundaries ('pure human') marked by separating materially as well as discursively – through socialization, sanitization and coercion – the animal life as impure and to be expelled. And yet, in order for both species to survive and have a productive life, each requires the other. Longevity, recovery from illness, immunity from the sun, are qualities that enhance the quality of life for human and vampire, and can proceed only when each species becomes-with the other. Vulnerability – of the vampires to the sun, and of the humans to sickness – is what both species share, and what is mitigated due to their becoming-with each other.

The recoding of biovalue is an important theme in critical posthumanist fiction, especially Butler's. Take, for instance, Butler's rejection of the gender binaries of reproduction in her works. Interspecies sex in *Xenogenesis* goes beyond the traditional notions of sex and gender (Miller 1998: 344). The Oankali mode of reproduction requires a male, a female and a neuter partner (Ooloi). Sex involves the penetration of both male and female by the neuter Ooloi. Indeed Butler points to the human male's revulsion at the changed gender roles when she chronicles how the men objected when they were 'taken like a woman' (1988a: 216). In Butler's *Patternist* series, Doro and Anyanwu can be either male or female, and therefore father or mother (Bruce Clarke is, however, correct in his assessment that, even with the 'biotechnological updating' in *Fledgling*, the vampirism evoked remains a 'form of posthuman transformation contingent upon premodern convictions about blood as the essence of life and racial identity' – 2008: 166). In Ursula Le Guin's *The Left Hand of Darkness* gender roles on the planet Gethen are not fixed and individuals can be male or female as they choose. In her story 'Vaster than Empires and More Slow' (1987) the modified human Osden merges with the plant life on the new planet because his empathic power relates to the 'feelings' emanating from the plants. The entire plant life on the planet, says Osden, 'is one big green thought' (122). In the case of Butler's *Dawn* Lilith is advised to 'bury uneaten food . . . "feed it to the ship"' – since the ship is organic and linked organically to the life forms on/in it (1988a: 62). Plants and animals 'aren't separate from the ship', Jhdaya tells her (33).

In the case of *Fledgling*, Shori's 'biovalue' and therefore her biological citizenship are at once merely corporeal and moral (her response-ibility toward other species). Now Ina–human biovalue is material–discursive because it is at once to do with the qualities and functions of Shori's body-matter but also with the discursive construction of these values. The 'meaning' of Shori's hybrid body is made possible through the material construction of difference (from other vampires and also humans) even as this materiality is itself discursive in that it emerges in the inter-action of apparatuses (genetic experimentation, Ina history, human history, Ina–human relations). Biovalue is a phenomenon, an emergent condition, of and within these intra-actions. Butler is, however, not simply valorizing a recoding of biovalue in hybrid lives, but is constantly aware that this new biology is always already a 'subject': to technoscience, gendered capitalism and corporate greed, whether human or alien. Butler's critical posthumanism is therefore not simply utopian, but realist utopian. Power for Butler marks all identities, matter and relations, even in an age of new biological citizenship. The human is a non-unitary subject.

Now, the Ina wish to invest in Shori's body for this particular biovalue. This worryingly proffers a new genetic fundamentalism, but Butler evades the charge by proposing the value of Shori as a moral agent, one who is genetically predisposed to responsibility, care and ethical behaviour. This is the critical posthumanism of Cary Wolfe and others. Biovalue inheres in the *moral* enhancement of Shori, and is the *result* of her multispecies citizenship. It is not Ina+ or human+. Rather, it is the multispecies quality effected through mergers and convergences – which of course are embedded in power relations across and within species – that constitute a moral enhancement. If every species is also difference instantiated, a congeries of species, then, in Butler's utopian vision, perhaps difference will not be penalized in genocides and ethnicides.

It must be kept in mind that Butler's vision of enhancement differs sharply from the moral transhumanism of Nick Bostrom and others (outlined in chapter 1), because it is not the innate or essential qualities of the human or the vampire that are to be enhanced in *Fledgling*. Rather, biovalues and ethics (of bodies) are emergent conditions in the dynamics of vampire–human relations. A better morality is a phenomenon made possible through the material–discursive construction of hybridity. The vampires and humans are constitutive of each other, and neither Ina nor humans are presented as possessing virtues, qualities and characteristics independent of the other: the vampiric Other is within the human, even as the human humanizes the vampire. If there is a moral enhancement, it is this emergence within Shori's hybridity.

Fledgling is situated firmly within the ideologies of posthumanism where theorists and philosophers like Matthew Calarco, Cora Diamond, Cary Wolfe, Jacques Derrida, Stanley Cavell, among others, have probed the anthropocentrism that characterizes western humanism. Posthumanism in Butler is the rejection of simple binaries (human/alien, human/animal), showing each as constitutive of the other. It is Shori's Ina – and animal – qualities that enable her to possess such ferocity and help her guard her human family. It is her human qualities that help her stay awake and guard the Ina. Productive subjectivity such as Shori's emerges out of a cooperation, co-optation and collaboration across species, where vampires, aliens, humans, plants and animals all demonstrate a species cosmopolitanism.

Species cosmopolitanism is the apotheosis of critical posthumanism because of its rejection of easy binaries, whether gender (male/female) or life form (animal/human, human/plant) or compositional elements (organic/inorganic). Species cosmopolitanism sees all species as *always already nodes and intersections along a continuum, full of borrowed characteristics, genes and behaviour.* What is enhanced is the dynamics of relations and borrowings, and in these dynamics something better will arise, in Butler's vision.

Our origins, like our future evolution, says the species cosmopolitan, are *multiple, diverse and uncertain.* Our histories, to use Donna Haraway's favourite word from *When Species Meet* (2008), are 'entangled'. Species cosmopolitanism and the companion species ideal manifest as the climax of an entire process that, starting with 'different' origin stories, progresses through new configurations of biological citizenship and the theme of a new response-ibility toward other species (involving a new ethics of care) and potentiality.

Species cosmopolitanism involves, as can be gathered from the above discussions, a fair amount of 'domestication' of the alien species. Domestication is essentially, first, a deracination wherein vampires, humans, animals and alien species are to become domesticated with another species, or to become-with another species. Shori becomes near-human (*Fledgling*), humans become animals (*Clay's Ark*) or plants ('Vaster than Empires and More Slow'). These interspecies connections produce new loyalties and new racial identities (as John Allen Stevenson (1988) argued in the case of Bram Stoker's *Dracula*). A second mode, also noted in the reading of Octavia Butler, is the vision of alternative histories that we are offered about the origins of vampires, aliens and humans. Symbiogenesis, I have argued, is this alternative vision in which species mixing is a bio-historical 'fact' (Lacey 2008: 388–9). Finally, technology enables the intervention in genetic and genealogical narratives of any/all species. Shori begins as a disenfranchised vampire because she is simply *zoē*. Lilith is African American, as is Anyanwu in *Wild Seed* (1980). Olamina is black, and cohabits with Bankole, another black (*Parable of the Talents*, 1998). In each case some mutation transforms these disenfranchised and powerless women into women of power, and progenitors of powerful breeds and new species. Their non-white features are also deracinated out so that they become more than just black or brown. It is this new technologically induced alteration that enables any species to determine its fate/future and, most importantly, to subordinate itself to new species and new alliances across species.

With mutation species cross species borders, detach themselves – displacement from points of cultural, ethnic and national origin is central to cosmopolitanism. As Amanda Anderson puts it, cosmopolitanism is a 'reflective distance from one's original or primary cultural affiliations, a broad understanding of other cultures and contexts, and a belief in universal humanity' (2001: 63). It is marked by 'overlapping allegiances' (Bruce Robbins' account of cosmopolitanism, cited in Anderson 2001: 78). Can we then think of a species movement away from an 'original' species identity and toward others?

As early as 1976 in her classic work *Interview with the Vampire*, Anne Rice had suggested this distancing (accompanying domestication–deracination) model for vampires. Louis, the vampire-protagonist, speaking of life after transformation from human to vampire, says (and I have had occasion to cite this before): 'It was detachment that made this possible, a sublime loneliness with which Lestat and I moved through the world of mortal men' (38). As I have proposed elsewhere, the invasive procedure of the bite results in a loosening of familial and species ties and a forging of new ones (Nayar 2011a, 2011c). In Stephenie Meyer's *Twilight* series, vampires are increasingly seen cohabiting with humans, marking the collapse of species borders again. The ethical engagement with the other – as we see embodied in the hyperempath Olamina, with Shori, with Osden – is the species cosmopolitanism of posthumanist thinking, originating in multiple species, recognizing their embeddedness within a variety of life forms that have helped them evolve, responding to several and responsible for several. Further, if genetic engineering can induce greater levels of empathy, which is, if contemporary neurobiologists like Christian Keysers are to be believed, 'wired' into our brains as mirror neuron activity, then our consciousness is connected to, embedded in and growing with others' consciousness and actions. Our empathic and ethical engagement with the other might have a biological basis, after all. If this is indeed proved to be true of the human species (mirror neuron activity has been proved conclusively in several primates), then it suggests that we are, through and through, cosmopolitan and is the final move, I propose, in the rejection of speciesism.

The rejection of 'speciesism' – as Cary Wolfe, writing about the politics of the human–animal divide, calls it (Wolfe 2003) – is posthumanism's politics and ethics. Speciesism is antagonistic to the new biological citizenship of which figures like Shori or the human–Oankali hybrids are the instantiation. This is the posthumanist vision where the form of life is '*immediately* translatable into politics so that politics might assume an *intrinsically* biological characterization' (Esposito 2008: 9, emphasis in original). *Bíos* is enhanced biovalue, but it is also a posthumanist biovalue where species boundaries do not matter and care, concern and cooperation cut across species in Butler's trans-species manifesto. If the destiny of animals is linked to man, then 'man' himself 'enters into a different relationship with his own species', and produces a 'biopolitics potentially different from what we know because it is in relation not only to human life, but to what is outside life, to its other, to its after' (Esposito 2008: 109).

This is Butler's Shori as well: now in a wholly new relationship with her 'own' species (if there is such a thing) and with those species 'outside' her own. This is the politics of a new biological citizenship in which instead of presenting humans and vampires as possessing antagonistic biovalues and different values of citizenship, Butler suggests that multispecies citizenship produces a new kind of biovalue that might be worth investing in. When Shori becomes the other to both Ina and humans, she also becomes responsible to/for both, and this is Butler's vision for a new (post)humanity.

The new biological citizenship of the species cosmopolitan variety rejects autonomy and favours connection, seeks difference but not xenophobia, prefers plurality over binaries. In Butler's texts where the dynamics of connection do not distinguish between human and non-human life forms, we see a critical posthumanist vision. What we see as unique to our species is an adaption from multiple sources, just as our consciousness, intelligence and sensoria have evolved through centuries of negotiating with ecosystems (as we have seen in preceding chapters on the body and consciousness). Critical posthumanism proposes a sentience and subjectivity that is constantly dynamic in its connectivity. The ethics of care and responsibility that characterizes a Shori is possible, Butler suggests, because of a reconfigured biological citizenship, in which the *bíos* is based neither in the human nor in the animal-vampire. Le Guin suggests that it is based neither in plants nor in modified humans. The structural prejudices of each species are *eroded* in this new biological citizenship which, in effect, becomes the posthumanist plea for a social adaptation of genetic engineering that might, finally, end all forms of racisms. In connections, one 'learned the love of the Other' (Le Guin 1987: 127). If humans were 'genetically inclined to be intolerant of difference', as Octavia Butler puts it in the final volume of *Xenogenesis, Imago* (Butler 1989: 185), then particular *dispositifs* and genetic modifications have to be deployed in order to make them understand that difference is what all species are, and contain.

This means opening oneself up not only to the non-human Other but to other 'species' *within* humanity as well. In other words, a critical posthumanism proposes a multispecies citizenship that involves *all* forms of life. Species cosmopolitanism is an openness toward the Other but also an opening up to uncertainty and possibilities of the not-yet. I see species cosmopolitanism's in-built uncertainty as linked to the general state of precarity (Judith Butler 2004) we all now experience. Our lives are determined, affected, altered by elements we cannot even conceive of. The fabric of our lives – suffering, joys, anxieties and equanimity – are the result of the criss-crossing of the everyday by multiple, diverse and often unknown entities, from bacteria, to animals and humans. 'Cosmopolitics', as the philosopher Isabelle Stengers defines it, is the 'question of possible non-hierarchical modes of coexistence among the ensemble of inventions of nonequivalence, among diverging values and obligations through which entangled existences that compose it are affirmed' (2011: 355–6). 'Entangled existences' that do not respect origins, boundaries or purity are the name of the posthumanist game. The sharing of consciousness and nervous systems, of thought and body, is the coming community. Individual borders break down and each individual gives up something in order to be a part of the community. Jodahs in Butler's *Imago* describes such a community connection that recalls Osden's 'wiring into' the plant consciousness of the new planet: 'I took their hands, rested each of them on one of my thighs so that I would not have to maintain a grip. I linked into their nervous systems and brought them together as though they were touching one another. It was not illusion. They were in contact through me' (1989: 122). If we share precarity with other individuals and other species, as Judith Butler suggests, then surely with species cosmopolitanism we can share more? From a race that suffers from xenophobia, can we 'grow', or engineer, a xenophilia once we recognize that the Other is already within us?

An affective posthumanism, where empathy resulting from and in connections and companionate histories constitutes the new community of strangers, is what we see emerging in Butler's fiction. This affective posthumanism which values the connections across species entails, no doubt, a detachment from 'origins' and gene sources – 'human', 'animal', 'plant', 'alien' – but concomitant with this detachment is the awareness of how each species is linked with these other species for both vulnerability and survival. The 'biological conscience' (as Butler calls it in *Parable of the Sower* – 1993: 102) toward others is the ethical–moral transhumanism that we have already mentioned. It marks a 'broader expression of a more normal level of empathy' (Bollinger 2010: 345). It is in this kind of connection with others – of the same or different species – that species cosmopolitanism emerges. The possibilities and potentiality within this reconnection with our ecosystem, other neighbouring forms of life – whether vegetable, bacterial or animal – are what critical posthumanism hopes for. As noted in the opening chapter, critical posthumanism emphasizes that, only by recognizing the link between speciesism and discriminatory practices like racism or sexism, and the shared vulnerability of all species, can we begin to rethink connectedness and mutuality with *all* forms of species and life. But if moral transhumanism emphasized the need to enhance the supposedly innate human qualities of compassion or care, a critical posthumanism of Butler's variety posits the human qualities as always already multispecies: that to be more human means to accept more of other-species within us. The Other within is what makes us vampire or human. However, as noted earlier, Butler's critical posthumanist vision is realist utopian in that she alerts us to the possibility of the instrumental use of cross-over, multispecies identities as well. The posthuman subject, in Rosi Braidotti's terms, is constituted 'in and by multiplicity' (2013: 49). Species cosmopolitanism is what enables species to survive, whether they are vampires, bacteria, humans or aliens. This is not about species *harmony*, as Sherryl Vint points out in connection with Haraway's work. Rather, it is about a 'more complex politics of how to live as omnivores among herbivores and carnivores, in relations of mutual consumption and mutual dependency, but without reducing some species to objects that can be ruthlessly exploited without ethical dilemma' (Vint 2010: 28). While gesturing at the instrumental possibilities of multispecies citizenship, Vint cautions us, like Butler's fiction, against a simplistic celebration of species cosmopolitanism.

The last word on the subject must belong, appositely, to Octavia Butler whose Jdhaya in *Dawn* tells Lilith: 'We *must* do it [genetic engineering]. It renews us, enables us to survive as an evolving species instead of specializing ourselves into extinction or stagnation' (1988a: 39, emphasis in original). Once we accept that we *are* difference, perhaps we will cease to be worried about difference as *Other*.

Notes

1 REVISITING THE HUMAN: CRITICAL HUMANISMS

1   In an essay on Tissue Culture and Art work, Louis Van Den Hengel calls for a 'zoegraphy' in which this vitality of life that transverses humans, animals and inanimate objects and life then might be envisioned as 'a continuous production of new relationalities' (2012: 8). This sense of relationality across species and forms is central to Haraway, Wolfe and the posthumanist vision in general.

2   Deleuze and Guattari come close to suggesting this posthumanist thought when they write in *A Thousand Plateaus*: 'Not all Life is confined to the organic strata: rather, the organism is that which life sets against itself in order to limit itself . . . There are also nonhuman Becomings of human beings that overspill the anthropomorphic strata in all directions' (2004: 554).

3   Even material exchanges involve the transmission of information and data, as Jöns notes, just as immaterialities, like beliefs or the imagination, use words and other such vehicles for the making and circulation of meaning (2006: 573).

4   For a recent development of the Eurocentric paradigm of humanism, see the discussion in Braidotti 2013.

5   Foucault argued that even radical thinkers like Freud and Marx endorsed humanistic ideals of a rational trajectory through which the human subject fulfils its essential nature. Marx believed that when the human subject re-appropriates its basic capacities, it fulfils itself. Freud believed that once a human subject is allowed to go through with its inherent drives and dispositions – that have been suppressed and repressed in the social order – it would fulfil itself.

6   Haraway focuses on companion species, such as dogs, that share everyday lives with humans. In the first part of her *When Species Meet* (2008), Haraway demonstrates how human / companion species interactions and relations have economic, historical and functional connections, from seeing-eye dogs to laboratory animals to pets. The human autobiography, Haraway shows, is often an animalography. For a reading of Haraway's animalography and autobiographical modes, see Huff and Haefner (2012).

2 CONSCIOUSNESS, BIOLOGY AND THE NECESSITY OF ALTERITY

1   'Consciousness' is taken to include a wide variety of events and actions: emotion, thinking, memory, intelligence and self-awareness.

2   The early cybernetic theories had an important tension written into them. One group argued that information might be considered a 'pure' thing: it could be transmitted across or into any medium as a stable entity. Information here was conceptualized as delinked from what it meant. Another group in the Conferences argued that information cannot be decontextualized: how it is received and what meanings are made of it are integral to the very idea of information.

3   Human beings start making distinctions when they enter language: different things are called different names. Over a period of time, the repeated use of these names ensures that the distinctiveness and differences of things stabilize and enter our consciousness. However, at no point do we not recognize patterns in differences. To use an example from Pepperell, we have different names for leaf and branch and thus understand these to be different things, yet we also recognize the pattern that tells us they are part of a larger whole, a tree (2003: 81).

4   For a useful online resource, see www.neocybernetics.com, with Heikki Hyötyniemi's *Neocybernetics in Biological Systems*, 2006, at http://neocybernetics. com/report151/ (last accessed 27 May 2012).

5   Empathy is defined in neurobiological terms as 'any process where the attended perception of the object's [the primary individual who experiences the emotion] state generates a state in the subject [the individual or observer who secondarily experiences the emotion or understands the object's emotion] that is more applicable to the object's state or situation than to the subject's own prior state or situation' (Preston and de Waal 2002). Preston and de Waal note that this response to the object reduces with age due to changes in the prefrontal lobe's functioning (taken by many as the seat of mirror neuron activity and hence the seat of empathy), increased segregation of the self and what they call 'learned display rules', essentially socialization.

6   It is even possible, Kaneko notes, that some of these fluctuations in the system have a certain directionality guiding their progress (2006: 62).

3   THE BODY, REFORMATTED

1   Although the characters in *Never Let Me Go*, writes Rachel Carroll, are nominally heterosexual, they are nevertheless at odds with heterosexual norms; more specifically, as the product of technologies of assisted reproduction but genetically engineered to be unable to reproduce, their relationship to reproductive sexuality is paradoxical (2010: 60). Carroll's work explores the politics of heterosexuality and reproduction in the novel.

2   URLs last accessed 17 March 2013.

3   'Everting' was a term Gibson appropriated in *Spook Country* (2008) from marine biology and mathematics to describe a condition in which the inside could be turned out without creases. He used it to describe the condition in which cyberspace is no longer an external, 'out there' state, but one which envelops us.

4   See Anker and Nelkin's study *The Molecular Gaze: Art in the Genetic Age* (2004).

5   Adriana Petryna (2004), who initiated the arguments around biological citizenship with her work on Chernobyl, notes how, in this form of citizenship, social welfare measures relied on bodily injury, graded along radiation indices, and

compensated for their institutionally determined, arithmetically computed suffering. The calibration of radiation exposure levels of workers and their categorization as 'sufferers' determined their welfare benefits in this biological citizenship. Injury determines their membership as citizens requiring welfare, Petryna argues.

4 ABSOLUTE MONSTROSITIES: THE 'QUESTION OF THE ANIMAL'

1   This leads critics to posit a 'gynaecological gothic' (Fischer 1992, Scahill 2010, Nayar forthcoming). On madness, sex, corruption and gender in medieval medical theory see Jose (2008).

2   In odd cases, monstrosities are utilized by political and cultural discourses for very different purposes. Thus Allison Pingree demonstrates how Chang and Eng, the Siamese twins, were exhibited in nineteenth-century America as freaks and monsters but also served to illustrate the American motif of unity and togetherness (1996)! In Victorian England the representation of Assyrian bull-headed humans invoked, predictably, an anxiety about hybrid species. But these representations were also 'domesticated' when English viewers, according to one critic, 'perceived a kinship between themselves and the ancient Assyrians' in the bull figure (Thomas 2008: 900).

3   Crake tells Jimmy in Atwood's *Oryx and Crake*, 'men can imagine their own deaths, they can see them coming' (2004: 139), and this, according to Crake, is what drives humans to reproduce.

4   Ethologists have cast doubt for some decades now on the assumptions about animal capacities. See, for a literary-cultural perspective, the essays by Wendy Doniger, Marjorie Garber and others in J. M. Coetzee's *The Lives of Animals* (1999).

5   Paradoxically, the animal rights philosophies also centre the human when they seek equal rights for animals. When, for instance, they propose that animals have rights, what they are implying is that it is the human who grants the rights to the animals, once again situating the human as the centre of the moral universe from where s/he grants rights and bestows recognition upon other life forms. Also, when animal rights campaigners show the animals' affinities with humans, they work on a logic of similarity, not difference, implying that animals deserve better treatment because they are, to a greater or lesser degree, like us.

6   Racism is the discrimination against and marginalization of particular races based on one criterion: racial identity. Speciesism, as defined by Cary Wolfe, is the 'systematic discrimination against an other based solely on a generic characteristic – in this case, species' (2003: 1). Joan Dunayer calls it 'an attitude and a form of oppression', a 'failure, in attitude or practice, to accord any nonhuman being equal consideration and respect' (2004: 5).

7   In much the same way that Derrida theorizes the animal-as-subject looking at the human, Katherine Dunn's novel *Geek Love* presents the world of the 'normal' human as seen by a 'freak'. The narrator is a 'freak', the dwarf Olympia. Victoria Warren reading Dunn argues that this shift in narratorial identity and focalizer identity reverses the traditional equations between normal and freaks: 'From the perspective of conventional society the physically different are simply

objects to look at with "superior knowledge", amazement, pity, or disgust, and the gazer is confident in his or her normalcy. In this novel, the physically different are not spectacle but subjects who look out at the normal world and find much to criticize' (2004: 329).

8   A quick list of these works includes: Erica Fudge, *Perceiving Animals: Human and Beasts in Early Modern English Culture* (2002); Fudge, Ruth Gilbert and Susan Wiseman, eds., *At the Borders of the Human: Beasts, Bodies, and Natural Philosophy in the Early Modern Period* (1999); Nigel Rothfels, *Savages and Beasts: The Birth of the Modern Zoo* (2002); Richard Nash, *Wild Enlightenment: The Borders of Human Identity in the Eighteenth Century* (2003); Bruce Boehrer, *Shakespeare Among the Animals: Nature and Society in the Drama of Early Modern England* (2002), and *Parrot Culture: Our 2500-Year-Long Fascination with the World's Most Talkative Bird* (2004); David Perkins, *Romanticism and Animal Rights* (2003); Karen Raber and Treva Tucker, eds., *The Culture of the Horse: Status, Discipline, and Identity in the Early Modern World* (2005); Nathaniel Wolloch, *Subjugated Animals: Animals and Anthropocentrism in Early Modern European Culture* (2006); Mark Blackwell, ed., *The Secret Life of Things: Animals, Objects, and It-Narratives in Eighteenth-Century England* (2007); Donna Landry, *Noble Brutes: How Eastern Horses Transformed English Culture* (2009); and Laura Brown, *Homeless Dogs and Melancholy Apes: Humans and Other Animals in the Modern Literary Imagination* (2010).

5 LIFE ITSELF: THE VIEW FROM DISABILITY STUDIES AND BIOETHICS

1   Melville was obsessed with disability. Tommo, the narrator of *Typee*, has a swollen leg that places him in a 'disabled condition'. The inhabitants of Hooloomooloo in *Mardi* are segregated because they were 'not symmetrically formed' and their king Yoky communicates with his fingers. Then there is the aphasic Isabel in *Pierre* and Pierre, who physically disintegrates. In *The Confidence-Man*, we have the deaf mute, the crippled Black Guinea, the man with a wooden leg, the coughing miser, the sick old man, the invalid Titan, the paralysed soldier of fortune Thomas Fry, and the mad beggar. For a survey of Melville's representations of the disabled, see Otter (2006).

2   Cary Wolfe (2010), reading the writings and work of Temple Grandin, foregrounds the relationship between disability and 'trans-species affinity', where, for instance, Grandin is able to relate better to horses and other animals precisely because she is autistic. Wolfe also notes the relationship between blind people and their service dogs, and proposes a 'shared trans-species being-in-the-World constituted by complex relations of trust, respect, dependence, and communication' (140–1).

3   Studies since the 1990s have noted that the literary and popular cultural representations of disability are usually embedded in their social and cultural contexts. In a fascinating study, Susan Schoon Eberly (1988) argued that the representations of changelings in European literature and folklore, for instance, drew upon current knowledge – and ignorance – about medical conditions such as Down's syndrome and cerebral palsy, so that children born with congenital disorders quickly became fantastic or freak children of popular culture. Likewise, Diane Price Herndl's work (1994) on modern American

representations of disability has demonstrated how cultural ideologies of the period produced particular kinds of popular representation.

4   Mitchell and Snyder note that it was because impaired individuals were seen as 'extracted' from the 'productive membership' in an economy that they were 'controlled' by 'new terms reflecting the emergent concepts of modern charity': 'named as members of a deficient population, disabled bodies were to be managed by private organizations as well as state and federal agencies. This historical transition marks a critical moment in American approaches to disability issues and disabled people' (2006: 35).

5   Studies of popular films show that anger, bitterness, self-destructive behaviour are frequently associated with disabled individuals. Their community integration and sociality were minimal (see Black and Pretes 2007). As early as the seventeenth century, Francis Bacon had indeed come up with this argument regarding the disabled's resentment of the world when, in his essay 'Of Deformity', he declared: 'as nature hath done ill by them, so they do by nature'. He claimed that due to their exposure to the 'scorn' of the world, they 'watch and observe the weakness of others, that they may have somewhat to repay'.

6   On freak bodies, see, besides Fiedler's classic, *Freaks* (1978), Rosemary Garland-Thomson's *Freakery* (1996).

7   R. Funk argued that the disabled group was itself divided internally through the making of disability-specific programmes and segregation of disabled people. This ensured, writes Funk, the making of a 'politically powerless and diffuse class of people who are unable to coalesce with other groups of disabled people on common issues, to vote, to be seen or heard. This class has accepted the stigma and caste of second-hand citizenship and the incorrect judgement of social inferiority' (1987: 24).

8   Rosemary Garland-Thomson (2008) shows how language works to normalize certain bodies and reject certain others.

9   Other defining features that constitute the person include: self-consciousness, a sense of the self, self-motivated activity, rational thought.

10 The anxiety that Ben might reproduce his own kind, like in a classic sci-fi film where the primary anxiety is about monsters reproducing, is voiced in a throwaway line toward the end of the tale: 'and perhaps Ben's genes were already in some foetus struggling to be born?' (Lessing [1988] 2001: 156).

11 Last accessed 17 March 2013.

12 For a critique of the ethics of moral transhumanism, see Koch (2010). Koch notes that what qualities of the human are good enough to be 'enhanced' are not clearly defined by its proponents (692). This, Koch suggests, recalls the eugenics of an earlier era which, while proposing enhancement, culminated often in the (logical) call for the elimination of 'bad' characteristics. For a prescient critique of Harris, see Joanna Zylinska (2009: 15).

13 Such a call, James Hughes notes (2010), echoes the liberal ideal of the perfectibility of mankind.

6   POSTHUMAN VISIONS: TOWARD COMPANION SPECIES

1   The posthumanist vision of species cosmopolitanism fictionalizes the vision of life forwarded by Margulis and Dorion Sagan: 'all organisms of greater

morphological complexity than bacteria . . . are also polygenomic. They have selves of multiple origins . . . comprised of heterologous different-sourced genomic systems that each evolved from more than one kind of ancestor' (cited in Clarke 2008: 195).

2   On Butler's familiarity with the work of Margulis, E. O. Wilson and other biologists, see Peppers (1995) and Clarke (2008: 169).

3   Lilith's condition, incarcerated by the Oankali, resembles the slavery of an earlier era of human history when black women, as chattels and slaves, bore their white masters many children. Butler clearly positions the African American woman as the progenitor of a new race of human 'constructs' (the term used throughout the trilogy). In *Dawn*, Lilith ponders about her condition: 'Was that what she was headed for? Forced artificial insemination. Surrogate mother-hood? Fertility drugs and forced "donation" of eggs? Implantation of unrelated fertilized eggs. Removal of children from mothers at birth . . . ? Humans had done these things to captive breeders – all for a higher good, of course' (1988a: 59). The woman's total lack of control over reproduction is what Lilith recog-nizes, even though the 'other' species here is not the human male but Oankali.

4   But if, as Eugene Thacker (2005) suggests, the genome and the global economy are linked, then the bodies of those females like Lilith or Shori are part of an interspecies, intergalactic economy.

5   That Butler had serious reservations about origin stories should be clear from this discussion. In *Parable of the Talents* (1998), Olamina says about Andrew Steele Jarrett, the Presidential hopeful: 'he wants to take us all back to some magical time when everyone believed in the same God, worshipped him in the same way, and understood that their safety in the universe depended on completing the same religious rituals and stomping anyone who was different' ([1998] 2001: 23). If remembering is also dismembering, as I shall shortly argue, then Olamina finds Jarrett's single narrative of origins problematic because it eschews different stories.

6   There has been a debate about whether vampires are humans. Nicolas Michaud argues that the vampires in *Twilight* meet all the five criteria that define the 'human': consciousness, reasoning, self-motivated activity, the capacity to com-municate, and the presence of self-concepts (2009: 41).

7   This 'vegetarianism' of the vampire in Meyer is not without its ethical prob-lems, as Jean Kazez points out, for it assumes that animals are meant to cater to humans, and vampires. Edward needs to kill to survive, and he opts for a non-human animal (2009: 25–7).

8   Of these, Butler did not reissue *Survivor*, and a 2007 compilation does not carry this one novel.

9   In Alan Moore's *Saga of The Swamp Thing* (1987), the memories of the dead Alec Holland are merged with the consciousness of the plant life of the swamp, creating the swamp thing who has a particular attitude toward humans as a result. More accurately, the plant consciousness absorbs whatever Alec Holland remains at his death. (Holland has imbibed some bio-restorative he has been experimenting with, and the remains of his body carry these into the swamp for the plants to absorb them as well, even though they have already had suf-ficient doses of the chemicals.) As Moore puts it: 'The plants whose hungry root systems are busily ingesting the mortal remains of Alec Holland . . . they eat him . . . and they become infected by a powerful consciousness that does

not realise it is no longer alive! . . . It builds itself a skeleton of wood . . . and constructs muscles from supple plant fibre . . . it was a plant that thought it was Alec Holland' (Moore [1987] 2009: I: 48–9). It is the organic memory – literally organic, since Moore suggests that memories are what make the 'elemental' monster of the swamp – that constitutes the creature as a posthuman.

10 Sandra Govan (1986) has argued that Butler's interest in historical fiction merges with her kinship theme in the *Patternist* series.

Bibliography

Abbott, J. 1993 'The "Monster" Reconsidered: *Blade Runner's* Replicant as Romantic Hero', *Extrapolation* 34. 4: 340–50.

Abu-Lughod, L. 1993 *Writing Women's Worlds: Bedouin Stories*. Berkeley, CA: University of California Press.

Agamben, G. 1993 *The Coming Community*. Trans. Michael Hardt. Minneapolis and London: University of Minnesota Press.

— 1998 *Homo Sacer: Sovereign Power and Bare Life*. Trans. Daniel Heller-Roazen. Stanford: Stanford University Press.

— 2004 *The Open: Man and Animal*. Trans. Kevin Attell. Stanford: Stanford University Press.

— 2009 *What is an Apparatus?* Trans. David Kishik and Stefan Pedatella. Stanford: Stanford University Press.

Amoore, L. 2006 'Biometric Borders: Governing Mobilities in the War on Terror', *Political Geography* 25. 3: 336–51.

Ahmed, S. 1996 'Beyond Humanism and Postmodernism: Theorizing a Feminist Practice', *Hypatia* 11. 2: 71–93.

Anderson, A. 2001 *The Powers of Distance: Cosmopolitanism and the Cultivation of Detachment*. Princeton: Princeton University Press.

Anker, S., and D. Nelkin 2004 *The Molecular Gaze: Art in the Genetic Age*. Cold Spring Harbor, NY: Cold Spring Harbor Laboratory Press.

Ansell-Pearson, K. 1999 *Germinal Life: The Difference and Repetition of Deleuze*. London and New York: Routledge.

Atwood, M. 2004 *Oryx and Crake*. London: Virago.

— 2009 *The Year of the Flood*. London: Virago.

Aubrey, J.R. 1993 'Race and the Spectacle of the Monstrous in *Othello*', *CLIO* 22. 3: 221–38.

Auerbach, N. 1997 *Our Vampires, Ourselves*. Chicago and London: University of Chicago Press.

Baker, S. 2003 'Sloughing the Anima'. In C. Wolfe (ed.) *Zoontologies: The Question of the Animal*. Minneapolis and London: University of Minnesota Press, 121–46.

Baldick, C. 1992 'Introduction'. In Baldick (ed.) *The Oxford Book of Gothic Tales*. Oxford: Oxford University Press, xi–xxiii.

Barad, K. 2003 'Posthumanist Performativity: Toward an Understanding of How Matter Comes to Matter', *Signs* 28. 3: 801–31.

Barker, P. [1988] 2003 *Michel Foucault: An Introduction*. Edinburgh: Edinburgh University Press.

Baudrillard, J. [1996] 2005 *The System of Objects*. Trans. James Benedict. New Delhi: Navayana.

Belsey, C. 1980 *Critical Practice*. London: Methuen.

Benefiel, C.R. 2004 'Blood Relations: The Gothic Perversion of the Nuclear Family in Anne Rice's *Interview with the Vampire*', *Journal of Popular Culture* 38. 2: 261–73.

Bergthaller, H. 2010 'Housebreaking the Human Animal: Humanism and the Problem of Sustainability in Margaret Atwood's *Oryx and Crake* and *The Year of the Flood*', *English Studies* 91. 7: 728–43.

Bess, M. 2010 'Enhanced Humans versus "Normal People": Elusive Definitions', *Journal of Medicine and Philosophy* 35: 641–55.

Black, R.S., and L. Prete 2007 'Victims and Victors: Representations of Disability on the Silver Screen', *Research and Practice for Persons with Severe Disabilities* 32. 1: 66–83.

Black, S. 2009 'Ishiguro's Inhuman Aesthetics', *Modern Fiction Studies* 55. 4: 785–807.

Bollinger, L. 2007 'Placental Economy: Octavia Butler, Luce Irigaray, and Speculative Subjectivity', *Literature Interpretation Theory* 18: 325–52.

— 2010 'Symbiogenesis, Selfhood, and Science Fiction', *Science Fiction Studies* 37. 110, Part 1: 34–53.

Bordo, S. 1993 *Unbearable Weight: Feminism, Western Culture, and the Body*. Berkeley and London: University of California Press.

Bostrom, N., and R. Roache 2007 'Ethical Issues in Human Enhancement'. In J. Ryberg, T.S. Petersen and C. Wolf (eds.) *New Waves in Applied Ethics*. London: Palgrave-Macmillan, 120–52.

Bradshaw, H.G., and R. Ter Muelen 2010 'A Transhumanist Fault Line Around Disability: Morphological Freedom and the Obligation to Enhance', *Journal of Medicine and Philosophy* 35: 670–84.

Braidotti, R. 1991 *Patterns of Dissonance*. Cambridge: Polity.

— 2006a *Transpositions: On Nomadic Ethics*. Cambridge: Polity.

— 2006b 'Posthuman, All Too Human: Towards A New Process Ontology', *Theory, Culture and Society* 23. 7–8: 197–208.

— 2007 'Feminist Epistemology after Postmodernism: Critiquing Science, Technology and Globalisation', *Interdisciplinary Reviews of Science* 32. 1: 65–74.

— 2013 *The Posthuman*. Cambridge: Polity.

Brown, W. 1995 *States of Injury*. Princeton, NJ: Princeton University Press.

Brox, A. 2008 ' "Every Age has the Vampire it Needs": Octavia Butler's Vampiric Vision in *Fledgling*', *Utopian Studies* 19. 3: 391–409.

Brueggemann, B.J., R. Garland-Thomson and G. Kleege 2008 'What Her Body Taught (Or, Teaching about and with a Disability)'. In N. Watson (ed.) *Disability: Major Themes in Health and Social Welfare*. London and New York: Routledge, 180–96.

Buchanan, A. 2011 *Beyond Humanity? The Ethics of Biomedical Enhancement*. Oxford: Oxford University Press.

Butler, J. 1990 *Gender Trouble: Feminism and the Subversion of Identity*. London and New York: Routledge.

— 2004 *Precarious Lives: The Powers of Mourning and Violence*. London: Verso.

Butler, O.E. [1979] 1988 *Kindred*. Boston: Beacon.

— [1984] 1996 *Clay's Ark*. New York: Warner.

— 1988a *Dawn*. New York: Popular-Warner.

— 1988b *Adulthood Rites*. New York: Popular-Warner.

— 1989 *Imago*. New York: Warner.

— [1993] 1995 *Parable of the Sower*. New York: Popular-Warner.

— [1998] 2001 *Parable of the Talents*. London: Women's Press.

— 2005 *Fledgling*. New York: Grand Central.

— 2007 *Seed to Harvest. Inclusive of Wild Seed, Mind of My Mind, Clay's Ark and Patternmaster*. New York: Grand Central.

Calarco, M. 2008a *The Question of the Animal: From Heidegger to Derrida*. New York: Columbia University Press.

— 2008b *Zoographies: The Question of the Animal from Heidegger to Derrida*. New York: Columbia University Press.

Calvino, I. 1983 *Mr. Palomar*. Trans. William Weaver. http://mit.edu/jot/Public/ Calvino,%20Italo/Mr%20Palomar%20(trans.%20Weaver).html.

Campbell, N., and M. Saren 2010 'The Primitive, Technology and Horror: A Posthuman Biology', *Ephemera* 10. 2: 152–76.

Campbell, T. C. 2011 *Improper Life: Technology and Biopolitics from Heidegger to Agamben*. Minneapolis and London: University of Minnesota Press.

Carroll, R. 2010 'Imitations of Life: Cloning, Heterosexuality and the Human in Kazuo Ishiguro's *Never Let Me Go*', *Journal of Gender Studies* 19. 1: 59–71.

Castricano, J. 2008 'Introduction: Animal Subjects in a Posthuman World'. In J. Castricano (ed.) *Animal Subjects: An Ethical Reader in a Posthuman World*. Ontario: Wilfrid Laurier University Press, 1–32.

Catts, O., and I. Zurr 2002 'Growing Semi-Living Sculptures: The Tissue Culture & Art Project', *Leonardo* 35. 4: 365–70.

Cavalieri, P. 2001 *The Animal Question: Why Nonhuman Animals Deserve Human Rights*. Trans. Catherine Woollard. Oxford: Oxford University Press.

Chaney, M. A. 2011 'Animal Subjects of the Graphic Novel', *College Literature* 38. 3: 129–49.

Channel, D. 1991 *The Vital Machine*. Oxford: Oxford University Press.

Chorost, M. 2005 *Rebuilt: How Becoming Part Computer Made Me More Human*. London: Souvenir.

Cixous, H. 1976 'The Laugh of the Medusa'. Trans. K. Cohen and P. Cohen. *Signs* 1. 4: 875–93.

Cixous, H., and M. Calle-Gruber 1997 *Rootprints: Memory and Life Writing*. London and New York: Routledge.

Clark, A. 2004 *Natural Born Cyborgs: Minds, Technologies, and the Future of Human Intelligence*. New York: Oxford University Press.

Clarke, B. 2008 *Posthuman Metamorphosis: Narrative and Systems*. New York: Fordham University Press.

Coetzee, J. M. 1999 *The Lives of Animals*. Princeton, NJ: Princeton University Press.

Cohen, J. J. 1996 'Monster Culture (Seven Thesis)'. In Cohen (ed.) *Monster Theory: Reading Culture*. Minneapolis and London: University of Minnesota Press, 3–25.

— 2003 *Medieval Identity Machines*. Minneapolis and London: University of Minnesota Press.

Coleman, S., and R. Hanley 2009 'Homo sapiens, Robots and Persons in *I, Robot* and *Bicentennial Man*'. In S. Shapshay (ed.) *Bioethics at the Movies*. Baltimore: Johns Hopkins University Press, 44–55.

Connell, R. W. 1987 *Gender and Power: Society, the Person and Sexual Politics*. Stanford, CA: Stanford University Press.

Corker, M. 2008 'Sensing Disability'. In N. Watson (ed.) *Disability: Major Themes in Health and Social Welfare*. London and New York: Routledge, 66–83.

Davies, T. 1997 *Humanism*. London and New York: Routledge.

Dawkins, R. 1976 *The Selfish Gene*. Oxford: Oxford University Press.

Deleuze, G., and F. Guattari [1988] 2004 *A Thousand Plateaus: Capitalism and Schizophrenia*. Trans. Brian Massumi. London and New York: Continuum.

Derrida, J. 1991 '"Eating Well" or The Calculation of the Subject'. In E. Cadava, P. Connor and J.-L. Nancy (eds.) *Who Comes After the Subject?* New York: Routledge, 96–119.

— 2002 'The Animal that Therefore I Am (More to Follow)'. Trans. D. Wills. *Critical Inquiry* 28. 2: 369–418.

— 2003 'And Say the Animal Responded?' Trans. D. Wills. In C. Wolfe (ed.) *Zoontologies: The Question of the Animal*. Minneapolis and London: University of Minnesota Press, 121–46.

Devereaux, M. 2008 'Cosmetic Surgery'. In B. Gordijn and R. Chadwick (eds.) *Medical Enhancement and Posthumanity*. Dordrecht: Springer, 159–74.

DiMarco, D. 2005 'Paradice Lost, Paradise Regained: *Homo faber* and the Makings of a New Beginning in *Oryx and Crake*', *Papers in Language and Literature* 41. 2: 170–95.

Dinerstein, J. 2006 'Technology and Its Discontents: On the Verge of the Posthuman', *American Quarterly* 58. 3: 569–95.

di Pellegrino, G., L. Fadiga, L. Fogassi, V. Gallese and G. Rizzolatti 1992 'Understanding Motor Events: A Neurophysiological Study', *Experimental Brain Research* 91: 176–80.

Diprose, R. 2002 *Corporeal Generosity: On Giving with Nietzsche, Merleau-Ponty, and Levinas*. Albany: SUNY Press.

Dolar, M. 1991 '"I Shall Be with You on Your Wedding Night": Lacan and the Uncanny', *October* 58: 5–23.

Dourish, P. 2001 *Where the Action Is: The Foundations of Embodied Interaction*. Cambridge, MA: MIT Press.

Doyle, R. 2003 *Wetware: Experiments in Postvital Living*. Minneapolis and London: University of Minnesota Press.

Dunayer, J. 2004 *Speciesism*. Derwood, MD: Ryce.

Dunn, K. 1989 *Geek Love*. London: Abacus.

Eatough, M. 2011 'The Time that Remains: Organ Donation, Temporal Duration, and *Bildung* in Kazuo Ishiguro's *Never Let Me Go*', *Literature and Medicine* 29. 1: 132–60.

Eberly, S.S. 1988 'Fairies and the Folklore of Disability: Changelings, Hybrids and the Solitary Fairy', *Folklore* 99. 1: 58–77.

Esposito, R. 2008 *Bíos: Biopolitics and Philosophy*. Trans. Timothy Campbell. Minneapolis: University of Minnesota Press.

— 2010 *Communitas: The Origin and Destiny of Community*. Trans. Timothy Campbell. Stanford: Stanford University Press.

Fanon, F. [1963] 2004 *The Wretched of the Earth*. Trans. Richard Philcox. New York: Grove Press.

— [1965] 1970 *A Dying Colonialism*. Trans. Haakon Chevalier. Harmondsworth: Penguin.

— 1967 *Towards the African Revolution*. Trans. Haakon Chevalier. New York: Grove.

Fiedler, L. 1978 *Freaks: Myths and Images of the Secret Self*. New York: Anchor.

Fingeroth, D. 2004 *Superman on the Couch: What Superheroes Really Tell Us about Ourselves and Our Society*. New York: Continuum.

Fischer, L. 1992 'Birth Traumas: Parturition and Horror in *Rosemary's Baby*', *Cinema Journal* 31. 3: 3–18.

Flusty, S. 2004 *De-Coca-Colonization: Making the Globe from the Inside Out*. New York and London: Routledge.

Ford, P. 2009 'Hacking the Mind: Existential Enhancement in *Ghost in the Shell*'. In S. Shapshay (ed.) *Bioethics at the Movies*. Baltimore: Johns Hopkins University Press, 156–69.

Foucault, M. 1972 *Power/Knowledge*. Ed. Colin Gordon. New York: Pantheon.

— 1973 *The Order of Things*. New York: Vintage.

— 1997 *Ethics: Subjectivity and Truth*. Ed. P. Rabinow. Trans. R. Hurley and others. *The Essential Works of Michel Foucault 1954–1984*. Vol. I. New York: New Press.

Fudge, E. 2002 *Animal*. London: Reaktion.

Funk, R. 1987 'Disability Rights: From Caste to Class in the Context of Civil Rights'. In A. Gartner and T. Joe (eds.) *Images of Disabled, Disabling Images*. New York: Praeger, 7–30.

Garland-Thomson, R. 2008 'Feminist Disability Studies'. In N. Watson (ed.) *Disability: Major Themes in Health and Social Welfare*. London and New York: Routledge, 197–224.

Gates, K. 2006 'Identifying the 9/11 "Faces of Terror"', *Cultural Studies* 20. 4–5: 417–40.

Gavaghan, C. 2009 '"No Gene for Fate?" Luck, Harm, and Justice in *Gattaca*'. In S. Shapshay (ed.) *Bioethics at the Movies*. Baltimore: Johns Hopkins University Press, 75–86.

Gazzola, V., L. Aziz-Zadeh and C. Keysers 2006 'Empathy and the Somatotopic Auditory Mirror System in Humans', *Current Biology* 16: 1824–9.

Gerschick, T.J., and A.S. Miller 2008 'Coming to Terms: Masculinity and Physical Disability'. In N. Watson (ed.) *Disability: Major Themes in Health and Social Welfare*. London and New York: Routledge, Vol. IV, 3–23.

Gibson, W. 1984 *Neuromancer*. New York: Ace.

— 2003 *Pattern Recognition*. New York: G. B. Putnam.

Gilbert, S.F. 2002 'The Genome in Its Ecological Context: Philosophical Perspectives on Interspecies Epigenesis', *Annals of the New York Academy of Sciences* 981: 202–18.

Goldberg, E. S. 2007 *Beyond Terror: Gender, Narrative, Human Rights*. New Brunswick: Rutgers University Press.

Goss, T., and J.P. Riquelme 2007 'From Superhuman to Posthuman: The Gothic Technological Imaginary in Mary Shelley's *Frankenstein* and Octavia Butler's *Xenogenesis*', *Modern Fiction Studies* 52. 3: 434–59.

Gottweis, H. 2008 'Biobanks in Action: New Strategies in the Governance of Life'. In H. Gottweis and A. Petersen (eds.) *Biobanks: Governance in Comparative Perspectives*. New York and London: Routledge, 22–38.

Govan, S.Y. 1986 'Homage to Tradition: Octavia Butler Renovates the Historical Novel', *MELUS* 13. 1–2: 79–96.

Graham, E.L. 2002 *Representations of the Post/human*. New Brunswick, NJ: Rutgers University Press.

Grandin, T. 2006 'Thinking Like Animals'. In S.J. Armstrong and R.G. Botzler (eds.) *The Animal Ethics Reader*. London and New York: Routledge, 184–6.

Gray, C.H. 2001 *Cyborg Citizen: Politics in the Posthuman Age*. New York and London: Routledge.

Griffin, G. 2009 'Science and the Cultural Imaginary: The Case of Kazuo Ishiguro's *Never Let Me Go*', *Textual Practice* 23. 4: 645–63.

Hahn, H. [1985] 2008 'Towards a Politics of Disability: Definitions, Disciplines and Policies'. In N. Watson (ed.) *Disability: Major Themes in Health and Social Welfare*. London and New York: Routledge, Vol. I, 57–78.

Hansen, M.B.N. 2006 *Bodies in Code: Interfaces with Digital Media*. New York and London: Routledge.

— 2009 'System–Environment Hybrid'. In B. Clarke and M.B.N. Hansen, *Emergence and Embodiment: New Essays on Second-Order Systems Theory*. Durham and London: Duke University Press, 113–42.

Hanson, C. 2007 'Reproduction, Genetics, and Eugenics in the Fiction of Doris Lessing', *Contemporary Writing* 1. 1–2: 171–84.

Haraway, D. 1988 'Situated Knowledges: The Science Question in Feminism as a Site of Discourse on the Privilege of Partial Perspective', *Feminist Studies* 14. 3: 575–99.

— 1991a 'A Cyborg Manifesto: Science, Technology, and Socialist-Feminism in the Late Twentieth Century'. In Haraway, *Simians, Cyborgs and Women: The Reinvention of Nature*. New York: Routledge, 149–81.

— 1991b 'Cyborgs at Large'. Interview with Constance Penley and Andrew Ross. In C. Penley and A. Ross (eds.) *Technoculture*. Minneapolis: University of Minnesota Press, 1–20.

— 1997 *Modest_Witness@Second_Millennium.Female Man©_Meets_Oncomouse™: Feminism and Technoscience*. New York and London: Routledge.

— 2008 *When Species Meet*. Minneapolis: University of Minnesota Press.

Haraway, D., with T. Goodeve 2000 *How Like a Leaf*. New York: Routledge.

Hardin, M. 2004 'Fundamentally Freaky: Collapsing the Freak/Norm Binary in *Geek Love*', *Critique* 45. 4: 337–46.

Harpham, G.G. 1982 *On the Grotesque: Strategies of Contradiction in Art and Literature*. Princeton, NJ: Princeton University Press.

— 1999 *Shadows of Ethics: Criticism and the Just Society*. Durham and London: Duke University Press.

Harris, J. 2007 *Enhancing Evolution: The Ethical Case for Making Better People*. Princeton, NJ: Princeton University Press.

Harris, J. 2011 'Moral Enhancement and Freedom', *Bioethics* 25. 2: 102–11.

Hartsock, N. 1990 'Foucault on Power: A Theory for Women'. In L. Nicholson (ed.) *Feminism/Postmodernism*. London and New York: Routledge, 157–75.

Hayles, N.K. 1999 *How We Became Posthuman: Virtual Bodies in Cybernetics, Literature, and Informatics*. Chicago and London: University of Chicago Press.

— 2005 *My Mother was a Computer: Digital Subjects and Literary Texts*. Chicago and London: University of Chicago Press.

Hengel, L.V.D. 2012 'Zoegraphy: Per/forming Posthuman Lives', *Biography* 35. 1: 1–20.

Herndl, D.P. 1994 *Invalid Women: Figuring Feminine Illness in American Fiction and Culture, 1840–1940*. Chapel Hill: University of North Carolina Press.

Heyes, C. 2010 'Where Do Mirror Neurons Come From?' *Neuroscience and Biobehavioural Reviews* 3. 4: 574–83.

Hollinger, V. 2006 'Stories about the Future: From Patterns of Expectation to Pattern Recognition', *Science Fiction Studies* 33. 3: 452–72.

Huff, C., and J. Haefner 2012 'His Master's Voice: Animalographies, Life Writing and the Posthuman', *Biography* 35. 1: 153–69.

Hughes, J. 2010 'Contradictions from the Enlightenment Roots of Transhumanism', *Journal of Medicine and Philosophy* 35: 622–40.

Hunt, P. [1966] 2008 'A Critical Condition'. In N. Watson (ed.) *Disability: Major Themes in Health and Social Welfare*. London and New York: Routledge, Vol. I, 25–35.

Ingram, D. 1994 'Foucault and Habermas on the Subject of Reason'. In Gary Gutting (ed.) *The Cambridge Companion to Foucault*. Cambridge: Cambridge University Press, 215–61.

Ishiguro, K. 2005 *Never Let Me Go*. London: Faber and Faber.

Jeannerod, M., and T. Anquetil 2009 'Putting Oneself in the Perspective of the Other: A Framework for the Self/Other Differentiation'. In C. Keysers and L. Fadiga (eds.) *The Mirror Neuron System*. Hove and New York: Psychology Press, 356–67.

Jewiss, V. 2001 'Monstrous Movements and Metaphors in Dante's *Divine Comedy*'. In K. Jewell (ed.) *Monsters in the Italian Literary Imagination*. Detroit: Wayne State University Press, 179–84.

Jöns, H. 2006 'Dynamic Hybrids and the Geographies of Technoscience: Discussing Conceptual Resources Beyond the Human/Non-human Binary', *Social and Cultural Geography* 7. 4: 559–80.

Jose, L. 2008 'Monstrous Conceptions: Sex, Madness and Gender in Medieval Medical Texts', *Comparative Critical Studies* 5. 2–3: 153–63.

Kaneko, K. 2006 *Life: An Introduction to Complex Systems Biology*. Berlin and Heidelberg: Springer.

Kauffman, S. A. 1993 *The Origins of Order: Self-Organization and Selection in Evolution*. New York: Oxford University Press.

Kazez, J. 2009 'Dying to Eat: The Vegetarian Ethics of *Twilight*'. In W. Irwin, R. Housel and J. Wisnewski (eds.) *Twilight and Philosophy: Vampires, Vegetarians and the Pursuit of Immortality*. Malden, MA: Wiley-Blackwell, 25–37.

Keith, L. 2008 'Encounters with Strangers: The Public's Response to Disabled Women and how this Affects Our Sense of Self'. In N. Watson (ed.) *Disability: Major Themes in Health and Social Welfare*. London and New York: Routledge, Vol. IV, 24–38.

Kerr, A. 2003 'Genetics and Citizenship', *Society* 40. 6: 44–50.

Keysers, C. 2011 *The Empathic Brain: How the Discovery of Mirror Neurons Changes our Understanding of Human Nature*. N.p.: Social Brain Press.

Keysers, C., and L. Fadiga 2009 'The Mirror Neuron System: New Frontiers'. In Keysers and Fadiga (eds.) *The Mirror Neuron System. Special Issue of Social Neuroscience*. Hove and New York: Psychology Press, 193–8.

Keysers, C., and V. Gazzola 2010 'Social Neuroscience: Mirror Neurons Recorded in Humans', *Current Biology* 20. 8: R 353–4.

Koch, T. 2010 'Enhancing Who? Enhancing What? Ethics, Bioethics, and Transhumanism', *Journal of Medicine and Philosophy* 35: 685–99.

Krimsky, S. 1982 *Genetic Alchemy: The Social History of the Recombinant DNA Controversy*. Cambridge, MA: MIT Press.

Kuhse, H., and P. Singer 2001 'What is Bioethics: A Historical Introduction'. In H. Kuhse and P. Singer (eds.) *A Companion to Bioethics*. Malden, MA: Blackwell, 3–11.

Lacey, L. 2008 'Octavia E. Butler on Coping with Power in *Parable of the Sower*, *Parable of the Talents*, and *Fledgling*', *Critique* 49. 4: 379–94.

Lauro, S.J., and K. Embry 2008 'A Zombie Manifesto: The Nonhuman Condition in the Era of Advanced Capitalism', *Boundary 2* 35. 1: 85–108.

Le Guin, U.K. 1979 'Is Gender Necessary?' In *The Language of the Night: Essays on Fantasy and Science Fiction*. New York: G. P. Putnam's Sons, 161–9.

— 1987 'Vaster than Empires and More Slow'. In Le Guin, *Buffalo Gals and Other Animal Presences*. New York: Plume, 83–128.

Lessing, D. [1988] 2001 *The Fifth Child*. London: Flamingo.

Levitas, R. n.d. 'The Imaginary Reconstitution of Society'. Inaugural Lecture, University of Bristol.

Lingis, A. 2003 'Animal Body, Inhuman Face'. In C. Wolfe (ed.) *Zootologies: The Question of the Animal*. Minneapolis and London: University of Minnesota Press, 165–82.

Lippit, A. 2000 *Electric Animal: Toward a Rhetoric of Wildlife*. Minneapolis: University of Minnesota Press.

Longmore, P. [1985] 1997 'Screening Stereotypes: Images of Disabled People in Television and Motion Pictures'. In A. Gartner and T. Joe (eds.) *Images of the Disabled, Disabling Images*. New York: Praeger, 65–78.

Lyon, D. 2009 *Identifying Citizens: ID Cards as Surveillance*. Cambridge: Polity.

Margulis, L. 1981 *Symbiosis in Cell Evolution*. San Francisco: W. H. Freeman, 141–70.

— 2000 'Symbiosis and the Origin of Protists'. In L. Margulis, C. Matthews and A. Haselton (eds.) *Environmental Pollution: Effects of the Origin and Evolution of Life on Planet Earth*. Cambridge, MA: MIT Press.

Maturana, H.R., and F.J. Varela [1972] 1980 *Autopoiesis and Cognition: The Organization of the Living*. London: D. Reidel.

McMahan, J. 2001 'Brain Death, Cortical Death and Persistent Vegetative State'. In H. Kuhse and P. Singer (eds.) *A Companion to Bioethics*. Malden, MA: Blackwell, 250–60.

McNeil, M. 2010 'Post-Millennial Feminist Theory: Encounters with Humanism, Materialism, Critique, Nature, Biology and Darwin', *Journal for Cultural Research* 14. 4: 427–37.

Meyer, S. 2005 *Twilight*. New York: Little, Brown.

— [2006] 2009 *New Moon*. London: Atom-Little, Brown.

— [2007] 2009 *Eclipse*. London: Atom-Little, Brown.

Meyerowitz, J. 2006 'A "Fierce and Demanding" Drive'. In S. Stryker and S. Whittle (eds.) *The Transgender Studies Reader*. New York: Routledge, 362–86.

Michaud, N. 2009 'Can a Vampire Be a Person?' In W. Irwin, R. Housel and J. Wisnewski (eds.) *Twilight and Philosophy: Vampires, Vegetarians and the Pursuit of Immortality*. Malden, MA: Wiley-Blackwell, 39–62.

Miller, J. 1998 'Post-Apocalyptic Hoping: Octavia Butler's Dystopian/Utopian Vision', *Science Fiction Studies* 25. 2: 336–60.

Mitchell, D.T., and S.L. Snyder 2000 *Narrative Prosthesis: Disability and the Dependencies of Discourse*. Ann Arbor, MI: University of Michigan Press.

— 2006 'Masquerades of Impairment: Charity as a Confidence Game', *Leviathan: A Journal of Melville Studies* 8. 1: 35–60.

Mitchell, W.J. 2003 *Me^{++}: The Cyborg Self and the Networked City*. Cambridge, MA: MIT Press.

Mittman, A.S. 2006 *Maps and Monsters in Medieval England*. New York and London: Routledge.

Moore, A., with Stephen Bissette and John Totleben [1987] 2009 *Saga of the Swamp Thing. Book One*. New York: DC.

Moser, I. [2000] 2008 'Against Normalisation: Subverting Norms of Ability and Disability'. In N. Watson (ed.) *Disability: Major Themes in Health and Social Welfare*. London and New York: Routledge, Vol. I, 287–319.

Mousley, A. 2010 'The New Literary Humanism: Towards a Critical Vocabulary', *Textual Practice* 24. 5: 819–39.

Nancy, J.-L. 2002 *L'Intrus*. Trans. Susan Hanson. East Lansing: Michigan State University Press.

Nash, R. 2011 'Joy and Pity: Reading Animal Bodies in Late Eighteenth-century Culture', *The Eighteenth Century* 52. 1: 47–67.

Nayar, P. K. 2010 'How to Domesticate a Vampire: Gender, Blood Relations, and Sexuality in Stephenie Meyer's *Twilight*', *Nebula* 37. 3: 60–76.

— 2011a 'Posthumanism and Vampirism in Octavia Butler's *Fledgling*', *Notes on Contemporary Literature* 41. 2: 6–10.

— 2011b 'Traumatic Materialism: Info-flows, Bodies and Intersections in William Gibson's *Pattern Recognition*', *Westerly* 56. 2: 48–61.

— 2011c 'Border Disputes, Ap/proximate Humans: Vampires, Posthumans and a New Humanism', *Margins* 1. 1: 65–84.

— 2012a 'A New Biological Citizenship: Posthumanism in Octavia Butler's *Fledgling*', *Modern Fiction Studies* 58. 4: 796–817.

— 2012b 'I Sing the Body Biometric: Identity, Identification, Surveillance and Biological Citizenship', *Economic and Political Weekly* 96. 32: 17–22.

— 2013 *Frantz Fanon*. London and New York: Routledge.

— Forthcoming 'From the Gynaecological to the Species Gothic: Doris Lessing's *The Fifth Child*', *Samyukta*.

Neill, M. 1989 'Unproper Beds: Race, Adultery, and the Hideous in *Othello*', *Shakespeare Quarterly* 40: 383–412.

Nelson, A., and J. Hwang 2012 'Roots and Revelations: Genetic Ancestry Testing and the YouTube Generation'. In L. Nakamura and P. A. Chow-White (eds.) *Race after the Internet*. London and New York: Routledge, 271–90.

Ness, P. 2008 *The Knife of Never Letting Go*. London: Walker.

— 2009 *The Ask and the Answer*. London: Walker.

— 2010 *Monsters of Men*. London: Walker.

Oliver, M. [1989] 2008 'Disability and Dependency: A Creation of Industrial Societies?' In N. Watson (ed.) *Disability: Major Themes in Health and Social Welfare*. London and New York: Routledge, Vol. I, 141–56.

O'Mathúna, D. P. 2009 *Nanoethics: Big Ethical Issues with Small Technology*. New York and London: Continuum.

Ong, A. 2003 *Buddha in Hiding: Refugees, Citizenship, and the New America*. Berkeley, CA, and London: University of California Press.

Osherow, M. 2000 'The Dawn of a New Lilith: Revisionary Mythmaking in Women's Science Fiction', *NWSA Journal* 12. 1: 68–83.

Otter, S. 2006 'Melville and Disability', *Leviathan: A Journal of Melville Studies* 8. 1: 7–16.

Outterson, S. 2008 'Diversity, Change, Violence: Octavia Butler's Pedagogical Philosophy', *Utopian Studies* 19. 3: 433–56.

Pearson, K. A. 1997 'Viroid Life: Machines, Technics and Evolution'. In K. A. Pearson (ed.) *Deleuze and Philosophy: The Difference Engineer*. London and New York: Routledge, 180–210.

Pedersen, H. 2011 'Release the Moths: Critical Animal Studies and the Posthumanist Impulse', *Culture, Theory and Critique* 52. 1: 65–81.

Peterson, C. 2011 'The Posthumanism to Come', *Angelaki* 16. 2: 127–41.

Pennington, J. 2000 'Exorcising Gender: Resisting Readers in Ursula K. Le Guin's *The Left Hand of Darkness*', *Extrapolation* 41. 4: 351–8.

Pepperell, R. 2003 *The Posthuman Condition: Consciousness Beyond the Brain*. London: Intellect.

Peppers, C. 1995 'Dialogic Origins and Alien Identities in Butler's Xenogenesis', *Science Fiction Studies* 22. 1: 47–62.

Persson, I., and J. Savulescu 2010 'Moral Transhumanism', *Journal of Medicine and Philosophy* 35: 656–69.

Petryna, A. 2004 'Biological Citizenship: The Science and Politics of Chernobyl-Exposed Populations', *Osiris* 2nd series 19: 250–65.

Pickering, A. 2010 *The Cybernetic Brain: Sketches of Another Future*. Chicago and London: University of Chicago Press.

Piercy, M. [1976] 1983 *Woman on the Edge of Time*. New York: Ballantine.

— [1991] 1993 *He, She and It*. New York: Ballantine.

Pingree, A. 1996 'America's "United Siamese Brothers": Chang and Eng and Nineteenth-Century Ideologies of Democracy and Domesticity'. In J.J. Cohen (ed.) *Monster Theory: Reading Culture*. Minneapolis and London: University of Minnesota Press, 92–114.

Pradeu, T., and E. D. Carosella 2006 'The Self Model and the Conception of Biological Identity in Immunology', *Biology and Philosophy* 21: 235–52.

Preston, S. D. and F. B. M. de Waal 2002 'Empathy: Its Ultimate and Proximate Basis', *Behavioral and Brain Sciences* 25. 1: 1–71.

Prograis, Jr, L., and E. Pellegrino (eds.) 2007 *African American Bioethics: Culture, Race, and Identity*. Washington, DC: Georgetown University Press.

Ramey, L. 2008 'Monstrous Alterity in Early Modern Travel Accounts: Lessons from the Ambiguous Medieval Discourse on Humanness', *L'Esprit Créateur* 48. 1: 81–95.

Reynolds, R. 1992 *Superheroes: A Modern Mythology*. London: B. T. Batsford.

Rice, A. [1976] 2010 *Interview with the Vampire*. London: Sphere:

— 2000 *Merrick*. New York: Ballantine.

Rizzolatti, G., and L. Craighero 2004 'The Mirror-Neuron System', *Annual Review of Neuroscience* 27: 167–92.

Robert, J. S., and F. Baylis 2003 'Crossing Species Boundaries', *The American Journal of Bioethics* 3. 3: 1–13.

Roelvink, G. 2012 'Rethinking Species-Being in the Anthropocene', *Rethinking Marxism*: 1–18.

Rohman, C. 2009 'On Singularity and the Symbolic: The Threshold of the Human in Calvino's *Mr. Palomar*', *Criticism* 51. 1: 63–78.

Roof, J. 2007 *The Poetics of DNA*. Minneapolis and London: University of Minnesota Press.

Rose, N., and C. Novas 2005 'Biological Citizenship'. In A. Ong and S. Collier (eds.) *Global Assemblages: Technology, Politics, and Ethics as Anthropological Problems*. Malden, MA: Blackwell, 439–63.

Ross, J. C. 2007 'Biometrics: Intersecting Borders and Bodies in Liberal Bionetwork States', *Journal of Borderlands Studies* 22. 2: 77–96.

Rothberg, M., and Y. Yildiz 2011 'Memory Citizenship: Migrant Archives of Holocaust Remembrance in Contemporary Germany', *Parallax* 17. 4: 32–48.

Rout, K. 2003 'Who Do You Love? Anne Rice's Vampires and their Moral Transition', *Journal of Popular Culture*: 473–9.

Rushdy, A. H. A. 1993 'Families of Orphans: Relation and Disrelation in Octavia Butler's *Kindred*', *College English* 55. 2: 135–57.

Sabin, J. E., and N. Daniels 1994 'Determining "Medical Necessity" in Mental Health Practice', *Hastings Centre Report* 24. 6: 5–13.

Sawday, J. 1995 *The Body Emblazoned: Dissection and the Human Body in Renaissance Culture*. London and New York: Routledge.

Scahill, A. 2010 'Deviled Eggs: Teratogenesis and the Gynecological Gothic in the Cinema of Monstrous Birth'. In R. B. Anolik (ed.) *Demons of the Body and Mind: Essays on Disability in Gothic Literature*. Jefferson, NC: McFarland, 197–216.

Schatzing, F. 2006 *The Swarm*. Trans. S.-A. Spencer. London: Hodder and Stoughton.

Schippers, M. B., A. Roebroeck, R. Renken, L. Nanetti and C. Keysers 2010 'Mapping the Information Flow from One Brain to Another during Gestural Communication', *Proceedings of the National Academy of Sciences* 107. 20: 9388–93.

Scott, J. 2010 'Octavia Butler and the Base for American Socialism', *Socialism and Democracy* 20. 3: 105–26.

Seaman, M. J. 2007 'Becoming More (Than) Human: Affective Posthumanisms, Past and Future', *Journal of Narrative Theory* 37. 2: 246–75.

Shakespeare, T. [1994] 2008 'Cultural Representation of Disabled People: Dustbins for Disavowal?' In N. Watson (ed.) *Disability: Major Themes in Health and Social Welfare*. London and New York: Routledge, Vol. I, 192–211.

Sharp, L. A. 2006 *Strange Harvest: Organ Transplants, Denatured Bodies, and the Transformed Self*. Berkeley and London: University of California Press.

Shiva, V. 1997 *Biopiracy: The Plunder of Nature and Knowledge*. Boston, MA: South End Press.

Siegel, D. J. 2007 *The Mindful Brain: Reflection and Attunement in the Cultivation of Well-Being*. New York and London: W. W. Norton.

Smith, S. A. 2007 'Octavia Butler: A Retrospective', *Feminist Studies* 33. 2: 385–93.

Smith Keller, L. 1992 'Discovering and Doing: Science and Technology, An Introduction'. In G. Kirkup and L. S. Keller (eds.) *Inventing Women: Science, Technology and Gender*. Cambridge: Polity, 12–32.

Soyinka, W. [1975] 1984 *Death and the King's Horseman*. In Soyinka, *Six Plays*. London: Methuen.

Spillers, H. J. 2003 *Black, White, and in Color: Essays on American Literature and Culture*. Chicago, IL: University of Chicago Press.

Spooner, C. 2006 *Contemporary Gothic*. London: Reaktion.

Squier, S. 1998 'Interspecies Reproduction: Xenogenic Desire and the Feminist Implications of Hybrids', *Cultural Studies* 12. 3: 360–81.

Stacey, J. 2005 'Masculinity, Masquerade, and Genetic Impersonation: *Gattaca's* Queer Visions', *Signs* 30. 3: 1851–77.

Stengers, I. 2011 *Cosmopolitics II*. Trans. R. Bonono. Minneapolis and London: University of Minnesota Press.

Stevenson, J. A. 1988 'A Vampire in the Mirror: The Sexuality of Dracula', *PMLA* 103. 2: 139–49.

Stiegler, B. 2003 'Technics of Decision: An Interview with Peter Hallward'. Trans. S. Gaston. *Angelaki* 8. 2: 151–68.

Sundar Rajan, K. 2006 *Biocapital: The Constitution of Postgenomic Life*. Durham, NC: Duke University Press.

Svenaeus, F. 2012 'Organ Transplantation and Person Identity: How Does Loss and Change of Organs Affect the Self?' *Journal of Medicine and Philosophy* 37: 139–58.

Sztybel, D. 2008 'Animals as Persons'. In J. Castricano (ed.) *Animal Subjects: An Ethical Reader in a Posthuman World*. Ontario: Wilfrid Laurier University Press, 241–58.

Thacker, E. 2004 *Biomedia*. Minneapolis and London: University of Minnesota Press.

— 2005 *The Global Genome: Biotechnology, Politics, and Culture*. Cambridge, MA: MIT Press.

Thomas, C. [2004] 2008 'How is Disability Understood? An Examination of Sociological Approaches'. In N. Watson (ed.) *Disability: Major Themes in Health and Social Welfare*. London and New York: Routledge, Vol. I, 378–94.

Thomas, D.A. 2008 'Assyrian Monsters and Domestic Chimeras', *Studies in English Literature 1500–1900* 48. 4: 897–909.

Thompson, E. 2009 'Life and Mind: From Autopoiesis to Neurophenomenology'. In B. Clarke and M.B.N. Hansen (eds.) *Emergence and Embodiment: New Essays on Second-Order Systems Theory*. Durham, NC, and London: Duke University Press, 77–93.

Tooley, M. 2001 'Personhood'. In H. Kuhse and P. Singer (eds.) *A Companion to Bioethics*. Malden, MA: Blackwell, 117–26.

Tucker, J.A. 2007 ' "The Human Contradiction": Identity and/as Essence in Octavia E. Butler's "Xenogenesis" Trilogy', *The Yearbook of English Studies* 37. 2: 164–81.

UIDAI 2009 *Demographic Data Standards and Verification Procedure Committee Report*. New Delhi: Planning Commission. http://uidai.gov.in/UID_PDF/Committees/UID_DDSVP_Committee_Report_v1.0. pdf. Last accessed 4 June 2012.

Varela, F. 2001 'Intimate Distance: Fragments for a Phenomenology of Organ Transplantation', *Journal of Consciousness Studies* 8. 5–7: 259–71.

Vehmas, S. 2008 'Ethical Analysis of the Concept of Disability'. In N. Watson (ed.) *Disability: Major Themes in Health and Social Welfare*. London and New York: Routledge, Vol. I, 399–420.

Vint, S. 2005 'Becoming Other: Animals, Kinship, and Butler's "Clay's Ark" ', *Science Fiction Studies* 32. 2: 281–300.

— 2010 *Animal Alterity: Science Fiction and the Question of the Animal*. Liverpool: Liverpool University Press.

Vita-More, N. 2007 'Brave BioArt 2: Shedding the Bio, Amassing the Nano, and Cultivating Posthuman Life', *Technoetic Arts* 5. 3: 171–86.

Waldby, C., and R. Mitchell 2007 *Tissue Economies: Blood, Organs, and Cell Lines in Late Capitalism*. Durham, NC, and London: Duke University Press.

Warren, V. 2004 'American Tall Tale/Tail: Katherine Dunn's *Geek Love* and the Paradox of American Individualism', *Critique* 45. 4: 323–36.

Weisberg, Z. 2009 'The Broken Promises of Monsters: Haraway, Animals and the Posthumanist Legacy', *Journal of Critical Animal Studies* 7. 2: 22–62.

Wills, D. 1995 *Prosthesis*. Stanford, CA: Stanford University Press.

Wilson, S., and N. Haslam 2009 'Is the Future More or Less Human? Differing Views of Humanness in the Posthumanism Debate', *Journal for the Theory of Social Behaviour* 39. 2: 247–66.

Winnubst, S. 2003 'Vampires, Anxieties, and Dreams: Race and Sex in Contemporary United States', *Hypatia* 18. 3: 1–20.

Wittkower, R. 1942 'Marvels of the East: A Study in the History of Monsters', *Journal of the Warburg and Courtauld Institute* 5: 159–97.

Wolfe, C. 2003 *Animal Rites: American Culture: The Discourse of Species and Posthumanist Theory*. Chicago and London: University of Chicago Press.

— 2010 *What is Posthumanism?* Minneapolis and London: University of Minnesota Press.

Zelazo, P.D., M. Moscovitch and E. Thompson (eds.) 2007 *The Cambridge Handbook of Consciousness*. Cambridge: Cambridge University Press.

Ziarek, E.P. 2008 'Bare Life on Strike: Notes on the Biopolitics of Race and Gender', *South Atlantic Quarterly* 107. 1: 89–105.

Zylinska, J. 2009 *Bioethics in the Age of New Media*. Cambridge, MA: MIT Press.

Index

relational 20
self 14
social 60
species 5, 87, 91, 96, 139, 145, 148, 153
immunity 45, 97, 121, 134, 146–7, 150
see also community
as identity 63 *see also* Nancy
impairment 7, 100–1, 102, 103, 105, 106, 108 *see also* disability
Interview with the Vampire 94, 130, 133, 134, 153 *see also* Rice
Irigaray, Luce 8, 17–18, 19 *see also* body, fluid; feminine
Ishiguro, Kazuo 1, 26, 33, 60–2, 87, 100, 122–3 see also *Never Let Me Go*

Jurassic Park 55

Kauffman, Stuart 43–4, 47, 48, 50
Keysers, Christian 41–2, 121, 126, 154 *see also* mirror neurons

language 3, 11, 12, 16, 17, 18, 19, 20, 24, 47, 57, 88, 91, 93, 158n3, 161n8
Le Guin, Ursula 1, 16, 17, 18, 33, 125, 126, 129, 150, 151, 155 see also *The Left Hand of Darkness*; 'Vaster Than Empires and More Slow'
The Left Hand of Darkness 1, 16, 17, 18, 150, 151 *see also* Le Guin
Lessing, Doris 33, 78, 85, 116–20, 124, 161n10 see also *The Fifth Child*
Lingis, Alphonso 46, 90
Lippit, Akira 82

Margulis, Lynn 9, 42–3, 47, 70, 91, 128, 137, 161–2n1, 162n2
masculinity 17, 18, 23, 102, 114, 115, 131
materiality 24, 25, 36, 52, 65, 67, 76, 79, 82, 93, 129, 151
biological 57–8
of the body 52, 57, 65, 67, 76, 129
Maturana, Humberto 36, 37–8, 50, 52, 91, 148 *see also* autopoiesis; Varela

Melville, Herman 100, 105, 106, 160n1 see also *Moby-Dick*
Merrick 132 *see also* Rice
Meyer, Stephenie 1, 33, 94, 126, 130–1, 132, 134, 153, 162n7 see also *Twilight*
Mind of my Mind 42, 133 *see also* Butler, Octavia
mirror neurons 40–2, 121, 126, 154, 158n5 *see also* Keysers; resonance
monster 82–6, 159n2, 161n10, 162–3n9 *see also* Cohen
body of the 80
clone as 86
studies 4, 79, 80–1, 83, 84, 85
theory 82–7
Moore, Alan 125, 162–3n9 see also *Saga of the Swamp Thing*
mutant 2, 11, 77, 78, 79, 81, 83, 85, 101 *see also* individual, with special powers

Nancy, Jean-Luc 63 *see also* identity, as immunity
neocybernetics 10, 36, 37, 39, 158n4
Never Let Me Go 1, 26, 60–2, 87, 100, 115, 122–123, 158n1 *see also* Ishiguro

Oryx and Crake 24, 25–6, 88, 89, 122, 143, 159n3 *see also* Atwood

Parables (*Parable of the Sower*, *Parable of the Talents*) 40, 42, 122, 136, 140, 142–3, 144, 153, 156, 162n5 *see also* Butler, Octavia
Pattern Recognition 66–9 *see also* Gibson
Pepperell, Robert 39, 53, 158n3
perturbation 38, 46, 49–50, 51
Piercy, Marge 1, 15, 33, 78, 87, 110–11, 111–12, 113–14, 115 see also *He, She and It*; *Woman on the Edge of Time*
poststructuralist anti-humanism 12–15 *see also* Foucault
postvitalism 59–60, 64 *see also* Doyle
potential/ potentiality 74–5, 126, 130, 145, 146, 147–9, 153, 156